NOW
ENJOY YOUR PLANTS MORE
BY GETTING YOUR PLANTS
TO ENJOY YOU!

Your garden will respond
to this system
with new health and vigor.

Jerry Baker looks upon plants as people, with their own personalities and special language. He advises anyone who wants to garden successfully to do the same.

While giving expert counsel on every gardening subject—from seed to fertilizer, from the tallest tree to the smallest herb—he shows that love and encouragement are as necessary for a plant as for a growing child.

Books by Jerry Baker

I Never Met a House Plant I Didn't Like
Jerry Baker's Back to Nature Almanac
Jerry Baker's Second Back to Nature Almanac
Jerry Baker's Third Back to Nature Almanac
Jerry Baker's Bicentennial Gardener's Almanac
Make Friends with Your Lawn
Make Friends with Your Vegetable Garden
Plants Are Like People
Talk to Your Plants

Published by POCKET BOOKS

PLANTS ARE LIKE PEOPLE

Jerry Baker

Literary Consultant, Dan Kibbie

Illustrated by Carl Chambers

A KANGAROO BOOK
PUBLISHED BY POCKET BOOKS NEW YORK

This book is lovingly dedicated to my wife, Ilene, who watched it "grow" and who makes my life bloom like a garden.

POCKET BOOKS, a Simon & Schuster division of
GULF & WESTERN CORPORATION
1230 Avenue of the Americas, New York, N.Y. 10020

Copyright © 1971 by Jerry Baker

Published by arrangement with Nash Publishing Corporation
Library of Congress Catalog Card Number: 70-143002

ISBN: 0-671-81426-5

First Pocket Books printing August, 1972

13th printing

Trademarks registered in the United States and other countries.

Printed in the U.S.A.

Acknowledgments

In writing this book, I had a great deal of help, advice, encouragement and inspiration—but I didn't use any of it. To these people, however, my special thanks:

To the television and radio crews, who have often asked me to go "write myself a book" (or something like that); to the captains and crews of American Airlines, who flew so steady while I scribbled away; to the man who built my leaky basement, where I completed this manuscript; to Myron and Thelma Schwartz (whoever they are) . . .

And, finally, to Dan and Mary Kibbie, who painstakingly pruned away some of the grammatical debris and mulched over my mistakes.

To Katheryn

from

Joure-no-Bugs
my buddy

Happeness on your
new Job

Foreword

When I was a nine-year-old boy, I had no idea that Mother Nature had already singled me out to become one of her students. As a matter of fact, of all the things that must have been on my mind at that time, gardening and growing things were far, far from the top of the list.

You might say that Mother Nature got me into gardening as a part of a rehabilitation program designed to make me turn away from a life of crime.

It happened this way. I woke up early one fine spring morning with nothing to do. Since we were a new family in a Kansas City suburb, I decided to get out and do a little exploring. So, off I went along the railroad embankment which was a short way from our new home.

I don't remember now when I first noticed the greenhouse, but there it was, down at the foot of the embankment with all those beautiful glass windows! And there I was, directly above it—with all those rocks! In no time at all, the great rock-throwing exhibition was on!

But before I even had a chance to break more than three or four windows, there was a noise in the bushes behind me; and before I knew what was happening, I was nabbed by the nurseryman who owned the greenhouse.

My embarrassed dad offered to pay the nurseryman for all the damage that I had caused, but the nurseryman and Mother Nature had other plans.

Everyone agreed that the best thing for all parties concerned was for me to work at the nursery until I had paid off all the damages. And the next day, I began my career as a nine-year-old weeder!

Along with pulling weeds, part of my new job was to

pick out the hundreds and hundreds of tiny glass particles that were in every flat of seedings. It was hard, painstaking work that lasted from sunup to sundown six days a week. And every Sunday afternoon my favorite program, "The Shadow," would remind me that, "The weed of crime bears bitter fruit."

Looking back now, I'm sure that Mother Nature was somewhere nearby, watching my every move and drumming one of her most basic lessons into my head: Getting rid of weeds is one of the primary functions of a good gardener.

Contents

Chapter 1   Lawns: The Head of the Garden   1

Chapter 2   Evergreens: Sentinels of Beauty   59

Chapter 3   Shade Trees: Your Monument   97

Chapter 4   Flowering Trees: The Candy Store   123

Chapter 5   Fruit Trees: Two for the Money   133

Chapter 6   Flowering Shrubs: The Kindergarten   145

Chapter 7   Roses: The Royal Court   159

Chapter 8   Annuals: Magic Land   175

Chapter 9   Perennials and Biennials:
             Top Management   187

Chapter 10   Bulbs: The Golden Nuggets   195

Chapter 11   The Vegetable Garden: Your Team   205

Chapter 12   Ground Covers: Something to Hide   219

Chapter 13   Small Fruit Are the Berries   227

Chapter 14   House Plants:
              Living Room Landscape   233

Chapter 15   Herbs and Other Things:
              The Spice of Life   251

Chapter 16   Solution to Pollution   259

Index   263

List of Tables

Seed Chart   38

Surface Insects That Plague Lawns   45

Soil Insects That Plague Lawns   47

Catalogues Available   84

Landscape Planning Guide   87

Patio Palms   110

Most Popular Palms   110

Trees with Fruit or Berries   112

Trees with Flowers   113

Standard Shade Trees   115

Citrus Varieties Available at Garden Centers   140

Softwood Cuttings   151

Hardwood Cuttings   153

Flowering Shrubs for Home Use   153

Hybrid Teas   167

Grandifloras   168

Floribundas   168

Climbers (Roses)   169

Enemies of the Rose and What to Do About Them   169

Annuals   181

Perennials   191

Vegetable Team Starters   213

Climbers (Ground Covers)   223

Ground Creepers   224

Strawberries   230

Raspberries   231

Blackberries   231

Boysenberries   231

Grapes   231

Blueberries   231

House Plant Identification   247

1
Lawns:
The Head of the Garden

Has there ever been a person who didn't admire and appreciate a beautiful, green, lush and healthy lawn? I don't think so. From a hobo to a tycoon, man, woman and child—for everyone, green grass creates an image of freedom and tranquility. To the homeowner, it means "green thumb success." If he is complimented on his lawn, or consulted about it by his neighbors, he is truly considered a success.

But to have a perfect lawn is virtually impossible for the average guy. Most of you can't spare the time, effort or money. Anyone who belongs to a country club is aware of the real cost of a near perfect turf. All this does not, however, mean that you can't have a beautiful lawn. To have the kind of lawn you'd like means that you'll have to exert the three "P's." The three "P's" are Pride, Persistence and Patience. Just to be sure you understand the importance of these three points—because they are the three most important gardening concepts that we will have to deal with throughout this book, I'll explain.

Take pride in what you are doing. Don't be satisfied with a halfway job. Make it the best you can possibly do or don't even attempt it. The pride you put into your garden will be reflected in the end result.

Persistence is another absolute must for "growing success." Mother Nature has a way of punishing anyone who quits in the middle of a gardening job—by making it twice as difficult to finish when he returns.

Perhaps the most important of the three "P's" is patience. You can't rush Mother Nature or her helpers, but you can sort of prod her on with a few tricks I've learned over the years.

Think of your lawn as if it were the hair on your head. People judge your hair, or your lawn, by its appearance. Your lawn is the first thing a stranger sees when he approaches your house. He can't know if you have fine furniture or nice clothes or even if you have a fancy car in the garage. What he can see is your lawn, so make your lawn look like it just came back from the barber—clean, combed and well cut. Good grooming is as important to your garden as it is to you.

Give Your Lawn a Dandruff Treatment

Lawn dandruff is known as thatch. It's an accumulation of grass clippings and debris that builds up over a period of time. When it's not removed, this thatch becomes a breeding place for various lawn diseases called fungus. If the fungus diseases are not curbed, the grass will simply fade away, and your lawn will become bald.

This lawn dandruff, or thatch, is also a thief. It robs your lawn of food, air and water. As it gets thicker, and packed tighter, it sheds water and won't let the weed killers and lawn medicines get down to the roots of the grass where they are needed.

There are several ways to eliminate and remove this dandruff problem, and the first is to catch all of your grass clippings when mowing. The type of grass doesn't mean a thing; catch the clippings of them all.

To remove the existing thatch, you have a choice of three methods.

The first is the use of a lawn groom rake. This rake is especially designed for this purpose. It consists of many fine half-moon shaped blades with very sharp edges and a small bar at the top of each to allow the rake to clean itself as you go. This is the hand method recommended for small lawns.

The second method is to purchase an attachment that converts your power mower into a power de-thatcher. This attachment is called a roto rake bar. I would like to caution you on the use of this tool. Start your lawn mower on a concrete surface and then proceed back and forth

across the lawn at a normal pace, not stopping on the turf area as this will cause extensive root damage. When you have done the entire lawn area back and forth in one direction, then do the same area in a cross direction. The roto rake bar should cost less than five dollars.

The third method is to use a power rake or power renovator, which can be rented from local business establishments specializing in this type of equipment.

The power machines are extremely effective, but they need your complete concentration.

Each of these methods is comparable to a human scalp treatment, and the result is the same. Improved circulation to the roots produces fatter, stronger, greener, healthier grass.

Do not be shocked to find that you have collected seven to eight twenty-gallon garbage cans full of thatch for each 1,000 square feet of lawn.

Now what are you going to do with all this excess grass? Start your first compost pile (to be discussed later). Remember, ecology has to do with the methods by which we return to earth, in one form or another, what we have removed.

The best time to give your lawn its dandruff treatment is just before each shampoo. In the cool weather states, that means April, June and September; in the West and South it means October.

You must de-thatch before you do any other job on your lawn, or the others will be all for nothing.

Shampoo Your Lawn

Since we are comparing lawn care to a scalp treatment that we would give to ourselves, the next logical step after removing dandruff from our scalps would be shampooing.

Why not do the same to your lawn? That's what I am recommending. Shampoo your lawn with soap and water.

Professionally, we refer to this soap treatment as a surfactant and use it regularly on greens and fairways to relieve surface tension.

To understand surface tension, you need only to recall your childhood days when you would sit and spit into the dust and watch it just sit there in a ball and not soak in. Surface tension prevented penetration.

When we spray our lawn area with a mild solution of soap and water, we break through this invisible barrier which causes lawns to burn up in hot weather or makes us disappointed with the brand of fertilizer we are using when we don't get the results we expect. It really is not the fertilizer's fault at all. Surface tension is preventing the nitrogen from getting down to the roots. Instead it is only going down into the sewers, causing algae and weeds in our rivers, ponds, lakes and streams.

The proper quantities are one ounce of liquid soap per ten gallons of water, applied from a hose-end type lawn sprayer. Ten gallons should be applied to each 1,500 square feet.

I use a bio-degradable liquid dish soap only. This is a mild soap that does not contain any oil or harsh detergents.

Shampoo the lawn soon after the snows melt in the North and East, and as soon as the rains stop in the West. In the southern states begin any time. Lawn shampooing should be repeated at least once a month throughout the growing season.

I have explained surface tension as being one reason for applying a surfactant, but it is just one.

This shampoo will wash off the airborne soot and dust that attaches itself to the surface of the blades, clogging up the pores and cells that permit the plants to manufacture their own food through the process known as photosynthesis. When these cells are plugged up, the plant becomes anemic, turns yellow and pale (as we do when we have anemia) and, if not checked, will die.

Next, since this soap is sort of sticky and constantly moist, it holds water moisture longer. This means we do not need to water our lawns as often.

This lawn-washing system makes your garden dollar stretch because it is a spreader-sticker, which catches the nitrogen in your fertilizer when it is washed out of its regular carrier. By "regular carrier" I mean the type of material onto which the manufacturer sprays the nitrogen so that the bag is full before the nitrogen can wash down the sewer.

The presence of the soap makes your weed killer more effective by helping it to stick to the foliage where it belongs.

We certainly can't forget insects. Yes, the simple shampoo will act as a preventative insecticide against soil insects: bugs aren't too much different from us humans when it comes to tastes. Soap wasn't designed to eat, and neither of us cares for the taste of it. When it is necessary to use an insecticide, this same soap will hold it in place to do the job effectively.

"Bio-degradable" should be explained here, so that you will understand that by using soap you are not adding to pollution, but rather improving the environment. A bio-degradable substance is one that will break down and become an active part of the soil, instead of causing damage.

Believe it or not, your lawn will fairly sparkle like your

favorite crystal and china when it has been washed properly. Remember, a clean lawn is a healthy lawn.

You are probably wondering how long this lawn-washing procedure has been used and recommended. At least the sixty-eight years that Grandma Putnam was alive. And I'll just bet that a lot of you can recall your parents and grandparents pouring dish and wash water which did not contain grease or bleach over the roses and other plants, as well as the lawn.

You will be amazed at the difference in appearance of your lawn after the first shampoo.

Jog Your Lawn to Health

To prevent the dandruff from building up and the surface tension from returning, it is necessary to massage the turf area, to give it a little exercise. No, I am not going to suggest that you get down on your hands and knees and literally massage your grass with your hands; I suggest that you stand up and use your feet. Many of today's doctors recommend—and with good reason—that we jog every day. So what do we do, we don our sweat suits each morning and run up and down the roadside, when what we really should do is put on a pair of track spikes, baseball or golf shoes and run around our own yards. The spikes are the secret. They punch holes in the soil which let water and air down to the roots and let fertilizer get deeper into the soil. Jogging on your lawn breaks up compaction, the pressing down of the soil which crushes and smothers the roots. If you are reluctant to engage in this strenuous activity just for your lawn's sake, I suggest that you wear your golf spikes whenever you are working in your yard and take a walk each evening through your garden and say goodnight to the many friends that you have invited to live permanently in your garden. If you have small children in the neighborhood, encourage them to stop by to play a little catch with you, but make sure they wear spikes. And remember, no sliding.

What we are really after is aeration, which is an important factor for root structure. You can rent a machine, called a lawn plugger, that will remove plugs from your lawn, or you can purchase a hand tool called a plugger. In any case, your lawn would appreciate this treatment once a year in the late spring after you have de-thatched and shampooed for the first time. When using a lawn plugger, leave the plugs of soil on the lawn. When you are finished, go back and break them up with the back of a rake and spread them around. This then acts as a top dressing. Again, you can see where you are practicing ecology by returning to the good earth what might well have been thrown away.

If you will just relax and tune in to Mother Nature's frequency, you will find that your gardening can keep you healthy as much as it does the garden.

Lawn Rolling: The Caissons Went Rolling Along

If you can shut your eyes and picture those big, heavy wagons rolling across Flanders Field, each loaded with the heavy weight of a cannon, you can imagine the damage done to the poor earth below.

Mother Nature does not send a huge log rolling across a meadow to flatten it out just because it has a hump or two, nor does she hurtle a huge rock around to pound a knoll or two back into place. No, she gently nudges it back into place with a few light rains and sends the gophers, moles or angleworms over to undermine it so there is room for it to settle down.

I am by no means suggesting that you call the moles and gophers over, and the worms don't understand your lingo so you must do the job for them—but not with a roller. Rollers are built and designed to compact surfaces for reinforcement and to eliminate the possibility of soil expansion. To wit, parking lots, hard, strong and firm. If you want your lawn to be a parking lot, use a roller. If not, go the gentle way.

If after a hard winter, you have some humps and lumps, use a plugger and remove some of the surplus soil so that when you water, the remaining surface will have somewhere to expand to. Sort of like the air out of a balloon.

Or you might use a sod spade and cut around the mound, lift it off, remove the surplus soil and replace the turf cover.

Gullies and tire tracks are repaired in reverse: lift, refill and replace.

On an established lawn, the weight of a roller causes the soil to be packed down, thus shutting out penetration when warm weather comes, and it crushes the roots, causing them to suffocate.

The only time I recommend the use of a lawn roller is when seeding a brand new lawn. And this is an empty roller, used only to seat the seed in the newly prepared soil, that it might get a firmer grip. The other use is when laying sod, and again, only enough weight should be added to allow the roots of the new sod to touch the new soil beneath firmly and push the joints and butt ends together to insure a good knit.

I am sure that I will not win the lawn roller manufacturers' award again this year.

No Brush Cuts

Lawn cutting is probably the most taken-for-granted job around the yard. It is also the most begrudging. There is, believe it or not, a right time and a right way to cut any type of turf, and if you do not adhere to these, you can defeat your whole purpose.

We do not just cut a lawn to make it look nice. The major reason is to stimulate branching. When there are more plant surfaces, more photosynthesis can take place, thus enabling the rhizome, or growing factory, to utilize food. This food is then changed into chlorophyll, which is sent back through the system, giving the grass a rich green color.

The next reason we cut is to keep the blades standing tall and straight. No one likes to see a proud person or plant stoop-shouldered. And when grass is allowed to grow too tall, it bends over onto the blade next to it, shading its neighbor's roots and causing it to get tired and lean on the next. You end up with everybody lying down on the job.

Yet another reason for cutting the turf is to stimulate the chlorophyll (blood) flow. When you cut the tops off the blades, the rhizome sends a rush of fluid way up top to seal the fresh cut.

By the way, never think of a blade of grass as being a weakling. It is probably stronger than you or I. It is said that a blade of grass forcing its way through the soil exerts the equivalent of 4,600 pounds per square inch of thrust. That is probably a good proportion of the space-shot power. By the way, be very careful where you decide to lie down for a nap. You might wake up with some funny looking hair growing on your chest.

To Cut or Not to Cut, That Is the Question!

Who would ever think there is a right time to cut a lawn? Any good grass grower! Let's cover why first. When grass is cut, it is exposed to elements that it has thus far been protected from, namely heat and surface winds. Secondly, the tunnels to the roots are also exposed for a brief period of time to these same elements, which come as a shock and a surprise. It is like working in an air-conditioned office all day and walking outside into ninety-degree weather. It shocks your system and takes your breath away for a moment or two.

I have found that the best time for cutting the lawn is in the evening when it has cooled down some and the dry winds have subsided. This will also make it more comfortable for you. The grass will then have several hours to adjust to the new haircut before the noonday sun reaches its peak.

Now another thing to take into consideration when attempting to cut is the moisture content in both the soil and the blade. A barber wants your hair dry when he cuts, so that it doesn't mat down or stick together. That would cause pulling and pinching, and you would end up with festered hairs at the roots. Grass will have the same problems if you attempt to cut it when it is wet. It will mat down, sticking to the blades and inside of the machine, thus causing the lawn mower to pull the ends off instead of cutting them clean.

When grass is pulled, it dislodges the roots or runners, as the case may be, and causes a festering condition, thus causing the rhizome to die. And you end up with what looks like lawn "mange." The grass will drop out just as your hair. The lawn should be dry when cut, and you should water it early next morning.

The frequency with which you cut your lawn is another factor which will determine both its quality and density. The blue grasses, Merion and Kentucky, will be the greenest and healthiest if they are cut one-and-a-half to two inches every two days, and the clippings removed each time. The ryes and fescues should be cut twice a week, bent grasses every other day, and dichondra once a week. That's right, once a week. Some think that dichondra should be cut only once a month, but that is not so.

By the way, there are commercial growth inhibitors available, but I recommend them only for commercial use. At no time do I recommend that you lower a blade in season and give your lawn a brush cut.

HOW TO MOW

Have you heard that you can mow a lawn in any direction you want? I am sure this is right to some extent. However, for the sake of the grass's health and your lawn's appearance, I suggest that we copy the approved method of the Greens Superintendent and the sod growers.

It is important that we not walk on the grass area we are about to mow, as this tends to make it lie down, and we do not get an even cut.

Mow around the exterior of your lawn area first, perhaps two widths. This means the flower beds that border your lawn. Do not enter the center yet. Each time you cut your lawn, reverse the starting direction of this exterior cut.

Now begin a normal cross-lawn cut. As you approach tree wells and center beds, mow two-width circles around these and proceed on with your normal cutting practice until you have finished. The next time you cut the lawn, you will cut in a totally different direction so that the grass is never forced to grow in one direction. There are eight directions to cut: from north to south, south to north, west to east, east to west, southwest to northeast, northeast to southwest, northwest to southeast, and from southeast to northwest.

If you alternate your mowing pattern, your lawn will look like a picture.

The type of machine you use to cut your lawn will also affect the health and appearance of the grass plants themselves.

It is important to understand that you must use a sharp blade at all times. A dull blade will rip, tear and beat the grass to death, shattering the ends of the blades and leaving the lawn with a tannish, filmy appearance where the ends have dried out.

I suggest that you buy a new blade for rotary mowers each year, alternating with last year's blade every month. Have the spare one sharpened when you change. A reel type mover presents a different problem; I run a flat stone over the blade edges before I begin to mow, to take off the nicks and bumps that could cause tearing, and I have it sharpened once a month by a professional.

There are now plastic blades on the market for rotary lawn mowers, which are just as effective as steel and safer. It is again advisable to buy two and switch off. These blades can also be sharpened and balanced in the normal manner by a professional mower shop.

The argument about which is best, rotary or reel, power or hand, will not be settled by my opinion or this book. However, I do intend to give my opinion. I recommend, for the sake of saving time, a self-propelled machine, no matter what type you use. Next, I do not drive or fly blind. I like to see what's coming or going, so I use a reel type, as do most golf courses and sod growers.

Rotary lawn mowers do a fine job if they are sharp, tuned and balanced, and, you keep the undercarriage free of grass. Do not stop and start any more than necessary, and then only on a solid surface, free from stones (when possible). Stopping may create settling circles where the mower is allowed to sit with the blade rotating.

Bent grass must be cut with a special reel mower containing seven blades, as must most southern and western grasses.

Do not allow grass clippings to lie on the lawn, as this will just increase the thatch buildup that you will need to remove later.

Grass clippings can be added to your compost pile or given to a farmer who is fattening up cattle. In either case, you are again practicing ecology.

Grass Can't Swim

The most important ingredient for proper growth of any plant is water. Without it, we all know that plants, like people, would dry up, or dehydrate. Too much water, on the other hand, tends to make us blow up, or bloat. It will do the same to grass, making it fat, soft and tender,

much like your hands after they have been in dishwater too long.

In this bloated state, both your hands and your lawn can easily be injured because the tissue is soft. The secret: keep your lawn strong, firm and healthy with proper watering.

Types of Water

Oh yes! There are different types of water. The basic scientific formula is H_2O, but then we go on from there with natural trace elements that may be added as the moisture falls in the form of rain or snow.

For instance, nitrogen. During an electrical storm, the rain particles are charged with as much as seventy-eight percent nitrogen, which accounts for the fresh, green look of a lawn after a thunderstorm. This then means that rain water is best.

Well water has trace elements that it picks up from the soil, like iron, the blood builder for you and me; but it does not pick up as much nitrogen as rain water.

Last we have tap water. This has many, many trace elements, plus chemical additives. One of these trace elements is fluoride, which, in small amounts, helps build strong teeth. One of the chemical additives is chlorine, which helps to purify the water. Some of these chemical additives hurt plants, and there is one that especially harms them and also sometimes hurts the human system. The same thing that bothers the human system bothers the grass: namely, salt. Who would ever water with salt? You do every time you turn on a normal faucet. There are sodium salt additives in the public water systems, put in for our good health, strong teeth, strong bones, etc. Well, salt in the proper form is healthy for the human system, but not for plants. As a matter of fact, it kills more lawns than anything else.

So what we look for in water is purity. Of course, the best water we could get is that that would be collected from the downspouts in the homes that our grandparents had, or in older homes where there was such a thing as a cistern. Or the other thing is the rain barrel, and I don't know why, with the antique-collecting rage that's going on right now, we couldn't just as easily have a rain barrel. I have one. That water is so pure that not only does it not have the impurities in the trace elements that plants don't like, but as a bonus, it contains the purest and mildest, yet strongest, fertilizer that there possibly is: 78-21-1. That's right, that's what is in the air right now above our heads. One pound of actual nitrogen for one cubic foot of iron, seventy-eight percent nitrogen, twenty-one percent phosphorus, one percent inert matter.

If we could collect that, we wouldn't need to water. But since we can't, we try to achieve the same results the best way we can.

The way we can purify the water going into our systems is by picking up a thing that was around a few years ago and is now returning. It's called a robot gardener. This was a plastic apparatus into which you put fertilizer cartridges or insecticide or pesticide cartridges. The robot dissolved the cartridges and then disseminated the fertilizer out onto the lawn. But now what we do is fill it full of agricultural charcoal (available at any garden center, any variety store, any place where garden supplies are sold), and as the water passes over the charcoal, it becomes purified and we get the least possible amount of salts.

The next best thing for plants, of course, would be the water collected from your dehumidifier or from defrosting your refrigerator. But since there wouldn't be enough for anything but your house plants or your garden, we can't count on that.

Therefore, we must depend on Jupiter Fluvius, Mother Nature's right-hand man, god of the rains, and on our own ability to use filtered water wherever possible.

The Time to Water

It's been argued by many experts in many ways. But judging from my experience, I would say that there *is* a right time and a wrong time to water. The best time is just after the sun comes up. While the dew is still on the lawn, turn on your sprinkler and water. You should allow the hose to run so that you get deep penetration, because that's what you want. Deep penetration means deep roots. Shallow watering, or shallow penetration, means that the roots will stay close to the surface of the soil and, therefore, that when you stop watering, the soil will dry out very quickly and the roots will dry out also. When the roots dry out, the rhizome is injured, and when that happens, the top of the plant dies. Soon you have a brown lawn.

Now the reason for early watering is to permit the lawn to dry out slowly and to be dry by the time evening comes when the night dews and coolness set in. If your lawn is wet when the evening dew comes on, it doesn't have a chance to dry out. When the lawn is continually soggy, there's a great probability that fungi or other lawn diseases will develop. The top of the grass is cool, and the earth, down inside, stays warm. The fertilizer, which has nitrogen in it, makes the soil warm. So if you add water late in the afternoon or evening, you create ideal incubating conditions for lawn diseases. My advice is to go a little out of your way to make sure that somebody's responsible for early morning watering.

A very good comparison and, I think, one that we can easily understand, would be the following: suppose on a very hot summer night, before you went to bed, your wife took off your bed sheets, soaked them in a bathtub of cold water, threw a couple of buckets of ice water on the mattress, took your pajamas and made them soaking wet, and put all of that back on the bed. Then, you climbed into bed, pulled the covers over you, leaving the windows open (we're trying to duplicate your lawn's living conditions), and went to sleep. I'll bet by the end of three days you'd have a little fungus-amungus too!

Because you couldn't dry out, your skin systems would itch, and you would scratch. That's what happens to the plant tissue. It itches, scratches and catches all of the diseases there are.

The argument that I receive most often on my opinion of early-morning watering is, "How come the golf courses water all night long and don't have a lot of diseases?"

Well, I think that's relatively simple. We don't collect green fees, so we don't have to worry about the lawn being watered. And, besides that, the golf courses spend a great deal of money spraying with fungicides, probably once or, in many cases, twice a week, to combat the disease of fungus. So, you see, that's not much of an argument.

How to Water

The job of watering seems simple, but it's misunderstood in many cases. I said earlier that we want to water deep. Well, how deep is deep?

For the average lawn, the cool grasses, such as Merion and Kentucky blue, the ryes (which are both cool and warm), the red fescues, *Poa trivialis,* or any other cool grass: water to a depth of about three inches. For dichondra, zoysia, and Bermuda, it's a good idea to water to a depth of two inches. Even though you are in sandy soil, water deep so that the roots get used to staying down there.

How do you know when you have two, three or four inches? That's simple. Take a coffee can or a used fruit tin can and place it out at the farthest point that the water reaches. When the can is full, three or four inches, or whatever you've determined you want, stop watering. The can acts as a homemade water meter.

It's a good idea to do this at least twice a week. It isn't going to do your lawn any good if you water a little every day, because a little every day doesn't help at all. As a matter of fact, it harms, because that's shallow watering, and the lawn will react by growing shallow roots, which weakens it and makes it susceptible to all sorts of damage.

Pick a Sprinkler

There are all kinds of lawn sprinklers, and for me to list or illustrate every type on the market today would take up the greater part of this book. The best system of course, if you can afford it, is an automatic one, with a water meter and timer, that goes on at a set time. It waters for a given period at a constant pressure, giving off a certain amount of water to the depth that you indicate. That's the best, and it's also the most expensive. But it may not be feasible, and a lot of people don't want to tear up their lawns. So they go to a regular sprinkler.

There are some home watering systems at your local department store or garden center that you can buy. They are do-it-yourself kits, and they are very effective and very good. And they cost only about one tenth of what the professionally installed system costs.

What type of sprinkler do you use if you can't afford the first and don't want to bother with the second? You use a regular lawn sprinkler. I've found that the one that puts down the most water and gets it out there the fastest and heaviest is the pulsator that goes, "chicka-chicka-chicka-chicka-chicka." You can regulate the spray to a small circle or a large one. They cover a large area, and four of them will do approximately 5,000 square feet at a time.

The wand sprinklers are good for those hard-to-get-at places. There are some with adjustable heads that do an oblong, square, circle or rectangle. There are all kinds of them, and any of them will work. It's just a matter of economics and how long you want to wait to get the water down.

Feeding with liquids at the same time you sprinkle is not highly recommended, at least not in my book, because I find that people have a tendency to forget, or overfeed, and this causes the lawn to burn. However, feeding with a hose-end sprayer is highly recommended. That's the jar that fits on the end of the hose, and you put the liquid fertilizer into it. That is very good, but it's not to be considered as a watering of the lawn. It would only be considered a light daily sprinkling, and this should be done after the lawn has been watered. The automatic feeders are definitely not for the amateur. I have never found them used successfully by an amateur.

The phrase, "Grass can't swim," is used more to bring to your attention the fact that plants, especially grass plants, are just like human beings. We all need a certain amount of water in our diet in order to keep ourselves healthy. But too much of it will get us in trouble. We humans, since we breathe, drown. Grass is the same way. It depends on oxygen, if too much water is used and the roots are kept under water or are submerged for a period of time, or if the top of the grass plant is submerged, then the plant smothers. Therefore we have to remember not to put down too much water.

You can recall seeing light yellow or soggy spots, in a lawn, that have become off-color as a result of drowning. So it's a good idea not to water all day and all night in soil that isn't well drained.

Clay soils, as a rule, are not well drained. Grass will drown in clay soil where there are pockets in the ground, and where the ground is not level or has not been graded to let water run off of it. So never make a swimming pool out of your yard and expect the grass to live.

Fertilizers: Feed Your Lawn or Forget It

As to the best kind of fertilizers, there are no best kinds. I'm sorry, Jupiter Fluvius, mighty mythical rain god—

your thunder brew, 78-21-1, is by far the best, but then it is not always available. I am referring to a manufactured product.

Your lawn doesn't give a tinker's darn what you feed it. It just wants to eat—for as long as possible and as often as possible. I have found the best results are attained, in every part of the country, if you feed monthly at half the rate suggested by the manufacturer. Switch formulas every other time to vary the lawn's diet, or it will get bored and will not react after a while, just as you and I would get bored by a repetitive, day-in day-out diet.

I also recommend that you begin and end each growing season with a complete feeding as prescribed by the manufacturer. In the cool parts of the country, do this just before the snow season and again just after. In the winter rainy areas, do this just before and after the rains. In the South, October and May seem to do the job, and in the dry West, October and February will fill the bill.

Formulas Are Confusing

The three most common trace elements that all plants need are nitrogen, phosphorus and potash. The numbers on the front of most lawn food bags indicate the percentage of each of these three elements that is contained in the particular product. You need only multiply each of these numbers by the weight of the bag to find out, in weight, what you are getting for your money. In most cases we are after all the nitrogen we can get. You may be wondering what the rest of the bag is full of. It is the carrier or filler that the manufacturer uses to fill up the bag so you can safely put it through your spreader.

How much should you buy? As professionals, we try to spread one pound of actual nitrogen per 1,000 square feet of lawn area each time we apply.

Here is a simple formula that you can use to determine how many bags of lawn food you will need to get one pound of nitrogen per 1,000 square feet in each application.

Multiply the length of your lot by the width, then

divide by ten. Then divide *that* by the amount of nitrogen
(the first number on the bag) and this will tell you
exactly how many pounds to buy. Example: using a
10-6-4 lawn food on a 50′ x 100′ lawn: 50 x 100=5,000
square feet ÷ 10=500 ÷ (N) 10=50 pounds. Try it
with your lot and your favorite brand fertilizer formula.

Don't forget, I suggested you only apply one pound of
nitrogen twice a year and one-half pound of nitrogen per
1,000 square feet each month.

SPREADING

I have seen the oddest patterns on some lawn, because
the garden buff either had a damaged spreader or poor
vision, or was drunk. Do not apply lawn food if any of
these is the case.

The type of spreader has a great bearing on the end
result. I find that the broadest type, which throws the food
in a flaring pattern, is the fastest, neatest and safest.

To avoid odd patterns, I cut the spreader recommendation in half and go back and forth over the area—first
in one direction, then the other. That way there are no
missed areas.

This chapter on lawn food may seem short for such an
important area of gardening, but that is only because it
is so simple. Just treat your lawn's appetite as you would
your own, and the end result will be the same.

Check with the local stores selling lawn food to see
what formulas are popular for your part of the country,
and then let your pocket book determine the purchase.

Beat the Weeds

The dictionary sums up the situation as it presently per-
tains to our precious lawn: "Weed, n. Any plant growing
uncultivated, useless or troublesome, offensive or hurtful."
If there is anything in this whole wide world that will make
the hair stand up on the back of my neck, it is to come
out into the yard some bright, sunny morning and find a
fresh, fluffy yellow head poking its way through the blades

of a bright green lawn. Today one dandelion, tomorrow hundreds. What is a green thumb to do?

The first thing to do is relax. All too often we get so upset that we begin to run around like a chicken with his head cut off, and we end up compounding the situation—wasting time, effort and money.

Weeds are not all that bad. As a matter of fact, I haven't found a weed I couldn't like. I don't always like it where I find it, but eventually we reach a mutual understanding on where we will both enjoy the other's company.

I grow, cultivate, feed, harvest and eat dandelion greens. I grow, cultivate, feed, harvest, brew and drink the golden nectar resulting from the yellow flowers of the dandelion. So, you see, t'aint all bad having such a versatile weed handy. I might also remind you that some of our ancestors worshipped the weeds. The gospel was called Herbal, and one of the most sacred of the weeds was the one we call plantain, because it brought the bad spirits out of a person. So you see, you're not just dealing with any old stray cat. Some of the weeds in your garden played a part in our history.

When a sod grower is looking for additional land to plant, or a golf course designer is seeking a location for a new course, they both look for land with a good weed cover, because this tells them that the soil is fertile and that they can overcome the unwanted weeds without much difficulty by using any one of the modern herbicides (weed killers).

Next, you should know what you are looking for and at. Many a poor soul has completely destroyed his lawn by purchasing the wrong type of control, one which destroyed the good grasses and left the unwanted plants to thrive.

IDENTIFYING WEEDS

For the sake of simplification, let's concentrate on the two categories that you will meet on your journey with Mother Nature.

The first will be the "monocot," or grassy weed, such as goosegrass, crab grass, nut grass, foxtail, dallis grass and witch grass. These few, the annual monocots, live one full season and reseed themselves. Then the old foliage dies, never to return. But the new seed sprouts a hundred-thousandfold—which can cause one heck of an Excedrin headache for someone who's trying to grow a good-looking lawn.

Tall fescues, timothy, orchard grass and nimble-will are perennial monocots, and they return each year from the rhizome.

The second category is the "dicot," or the broad-leafed weed. In this category we find our most persistent pests. Purslane, chickweed, dandelion, henbit, oxalis, thistle, plantain, buckhorn, clover, ground ivy and knotweed are all dicots.

Now walk out and look at your lawn and its weedy inhabitants. Can you recognize them? What next?

CONTROL

I have found that when a lawn is de-thatched properly and often, shampooed, aerated, fed well, watered and mowed often, weeds are at a minimum, and very few chemical controls are necessary. So obviously this is the best method of control.

If your lawn is less healthy and you have a weed problem, try the following. Broad-leaf weeds can be controlled with 2, 4-D, a growth stimulator hormone that makes the plants grow themselves to death, combined with banvel, an herbicide. These weed killers are packaged under various brand names and are extremely effective when used as directed.

The monocots, or annual grassy weeds, are best controlled with a pre-emergence treatment which kills the seed when it is dormant, before it can germinate or sprout in the spring. The chemical compound bandane has been a safe and effective one for me, and can be purchased under many popular brand names.

But beware! Not all lawns are grass, as some unsuspecting easterners have discovered when they moved west and south and met dichondra, a ground-cover substitute for grass and a member of the morning-glory family. If you use a common weed-killer on this type of lawn, you can kiss it all goodbye.

When you move in and can't identify your variety of lawn, visit your local nurseryman with a sample of the turf area. It sure is better to be safe than sorry.

Time is of the essence. The secret to successful weed-control is timing. The broad-leaf weeds (dicots) can be effectively destroyed by a combination of 2,4-D and banvel applied while the weeds are growing their best in the early spring, not when it is hot and dry. Secondly, a liquid spray is more effective than a dry application. Any of the dry weed-killers and feeds will also give you great results, but they take a little longer in most cases. Remember, when using a liquid weed-killer, make sure there are no winds—or damage will occur to neighboring shrubs and flowers.

When using a dry weed-killer, apply it with the criss-cross method described in the lawn-feeding section.

The monocots, crab grass being the most devastating, are best controlled by applying a pre-emergence killer which contains the chemical bandane early in the spring before the evening temperatures get to fifty degrees, in a criss-cross pattern. To win this battle, you need only remember that you must concentrate on killing the seed, not the plant (as you do in the case of the grassy weeds).

I agree with my friend, Bob Hynes, who says he's never read so much folderol and confusing gardening poppycock as he has about weed control. He says it discourages him before he ever begins—and then he never does.

Lawn Diseases

Most lawns are grown under unnatural conditions. That is, they are expected to perform in soil, light and moisture conditions that are totally foreign to their natural habitat. These conditions make your lawn an ideal target for the many fungus diseases that attack a weak stand of grass.

The best defenses against these lawn diseases are, of course, the good cultural practices that we have discussed throughout this chapter. De-thatch and shampoo regularly to destroy the destructive spores. Aerate the soil with spikes whenever you're working on the lawn. Always remove the grass clippings when mowing. Water before 2:00 p.m. to allow the grass to dry out before evening. And feed regularly.

I have found that an application of garden gypsum—a natural soil conditioner, salt neutralizer, clay breaker-upper, nitrogen catcher, dog-urine-damage preventative and repairer, dry-spot firmer, and alkaline-soil neutralizer—certainly saves a lot of grief and aggravation. Gypsum will check any of the problems that are often mistaken for lawn diseases, as well as fertilizer burn.

Your very first step, however, should be to consider all of the possibilities before treating. Fungus diseases can be expensive, my friend, since the same type of antibiotics are used on the lawn as are used by your doctor to cure a fungus disease you might get.

Last, but not least, check for insect damage, which might be the cause of spots, specks, patches and bruises. You may now proceed with the identification of your lawn's particular infection.

The names, symptoms and suggested control of the following fungus diseases are designed to educate, not confuse. I am merely going to acquaint you with the time of the season you might expect one of these problems.

Leaf spot: This attacks Kentucky bluegrass in the early spring and fall when it is cool and damp. Reddish-brown to purplish spots appear on the leaf stem. Wash with soap and water and spray with Acti-Dione. Remove glass clippings and hold up heavy feeding until cured.

Fading-out: This attacks fescues, Kentucky blue, Merion blue, and bent lawns. It occurs in hot, humid weather. Lawns having this disease begin to turn yellow-green, as though they need iron or a good fertilizing. De-thatch, aerate, shampoo, and spray with Acti-Dione.

Brown patch: Brown patch attacks St. Augustine grass, rye, Kentucky and Merion blue, fescue, bent, and centipede grass. It occurs in humid regions during hot, wet weather. Brown patch will show up right after a heavy application of fertilizer during such weather, as it attacks new, lush growth. The grass will turn a brownish color in narrow streaks. Do not feed during these weather conditions; water early in the day. Apply Panogen Turf Fungicide as directed.

Rust: Rust attacks Merion and Kentucky bluegrass in the late summer, when heavy dew is present, and continues until frost. Reddish-brown or yellow-orange pustules develop on the leaf and stem. To control, shampoo and apply zineb. One repeat will probably be necessary.

Grease spot: This attacks most all grasses on poorly drained soil. It is most noticeable in the early morning. Circular spots, black in color and slimy, appear. Cut down on water, apply gypsum, and spray with captan.

Dollar spot: Attacks bent grass and fescue in the humid northern part of the country, but also occurs farther south and in northern California. It occurs in the cool, wet weather and on turf that is low in nitrogen. The grass will appear to have been damaged by a dull lawn-mower blade and to be bleached-out in color. When the disease is at its peak, a white web will be visible early in the morning when the dew is on the lawn. Control with soap and water and apply Acti-Dione.

Snow mold: This disease naturally attacks the grasses of the North. Greenskeepers dread it, as it loves the bent grasses, although it also attacks most of the bluegrasses. It occurs when snow covers the turf for a long period of time, under drifts, and where poor surface drainage is present. It looks like cotton on the leaves, or a slimy, pink growth. Apply gypsum in the fall and feed heavily in October with Milorganite. Shampoo and aerate.

Toadstools: They will grow wherever decayed organic material is buried. Tree stumps, builders' refuse, and peat moss deposits are some of the toadstools' food supplies. To control, you should, if possible, remove the source of food. Next, punch holes eight to ten inches deep all around the area and water well. Spray with soap and water and follow with a spraying of Panogen Turf Fungicide, applied directly down the holes. At least two applications will be necessary.

Fairy rings: These occur coast-to-coast, border-to-border, and get to about all the grasses. They are enlarging rings that continue to expand two to three feet a year, with toadstools growing in the edges of the ring. To attempt control, punch lots and lots of holes eight to ten inches deep inside the circle and half the distance to the outside. Water well, apply soap and water, and spray the surface with Acti-Dione. Repeat this a week later. Repeat again and pray!

In the case of lawn diseases, it is an absolute must to do everything possible to prevent their emergence, as the cure is costly and slow.

Insect Control

What's a body to do? You work hard to maintain a good-looking lawn, and just when it looks its best, wham! A brown spot appears here, a yellow patch there. You can't seem to win.

Hold on! Winners never quit and quitters never win. You have heard this most of your life. When you are fighting the insect armies you must keep this slogan in mind at all times. In order better to fight your enemies, the lawn insects, you must realize one thing: they appreciate you a lot more than you do them. As a matter of fact, they are probably your greatest admirers and praise your abilities to all of their friends. After all, you are their provider. You grow healthy, tender foliage to provide them with gourmet delights.

A good, strong, healthy bug would not think of eating old, tough, diseased grass and roots when he can have the best at your expense. I am sure that you now get the picture.

The healthier and better-looking your lawn is, the greater the possibility there is of an invasion by all of the bugs in the neighborhood.

By this time you are thinking, "To hell with a good-looking lawn, I think I'll tear the whole thing up, pour concrete and paint it green." Many a home gardener has had this thought, but soon passed it up when he discovered he could win.

I do not mean to bore you by continuing to remind you that the good cultural practices must be adhered to if we are to win. De-thatch, aerate, mow, water and shampoo.

Remember when parents used to wash a child's mouth out with soap? Well, try that on garden bugs. Believe me, it's just as effective. Pests and people have one thing in common: taste. They both like things that taste good, and neither the insects nor we like the taste of soap in any way, shape or form. Therefore, it is absolutely necessary that you use the mild shampoo on a regular basis to discourage the return of the insects.

Next, by applying Grand Prize Lawn and Garden Gypsum, which I have described as being the "Hadacol" of the garden kingdom, you are dealing those unwanted visitors yet another discomfort. This substance contains a considerable amount of natural sulphur, which acts as a preventative soil insecticide in the spring and fall.

Soon the bugs will ruin your reputation for being a good host throughout the insect kingdom, by saying you are a grower of bitter foliage. It doesn't matter where you live or what kind of lawn you have, gypsum and soap will act as safe preventative insecticides without changing the environment.

From time to time it will be necessary, to utilize a chemical control. When this becomes necessary, then *isolate* your problem, really dig into it, *identify* it as an insect problem and really look at the bug. Don't just take someone else's word for it simply because he once had a spot or brown patch like yours, which turned out to be insect damage. It could be one of the other problems that I have already acquainted you with, and by not knowing for sure, you could treat for the wrong thing with the wrong chemical, destroying all your hard work. Or you may endanger your health or that of your pets or the birds.

Now, treat your problem! Go to your local nurseryman with the intruder in a jar and confirm your identification if there is the least bit of doubt in your mind. Ask him for a recommendation as to what chemical will be necessary to treat the problem. Then read every single word on the label, including the copyright symbol. Buy only enough for the present application. Do not buy for the future. When applying the chemical control, use it only at the strength recommended by the manufacturer and for the period described. You see? We don't treat the plant world any differently from the way we would treat ourselves.

When I run into an insect infestation on a lawn, I follow these steps:

1. I remove the thatch in the infected area and for the same distance beyond.

2. I aerate the area with golf shoes and a pointed stick or other sharp object.

3. I water lightly.

4. I shampoo the area.

5. I apply the chemical prescribed as recommended.

6. I cover the treated area with a thin mesh cloth, such as a cheesecloth to discourage pets and birds from entering the area.

7. I keep adults and children from the area.

I follow these steps for the purpose of protecting the

plant area that is weak and ill and needs rest just like any other patient, and for the protection of any visitors that wander by.

Because I haven't come out against hard pesticides, I'll probably get many letters and cards from would-be conservationists and self-styled do-gooders who do not practice what they preach, but rather live by the adage "You do as I say, not as I do."

I have received so many pre-printed cards berating the hard pesticides, some signed and some not, that I could probably return next year's supply free to the sending organization.

We use and abuse medicine on ourselves and our loved ones, man and beast, day in and day out, in the form of both patented and prescribed medicine. We ballyhoo their benefits through advertisements in the press, on TV and over the radio. Take "Aspirin A," or drink "Solution B," or take "Zap" and sleep. Any one of these I am sure, is misused and kills many hundreds of people each year. Why isolate DDT for attack, when it has increased the yield per acre over the years so that we are now feeding millions more than we were formerly? The so-called hard pesticides have provided us with many benefits over the years. Banning them outright is somewhat like throwing out the baby with the bath water. I will leave this subject for you to digest and decide with one parting headline from a midwest newspaper editorial: "If DDT is so deadly, where are the bodies?"

Chemical types: When we have an insect problem and must use a chemical control, we will be dealing with one of two types. The first is a *contact killer,* which paralyzes the insect on contact. The second is a *stomach poison,* and this he must eat.

In the case of soil insects, such as grubs, I use Chlordane as recommended. When controlling the lawn moth and flying, crawling bugs and beetles on and around my lawn, I use a combination spray containing pyrethum and malathion.

Ants are best controlled with chlordane when the gypsum and soap solutions fail.

Be an Alert Gardener

If you are alert when working on your lawn, you can detect trouble when it begins and treat a small problem with as small an amount of chemical as is necessary. If you wait and hope, or expect it to go away by itself, you are asking for a much larger problem, needing much more expensive and time-consuming chemical control over a larger area.

I am reminded of the story my Grandma Putnam told me of the Indian brave who would not stamp out a small fire for fear of burning his new moccasins. He ran for help from a brave with old, worn moccasins. When they returned the little fire had grown into a big one that neither could stamp out. His moccasins did not burn, but his tepee burned to the ground with all the rest of his blankets and skins for clothes. Grandma Putnam reckons he was the first American to go south for the winter—without furs.

Fire is a good thing when used properly. Medicine is a lifesaver when used properly. Both are killers when abused. In the same way, when properly used, pesticides account for the agricultural abundance and our good health through the control of disease-spreading insects.

Pick a Winner: Seed Selection

Picking the right kind of grass seed for a lawn is just like picking a horse at the race track, or at least some folks use this system. If they like the name, that's what they plant. The result is usually the same in both cases—they run last.

Next, you can always find a "tout" handy to give you a little free advice. Sometimes it's very costly advice, because this horse usually runs out of the money. If the tout was so sure, he would bet on it himself.

The lawn tout is the vendor of the super-duper seed blend that he is selling at rock bottom prices. He implies it is so powerful that it will soon burst the seams of the bag it is in, it wants to grow so bad. But when you let it out to "run," it only lies there or "runs" down the sewer with the first rain, because it won't sprout in the soil.

Be a grass seed handicapper. Study the performance record and the breeding. Stick with thoroughbreds; they win more often.

No matter where you live or move to, you will find that a certain strain is a real stand-out, the growing champion of that area. That's the one for you.

When you have decided what variety will grow best in your area and your soil (for this you will need to know the drainage of your soil and how much sun and shade will be available), look for the action. Avoid buying grass seed or blends where they would not be likely to be found: drug stores, gas stations, liquor stores, etc. I have even had a barber try to hustle me on a special buy that he got. I am not saying that these people are not honest; in most cases, however, they themselves do not know that much about what they are buying. It could be old, poor germination, high weed-count or some other lame leg.

I suggest that you go to a garden center or section of a reputable merchant who has a specialist buying for him. *Read the labels.* The germination label is attached to the individually packaged seed and is (or should be) hanging on the bulk seed bin or bag. This special label will tell you the whole breeding record of the seed, much like the pony players' scratch sheet.

Germination: The percentage figure indicates what percent of the seeds in the bag will sprout. You want as close to one hundred percent as possible.

Purity: This tells you what percent of the seed is true to its name. Again, get as close to one hundred percent as possible.

Other grasses: This can be a real problem if you get the wrong grasses, especially tall fescue. Here you want as close to zero percent as possible. Then comes the big, bad wolf—weed-count. Be careful and again get as close to zero percent as possible. And lastly, inert material: this is chaff and shells.

Not all lawns are started from seed. Some begin as plugs of grass, sprigs or runners. Bermuda grass, some of the bents, St. Augustine grass and zoysia are planted from small plants and sprigs.

Dichondra, which is used as a lawn in California, is not a grass, but rather a ground cover, akin to the morning-glory. It can be grown from seed or plugs. Dichondra is reasonably easy to take care of but can keep you hopping if cut worms get a foothold.

When seeding a new lawn, I highly recommend that you use as high a percentage as possible of the permanent variety you have selected. I do not recommend that you buy a premixed blend. I would rather you do the mixing yourself. The same holds true when reseeding an old lawn. In the case of overseeding an established lawn, it is important that you use only the variety that you are trying to match up: Kentucky blue to Kentucky blue, Merion to Merion, Windsor to Windsor, and so on.

When overseeding in the Southwest, some of the South and Southern California, you will use an annual grass and not a blend. For instance, use only NK-100 rye straight, no combination.

It is possible to buy the purest seed—with the highest germination and lowest weed-count, no other grasses and not an ounce of inert matter—sow it into the richest soil, and not get a single blade of grass.

Grass, as you will discover, has a mind of its own, just like some horses that "tolerate" the jockey on their backs, but run their own races. They know when ; time to run, and they know how. Grass knows when it's time to grow and how, and if you rush it, it will balk. August 15 to September 20, give or take a few days, is the best time to sow seed in most every location of this big, beautiful land of ours, as this is the beginning of the harvest moon. The stars are in the right places and Mother Nature is calm and happy. The evenings are beginning to cool and more mois-ture is in the air. Now your new lawn will get up and grow!

But grass, like horses and people, can be fooled, and made to do something out of the ordinary. You can put blinders on a horse and lead him almost anywhere. People? Well, they put blinders on themselves and walk anywhere. Grass seed is no different. If you want to patch a dead spot, or speed up germination of a slow seed type like Merion, you must fool it into thinking it's fall!

To fool grass and get the garage floor or basement swept, add one cup of water with two tablespoons of tea (not leaves) to each pound of seed, mix well, place in a covered container and let stand in the refrigerator for five days. Remove from the refrigerator and spread out on the garage or basement floor and allow partial drying. Sweep the floor well, getting into all the corners and underneath cabinets and chests, being careful not to include glass, nails or grease. You are now ready to spread this combination of seed and dirt on your lawn.

You have accomplished two tricks at the same time. First, you have fooled the grass into believing that it woke up late from a cold damp winter and will have to rush now to take root and grow. Secondly, you have fooled whoever you got to sweep out your garage. He could have dried the damp seed some easier way!

Grandma Putnam used to call these her Honey-do jobs: Honey do this and Honey do that. She was a sweet soul and smart too, eh?

Starting from Scratch: Building a New Lawn

As the moving van pulls away and you stand on the porch surveying your very own piece of property, you are suddenly struck with a thought . . . "What am I going to do with this sand patch surrounding me?"

In many cases, as the moving van pulls away it also is taking your last buck. When many of us move into a new home, we have used up just about all our savings. Plus, by the time you make the down payment, the closing costs (which no one can figure out), and pay for the gas, water, phone, electric hook-up, the mover and the miscellaneous items needed for privacy, you're lucky if you can buy a loaf of bread and a quart of milk, let alone think about a lawn, trees, shrubs, evergreens or flowers. But since you have a reputation to build in your new neighborhood, you decide to build a lawn. Where do you start and what do you do?

You usually begin by swearing at the builder, whom you don't like anyhow, because you expected the Taj Mahal and he built a house that you are sure isn't as well constructed as the clubhouse you built in the back yard when you were only twelve years old. And now, with your shovel in hand, you begin to dig and find that he must have contracted with the city sanitation department to dump all of the old trash in your yard to get what he called a "finished grade," and you figure it is the movie location for the Battle of Italy, because the ruts are so deep. Nonetheless, it is yours, all yours, to do with as you please.

It would please you to have a beautiful lawn, so simmer down and let's get at it—you, me and Mother Nature. (By the way, don't expect too much from either her or me. We will just give a little advice here and there.)

Contrary to the beliefs of many, you can have a good, healthy, lush, green lawn, no matter what the soil content is, unless there is some chemical present. For instance, sometimes fill is brought from a construction site that had a heavy overflow of gasoline, oil or salt deposits. To make sure that this is not the case, smell the soil from various locations in your yard. If there are any strange smells that you cannot identify or that resemble petroleum, go to your local nurseryman and ask if he does soil tests or can get one done for you. If the soil turns out to be dead, by which I mean sterile, and nothing will grow as a result of the presence of a foreign chemical, contact your attorney. This little advice has come in handy for many of my clients.

Assuming that all is well, let's proceed. Put down your shovel. You won't need it for a day or two. Begin by picking up every loose object that you can lay your eyes and hands on: stones, bricks, tar paper, lumber, tree stumps, and glass. Do not pass over anything. If just a corner is in sight, work it out of the soil or it will haunt you later.

When you are sure you have picked up every rock, stone and pebble, ask your wife and mother-in-law to look it over. With their eyesight, you'll be amazed at what you missed.

Now I want you to apply fifty pounds of Grand Prize Garden Gypsum per 1,000 square feet of soil to the surface, any soil, clay, sand or loam matters not. Next, in snow country, add one hundred pounds of peat moss per 1,000 square feet. In the South, Southwest and West you can use old sawdust, leaf mold or steer manure in the same proportions. Finally, add fifty pounds of any garden food with a low nitrogen content—4-12-4 or 5-10-5 will do nicely. You don't want a big burst of growth; you want fat grass and healthy roots.

Here is where you will have to stretch your budget and rent a power tiller to grind up thoroughly the soil and the material that we have spread on top. Mix this all down from six to ten inches. Till back and forth, then criss-cross the area. When that's done, go over the same area from corner to corner and criss-cross that also. The secret is to get the soil as fine as possible in order to save you a lot of hand work.

Before you do anything else, take the rented machine back to save money. I have received mail galore for that simple suggestion. The rent goes on whether you use it or not.

You may now pick up the shovel and begin to work on your grade. Work the soil up around the foundation of your home, garage, sidewalks, drives, flower beds and trees. This is to force runoff and have proper drainage.

Look around. Any high mounds should be shaved, and any low pockets should be filled.

Getting the proper grade is going to take a little effort on your part. I suggest that you see if you can find an old bed spring from a local junk dealer or, perhaps, a neighbor. It won't hurt to ask. Tie a rope on the springs the way you would on the front of a sled, long enough so that you can put it around your waist and walk with it and it won't whack against your heels. Now walk in a large circle, overlapping as you go. Continue to drag, stopping only to fill in or shave off spots. When you are perfectly satisfied that you are level and that the grade runs away from trees, beds, buildings and drives, you may take up your rake and begin from the house and other buildings, trees, beds and walks, raking to the lowest point of the property all the stones and clods of earth that have not broken up.

You are now ready to seed. If it is late August or early September, you need not soak your seed or refrigerate it. I always do, however, to give myself an advantage. Just plan the seed venture a week ahead, and if it has to stay in the refrigerator a day or so longer, it won't hurt. Make sure that you dry the seed only enough to handle it and so it will separate. The quantity of seed can be determined from the grass seed chart.

To spread the seed for the best coverage, I have always found that hand broadcasting did the best job. First, I check the wind direction by throwing a few small scraps of paper into the air. Having done this, I back across the property with my back to the wind and throw the seed out ahead of me. When I have covered the area, I then go back and re-broadcast cross-wind. I have then crisscrossed and laid down a heavy cover.

Seed has been spread, so I then use the back of my bow rake to cover the seed just enough to discourage the birds from taking it and the wind from blowing it away.

With an empty roller, roll the area to make the seed come in contact with the soil. Do not use a full, heavy roller or you will compact the soil; if you do that you can kiss your lawn goodbye before it even gets a start. Watering is the only thing left to do in order to get your lawn started. Keep the newly seeded soil moist at all times. During warm, windy weather you may have to sprinkle several times a day. Moisten, do not soak or drench the area, or the seed will wash away.

Cutting will begin as soon as the new grass is one and one-half to two inches in height. Mow with a sharp blade at a height of one and one-half inches.

Feed the new lawn as soon as it has been cut four times. Use a light-weight, non-burning, balanced lawn food, and then continue on a normal lawn program.

When planting stolons, sprigs or small plants, I find that I get a better start and hold if I dip the roots into water before I place them in the ground. When planting the warm grasses, I do not plant in straight lines; I make odd patterns and plant extremely heavily. When you purchase your grass stolons, buy about twenty-five percent more than is recommended. Water, mow and feed just like a seeded lawn.

Seed Chart

COMMON LAWN GRASS SEEDS	RATE 1000 FEET	TONE OF GREEN	LOCATION AND USE
KENTUCKY BLUEGRASS (*Poa pratensis*)	2 lbs.	Medium	Sunny, will tolerate slight shade. Medium texture.
MERION BLUEGRASS (*Poa pratensis*)	1 lb.	Dark	Sunny, will tolerate slight shade. Medium texture.
ROUGH STALK MEADOW (*Poa trivialis*)	2 lbs.	Light	Wet, shade. Shiny leaf.
CHEWINGS FESCUE (*Festuca rubra*, var. *fallax*)	3 lbs.	Medium	Dry, shade and poor sandy soil. Fine texture.
CREEPING RED FESCUE (*Festuca rubra*)	3 lbs.	Medium	Sandy soil. Fine texture.
HIGHLAND BENT (*Agrostis tenuis*)	½-1 lb.	Dark	Sun and light shade. Fine texture.

COMMON LAWN GRASS SEEDS	RATE 1000 FEET	TONE OF GREEN	LOCATION AND USE
TALL FESCUE (*Festuca elatior*)	6-10 lbs.	Light	Athletic fields, etc. Coarse, striated leaf.
ASTORIA BENT (*Agrostis tenuis*)	½-1 lb.	Bright	Sun and light shade. Fine texture.
SEASIDE CREEPING BENT (*Agrostis maritima*)	½-1 lb.	Medium	Sun and light shade. Fine texture.
PENNCROSS CREEPING BENT (*Agrostis palustris*)	½-1 lb.	Dark	Sun and light shade. Fine texture.
RED TOP (*Agrostis alba*)	1-1½ lbs.	Medium	Used in mixtures. Medium texture.
ANNUAL RYE GRASS (*Lolium multiflorum*)	3-4 lbs.	Medium	Temporary lawns and in mixtures. Coarse texture.
PERENNIAL RYE GRASS (*Lolium perenne*)	3-4 lbs.	Dark	Temporary lawns and in mixtures. Coarse, shiny leaf.

COMMON LAWN PLANTED PLUGS	RATE PER FOOT	TONE OF GREEN	LOCATION
BERMUDA	1 sprig	Medium	Sun and dry. Coarse texture.
ST. AUGUSTINE	1 plug	Medium	Sun and dry. Coarse texture.
ZOYSIA	1 plug	Medium	Sun and dry. Coarse texture.

Face Lifting: Rebuilding an Old Lawn

For one reason or another, a lawn can get old. We won't even bother to ask why. But like a plastic surgeon, we can take the sag out of the old face and make it look as good as new.

If you have just moved into a home, and the lawn has been neglected, or if you suddenly get interested in a little home gardening, here is a good way to get started.

The best time to rebuild is in the fall, around September,

just after the children have returned to school. This will give the lawn even odds for survival—without the pounding of little feet.

Refrigerate your seed at this time, referring to the seed-selection section of this book for instructions.

Begin by either renting a power renovator or purchasing a roto-rake bar that converts your rotary lawn mower into a de-thatching machine. Go over your entire lawn using the criss-cross method. Then rake up all of the debris that the machine brings to the surface, power rake it again, and remove the balance of the thatch.

Apply fifty pounds of gypsum per 2,000 square feet, and follow with an application of low-nitrogen lawn food. Some of these foods are called Winter Green or Winter Survival, but any will do. Apply at the recommended rate.

Overseed the rebuilt lawn at the same rate as a new lawn, referring to the chart for seed recommendations. Remember, your seed has been, or should be, germinated first for a week in the refrigerator.

After you have overseeded, apply a thin top dressing of half soil, half peat to the lawn area and roll with an empty roller just to make contact.

Water down lightly with a soap solution of one ounce Palmolive Green dish soap to ten gallons of water, over 2,000 square feet. This is to insure penetration and prevent compaction of the top dressing.

When new grass is two inches tall, mow and remove clippings. Continue to mow until grass stops growing.

Crab grass control can begin in early March in the North and in February in the West and South. Use any of the locally recommended pre-emerge chemicals and apply as recommended.

Begin a normal and well-planned lawn program in the spring and continue to follow it to a successful lawn.

New Blood Seeding

There have been many discussions among gramonologists (grass specialists) as to the advisability of introducing strangers to an existing lawn.

Some say you are asking for trouble, because the new seed can carry diseases to the already healthy present grasses. Others argue that if you do not add new seed, the old will become weak from inbreeding.

I am a believer that plants communicate with each other —that they discuss the events of the day. And I believe that after so many years of living with each other in the same spot, they run out of conversation and get bored with the same old faces day in and day out. Consequently, they become short-tempered with each other, like children that have been cooped up all winter, and they begin to squabble over little things.

When you overseed, you are bringing a stranger into the neighborhood from another part of the country with tales of new places: Oregon, Washington, or any of a number of places where grass seed is grown. The old grasses soon make new friends, learn some new ideas and, perhaps, change fashions.

There is also another factor that shows up: romance. There might just be a tall, dark stranger in the crowd. After all, grass doesn't just happen, although I will admit that some of the grass babies do arrive by stork. Also, by pigeon, sparrow, crow and most other birds. But while the babies arrive this way, so do hobos such as crab grass, quack grass and some other unwelcome visitors. When *you* pick your lawn's friends, there is a much better chance that they will be compatible. For this reason alone I recommend overseeding.

Overseeding is best done in the fall of the year, during the same period as recommended for new seeding: August 15 to September 20 in the snow country, and August 15 to October 15 in the West, South, and Southwest. Refrigerate the seed in the same manner and for the same period of time.

Before overseeding the cool grasses, you should follow these few rules:

1. De-thatch. Remove all old grass clippings and accumulated debris with the use of a lawn groom rake for the small lawn. The roto-rake bar, the conversion unit for

your rotary lawn mower, or a power rake (which you can rent) should be used on larger lawns.

2. Sow the seed by hand at half the rate recommended by the seed chart. Where you are trying to build up an existing stand of grass, like Merion or Kentucky blue, overseed with the same variety. Do not use a blend or mix, but use the purest seed with the best germination you can possibly buy. Do not buy any bargains, even though you may be turning down a real steal.

If you have an all-American lawn, a little of everything, then you can buy a blend, but make sure of the germination factor. After all, even if we buy weed seed, we want to know how much of it is going to grow.

If you are overseeding Bermuda or any of the warm grasses for winter color, you still germinate the seed by refrigerating it. Use only the best rye grass seed you can buy. The new NK-100 has turned out to be a good, strong grower.

Dichondra lawns, more than any other, need an annual overseeding to keep their nice, bright color and replace the plants that die out.

3. Top dress the turf area if it is in a sparse condition. Use a mixture of half garden soil and half peat moss. Spread the top dressing over the area at a rate of about one-eighth of an inch, I know that's pretty thin, but that's all that will be needed.

4. Feed the lawn and new seed with a low-nitrogen fertilizer. One of the Winter Green or Winter Guard types will do nicely.

5. Water well, but not heavily. As a matter of fact, until the new grass sprouts, which should be in a week or less, only dampen the lawn in the early morning. After the grass has sprouted, water heavily as described earlier.

6. Mow the lawn just before you start this project and then do not mow for at least seven days. Be sure to pick up the clippings.

For those of you who have heard that a lawn can get too thick, there isn't a golf superintendent who would not like to have that problem. If you de-thatch and aerate as I have recommended each fall, your lawn will be fat and sassy.

Instant Lawn: Sodding

In the last few years, the pre-grown lawn business has grown into a billion-dollar business. This affluent generation, seeming to want instant results in everything, rushes out and buys sod because it seems like the answer to an instant, trouble-free lawn. I am by no means criticizing this attitude, if you can afford it, but I do find fault with a great number of new homeowners who go to the expense of having a full-grown, mature landscape job done on their new homes. They begin with sod and end by planting fifteen to twenty-foot trees. Then, they let the whole works become diseased or die because they don't know how to take care of their "instant landscape" after they get it.

If you truly want to get involved with the good earth, preserve what we have, and build to repair and replenish what we have abused and neglected in the past, then I will go along with anything that you wish to do in gardening. But to think that something like sod comes to you as a full-grown adult and can take care of itself—*that* grinds me no end.

Sod is the flesh of the earth and is comparable to a skin graft. Before the plastic surgeon applies a skin graft to the human body, he removes the old and dead flesh. He repairs any other damage and makes any structural changes that are needed. Then he takes patches of flesh from another part of the body, similar to the area which needs repairs and grafts them. This bit of information is necessary so that you might better understand the points I am going to make in reference to laying sod.

If you are planning to lay sod instead of sow seed, then you must make up your mind what kind of grass you want.

There are many kinds and mixes available from border to border and coast to coast. Kentucky and Merion blue, Windsor, fescue sods, field sods for road construction, bent sod and mixed sod.

The prices will vary in most locations and for various reasons. Oh yes, you can be had, the same as with seed.

Here are a couple of ways they can get you. In a new sub-division, a truck will pull up, or a man dressed in work clothes will knock on your door and say that they are just finishing up a big apartment complex and have some good sod left over, and he will sod your lot for only sixty-five cents a roll, including labor. Now let me tell you, McGee, that ain't a bad deal in anybody's book, but you don't have the lot graded.

Well, the man has his equipment there, so for twenty-five dollars he will grade it for you. Oh what a deal! For whom? Here is what you get. Ten minutes later, the tractor arrives, drops the grading blade and levels off the lawn. They don't pick up the junk, they just push it around until it falls into a rut somewhere. They don't build up your grade away from the house, trees, buildings and drives. They don't add compost, feed or soil conditioners to the weak soil for good rooting action.

Next the truck arrives with about four helpers and the driver, and they begin to unroll and unload the sod so fast that you get dizzy just watching; but you can't smell a rat yet, eh?

What they are or could be laying in your yard is a buy-out. This is a stand of sod that may, for instance, have been grown on a peat or muck bog where a weed infestation occurred. In order to control that kind of infestation, they would have had to destroy the sod. So the grower offered it for some ridiculous price, from a nickel to fifteen cents a roll, and the buyer had to cut and load it himself. The grower also stays close by when it is being cut to make sure that the buyer doesn't cut too much top soil with the sod. So you are getting a thinly cut, weed-infected turf that is not worth the powder to blow it to H***.

The men end up by sweeping the walk, turning on your sprinklers, and telling you to keep it wet.

You pay the dough by cash or check and feel great. In the meantime, the operator goes to your bank to cash your check.

Here is what you end up with. Because of the poor

grade job, water runs into your basement, the buried treasure that they didn't remove will rot or work through the turf, the ruts will settle and you will have an uneven lawn with water pockets. They didn't roll the sod, so it separates and dries out on the ends. So all in all, what deal?

To lay sod, buy from a reputable dealer. Next, prepare the lawn in exactly the same way as you would for seeding a new lawn—including rolling, watering for the first week, mowing at the end of ten days, feeding at the end of the first month and continuing a regular lawn program.

To determine how many rolls of sod you will need for your yard, multiply the length by the width and divide by nine. The answer is how many rolls to buy. Be sure to subtract the area of buildings and walks.

Surface Insects That Plague Lawns

INSECTS	DAMAGE	CONTROL
ANTS	Annoying pests. May sting or bite. Attracted to food served outdoors.	Treat soil surface or individual mounds. Wash chlordane into soil after application.
ARMYWORMS	Feed on blades of grass near soil surface.	Treat lawn surface with garden soil.
BOX ELDER BUGS	Do not damage grass, but travel over lawns to enter homes, garages, etc.	Spray or dust basement and living areas as well as box elder tree trunks and plants where bugs congregate. Also treat breeding and hiding places.
CUTWORMS	Feed on blades of grass, cutting them off at soil surface.	Treat lawn surface.
CENTIPEDES	Live in lawns, but do not damage grass. Some species have a painful bite.	Treat lawn surface.
CHIGGERS	Bite causes severe itching and raises a welt.	Treat lawn surface.

INSECTS	DAMAGE	CONTROL
CHINCH BUGS	Feed on grass blades. Yellow spots appear in lawn and rapidly turn into brown, dead grass.	Mow lawn and remove thatch. Water grass thoroughly prior to applying chlordane spray. Apply chlordane spray and wash into soil surface. Repeat application within ten days and after next mowing of lawn. If a substantial population of chinch bugs cannot be seen prior to spraying, then the problem may be caused by white grubs or fungi.
EARWIGS	Travel over lawns to enter homes.	Treat lawn surface and trash areas, along foundations and around compost heaps.
GRASSHOPPERS	Eat blades of grass.	Treat lawn surface.
LAWN MOTHS (Sod Webworms)	Fly over lawns depositing eggs, which later hatch into damaging larvae. (See Sod Webworms.)	Apply control later in the evening. Use 5-10 gallons of water per 1,000 sq. ft.
MILLIPEDES	Live in lawns, but do not damage grass. Annoying pests.	Treat lawn surface.
MOSQUITOES	Hide and may breed in lawns.	Treat lawn surface, shrubs, and other foliage, low spots that collect water, trash areas, etc.
SLUGS	Annoying pests. Do not damage grass, but may damage garden plants.	Treat lawn surface.
SNAILS	Same as slugs.	Treat lawn surface.
SPIDERS	May hide in or travel over lawn. Nuisance.	Treat lawn surface and other areas in

INSECTS	DAMAGE	CONTROL
SPIDERS (continued)	Some species have painful or poisonous bites.	which spiders are observed.
TICKS	Live in lawns and attach themselves to passing humans and animals. Some species carry disease.	Treat lawn surface.

Soil Insects That Plague Lawns

INSECTS	DAMAGE	CONTROL
ANTS	Make unsightly mounds and bare spots.	For overall treatment, apply on soil surface and along runways for most varieties of small ants. For carpenter ants and other nest-forming ants, locate the nest and saturate the nest area with a chlordane liquid formulation.
ASIATIC GARDEN BEETLE LARVAE	Stunt or kill grass in patches, by feeding on roots.	Apply to surface of soil. Water-in thoroughly.
EUROPEAN CHAFER LARVAE	Feed on roots of grass, causing patches of stunted or dead grass to appear in lawn.	Apply chlordane to soil surface and water-in to the upper two inches of soil. Heavier applications are necessary if the soil is compact and/or infestations are extremely heavy. Refer to additional information under the heading "Soil Insects."
JAPANESE BEETLE LARVAE	Same as European chafer larvae.	Same as European Chafer Larvae.

INSECTS	DAMAGE	CONTROL
MOLE CRICKETS	Feed on underground portions of plants. Tunnel through the ground, leaving raised burrows on the surface of the soil.	Water lawn before application, to make mole crickets move around in soil. Then apply chlordane to soil surface.
SOD WEBWORMS	Feed on grass blades. May cut grass and pull it down into their burrows in the soil. Damage results in uneven grass, dying back of new shoots, and irregular brown spots.	Water lawn thoroughly before treatment. Apply chlordane to soil surface. Do not water again for several days.
WHITE FRINGED BEETLE LARVAE	Feed on grass roots. Result in brown, dead patches of grass.	Apply chlordane to soil and water-in thoroughly.

Questions and Answers

Q. What can I do about the damage the neighborhood dogs do to my lawn?

A. Dog damage or urine burn can be repaired by applying a handful of gypsum to the affected area after scratching up the soil, then reseeding. To prevent this damage, apply gypsum at a rate of fifty pounds over 1,000 square yards where the animals run, in early spring.

Q. What can I do to prevent the lawn damage by the salt that the city puts on pavements in the wintertime?

A. To prevent salt damage, apply a five-foot band of gypsum around all walks and drives. This will preserve the lawn against melting rock-salt.

Q. My lawn has some soggy spots caused by water damage. What can I do?

A. Repair soggy spots by cutting through them on three sides of the sod, and gently roll the sod back and fill it with top soil. Press this down firmly, then roll back the sod and press it firmly to the new soil.

Q. I have a portion of lawn that is continually in the shade. Is there a type of grass that will grow there?

A. I have never yet found a grass that I can guarantee will grow in the shade, not even the ones that claim to do fairly well. You might try sowing a variety of the rye grasses under trees and then adding a small amount of new seed every couple of weeks.

Q. The soil in my yard is extremely sandy. What can I do?

A. For sandy soil, add gypsum at fifty pounds per 1,000 square feet along with one yard of clay loam per 1,000 square feet.

Q. It seems as though my yard is only good for making clay pots. Is there anything I can do about it?

A. For clay soil add gypsum at fifty pounds per 1,000 square feet and one yard of sand per 1,000 square feet.

Q. How can I get rid of moles?

A. Moles are nearly blind, but they have a supersensitive sense of hearing. You can control them by creating a noise that is offensive. To do this, bury wine bottles in the mole runs with the necks sticking out at angles. The wind passing over these sends the noise through the runs. The moles are after grubs that are in your soil. Spray the lawn with chlordane to kill the insects.

Q. How can I correct green moss?

A. Green moss is usually found on the north side of trees and buildings and is the result of lack of sunlight or poor drainage. Punch holes in the area and apply gypsum at fifty pounds per 500 square feet. It may be necessary to tile the area if the water problem is too bad.

Q. Parts of my grass turn dusty white. What causes this and what can I do about it?

A. Mildew-white dust will appear on the grass blades in a

shaded area. Wash this area often and apply turf fungicide.

Q. I apply large amounts of insecticides to my grub-infested lawn, but nothing seems to work. What am I doing wrong?
A. Insecticides can be made more effective by poking holes in the infested area before applying the chemical.

Q. I have used weed killer in my sprayer. How do I clean it so that it's fit for other uses?
A. To clean out lawn sprayers, wash out with lukewarm soapy water allowing some to spray through the tip, Follow with two tablespoons of baking soda in a quart jar. Back-flush and spray.

Q. Is there any way to conquer devil grass?
A. I have found that the best way to beat it is to join it and make a whole lawn out of it. However, it can also be controlled with most any of the spot grass and weed killers.

Q. When is the best time to destroy crab grass?
A. For some reason, folks seem to think they should destroy the plant, which is a waste of time and effort. To beat crab grass, kill the seed before it germinates. In most parts of the country this should be done in February or March. Use a pre-emergence killer.

Q. Can clover be killed without hurting good grass?
A. Sure. You can use any one of the chickweed and clover killers on the shelf of your local garden center.

Q. When is the best time to kill general lawn weeds?
A. At the time when weeds are growing their best, not when it is hot and dry.

Q. How long are weed killers good?
A. Like any garden chemical you use, you should never purchase more than you can use. The vapors of 2,4-D

weed killer can kill flowers and evergreens without your even opening the bag.

Q. Should quack grass be dug out, or can I use a spray of some sort?

A. Dig, dig, dig, is about the only way, if it is growing in your yard. There are weed killers that can be used for quack grass control in special crops. Check with your nurseryman.

Q. Can I use the same weed killer to control weeds just off shore at a cottage?

A. No, no, a thousand times no. Your neighbors might even tar and feather you. Fish can be destroyed by ordinary weed killers. For aquatic weeds use a diquat weed killer.

Q. I absolutely refuse to use any weed killers on my lawn. They kill birds and our furry friends. What can I use in place of them?

A. You can feed the lawn extra special, de-thatch, and dig out what few weeds you do have.

Q. What kind of weed killer do I use to kill green moss?

A. You don't need any weed killer for this purpose. Improve the drainage by punching holes, apply gypsum or let the sun shine in—if possible by thinning out a few limbs.

Q. Can all weeds be destroyed with one kind of weed killer?

A. The 2,4-D's and banvel can control most broadleafed weeds.

Q. I just can't afford these expensive fertilizers, but I want a pretty lawn. What can I do?

A. If you will follow the good commonsense, human cultural practices, like removing grass clippings, shampooing, mowing often, aerating and feeding a minimum of twice a season, a cheap lawn food will give you passable results. But it takes a well-balanced diet to have a fat and sassy lawn.

Q. How good is expensive lawn food?
A. Very good! The more types of nitrogen combined in a lawn food to spread the meal over a long period of time, the longer your lawn will stay a deep green.

Q. Is liquid lawn food, applied by these lawn companies, worth the money?
A. A call to the Better Business Bureau will tell you if the company is reputable. As to the results, I have had just as good luck with liquid fertilizers as with the dry ones, but the cost is a little higher.

Q. Is there a good way to spread fertilizer?
A. You bet your lawn there is. Always use the crisscross method. Apply the dry fertilizers and weed killers in dry form at half the rate recommended, back and forth in one direction, and then the other way.

Q. What is meant by dormant feeding?
A. In snow country, you can and should feed as early as possible in the spring. The best time is when there is still a little snow on the ground and more to follow. This is called dormant feeding.

Q. Is there any one good formula in a lawn food?
A. Not really, because different grasses and different soils require different quantities of the basic and special trace elements to grow good grass. I find that the ads in your local paper will soon tell you what formula is needed in your neighborhood.

Q. How much lime should I feed my grass?
A. None. Lime is not a food. Lime is merely used to change the acidity of the soil and should only be used if a soil test indicates that your soil is sour.

Q. How good is good old-fashioned manure for a lawn?

A. Raw manure is so harsh that it will burn an established lawn out, and it is full of weed seed. Driconure, a commercial product that is a blend of many manures, has been dried and the damaging salts and fertile weed seed have been destroyed, making it a gentle and effective product. Raw manure can be used when building a new lawn, because the heat it creates helps the new seed to germinate.

Q. Can I feed my lawn with a liquid fish fertilizer?

A. You can, but I'm sure your neighbors would rather you didn't, and I think you will find it a little too expensive.

Q. What good is iron, and how often should you use it on the lawn?

A. Iron builds blood, in humans and in plants. I have found that at least one application a season, just before the hottest part of the summer, keeps the color dark and fresh and eliminates the possibility of chlorisis.

Q. Do you recommend a sprinkler system?

A. I sure do if you can afford it and use it properly. A built-in sprinkler system, however, cannot just be left to look out for itself. You must still water early and deep.

Q. Is irrigation bad for a lawn?

A. In many of the southwestern states lawns are irrigated at night. It is a bad way to water, as it causes compaction and carries diseases and weed seed from one lawn to another. I prefer controlled watering with a sprinkler.

Q. Would it do any good to mix rain water with my regular tap water?

A. I would say so if you didn't cut it down more than fifty-fifty. This can be done with an inexpensive attachment called a hose-end.

Q. How effective is underground watering?
A. I have seen several systems, and I wouldn't give you a dime for them. The roots usually end up plugging up the system, or the soil remains soggy.

Q. How efficient are automatic feeding systems?
A. Not very. These pieces of equipment are designed for the use of professionals, not that of homeowners.

Q. I have heard that riding lawn mowers are bad for lawns.
A. The only person who would say this would be someone who couldn't afford a rider. However, any mower must have a sharp blade.

Q. How effective and practical would it be to lay drain tile in a lawn area?
A. If drainage were a real problem, I would say that it would be extremely practical, but I have never found an average home lot that I couldn't improve for a lot less money and work just by altering the grade.

Q. I have a syphon hose that hooks on the faucet and meters liquids into my water stream. Can I use a weed killer through this attachment?
A. Not if you cherish your other plants and your own health. When using any kind of attachment that hooks into your drinking water, be careful. Stop at a plumbing supply shop and purchase a back-flow valve. This keeps anything from flowing back into your drinking water. Do not use chemicals through a hose that something or someone might drink from.

Q. I have no one that can turn the water off for me during the day, so I must water at night. What should I use to prevent lawn diseases?
A. Some expensive and strong chemicals. But I have another suggestion. You can buy an automatic water timer that you can set to start when the sun comes up,

and then you can shut it off on the way to work. It's a lot less expensive than fighting a sick lawn.

Q. All professionals have a preference in equipment: ball players, hockey players, football players, racing drivers, etc., and since their livelihood depends on that piece of equipment, you can be sure that it is the best. Now, what is the best constructed, most efficient, least expensive lawn mower available?

A. Eight sheep to the acre. The average homeowner or sportsman would not pay what we pay for our equipment, because it isn't his livelihood.

Q. I have been told that it is a good idea to lower the blade of your lawn mower in the fall. Is this true?

A. As long as the grass is growing, you do not change your cutting height. I do, however, recommend that you cut your lawn at one inch in the early spring to cut off the dead, brown grass and to let the new rhizomes through.

Q. Zoysia grass is called a southern grass, but we receive advertisements saying that it is good for northern zones. Can I use it at my cottage in northern Wisconsin?

A. It will grow in the North, but will turn straw brown at the first hint of frost and stay that way until the temperature hits 75-80° and stays there. I have a friend who sprays it green. He lives next to you in Wisconsin.

Q. Will turf dye hurt grass?

A. Not at all. Turf dye is used more than you can imagine. In the fall of the year, when a pro football team is sharing the same stadium with a baseball team that is still in action, the turf superintendent uses plenty of grass dye on Monday morning. In most cases it is food coloring. You can also buy a professional product called Links Turf Dye.

Q. If you bought a used home and the lawn was overrun with weeds, would you use a garden cyanamid to sterilize it? And what is cyanamid?

A. Since you don't know what it is, or even how to use it, no! Do not use hot stuff unless you know what you are doing. Now, cyanamid is calcium cyanamid, a strong and effective sterilant. It kills everything that is living for six to eight weeks and then allows rhizomes to return—sometimes. I personally never use it in turf areas, although I do use it on my garden patch.

Q. What is Kentucky 31 and where do I use it?
A. On someone else's lawn. Thirty-one is known in weed circles as tall fescue, and it's a real tough customer to destroy. However, if you live the summer on a lake with lots of child traffic or a play area and want the world's toughest grass, plant Kentucky 31, tall fescue.

Q. I have heard that it is a good idea to burn off a bad lawn in the fall, so that a good one will return. True or false?
A. Smokey the Bear will haunt you the rest of your days if you miss. I have on occasion used fire, but then I am very careful. And I only use it where I am not concerned with the texture of the grass. For this reason it is best used on field grasses only.

Q. What harm can earthworms do to my lawn?
A. None, unless you have a bent lawn. Then the night-crawlers push up little mounds on the turf. I find that when I use a surfactant (shampoo), they go away but don't die.

Q. Is it true that weeds and lawn diseases are brought to my yard by my landscaper?
A. A good, well-trained landscaper and maintenance man doesn't have any sick lawns in his care, and if he does, it is usually the last one tended of the day, and his machines are cleaned that night. If he is not well-trained, and his equipment is dirty, I would change men, because he can transport trouble on his machines.

Q. If I have a landscape company take care of my yard, what questions can I ask to make sure that I am not being taken?

A. None. You wouldn't know if the man was giving you fact or fiction. Enjoy your yard and garden and learn something about your permanent visitors; they know a lot about you. If you make friends with your garden, it will tell you what ails it.

Q. Is it true that no one should walk on a lawn when there is snow on the ground?

A. That is right, and when the snow thaws, you can see the footprints for weeks, where compaction occurred. The same applies to a wet lawn in the East, South or West.

Q. Is there any one fungicide that will cure most lawn diseases?

A. There are so many that I won't even begin the list. I will only advise you to look on the shelves of your local garden center and ask your nurseryman when you have the problem.

Q. Can I make my own fertilizer cheaper than I can buy it?

A. I daresay that you could, but it would be more work than it was worth, unless you are a bull, horse, sheep or chicken.

Q. How much egg shell would it take to put calcium into my lawn?

A. More than the egg shells collected each day for a week in three of the suburbs of any one of our large cities.

Q. Where is the best place to get information when you have a lawn problem?

A. This book first, then your local nurseryman, and third, your county extension agent (check the yellow pages).

Q. How can I keep the water from my swimming pool from killing my grass?

A. Put a six-foot band of cement where the wet little feet run.

Q. Can a chemical like chlordane, malathion or sevin be used with the same effect in any part of the country?

A. Yep! They are all the same.

Q. Should you burn weeds when you cut them down or pull them?

A. No! Add them to your compost pile along with the grass clippings and leaves.

Q. Dichondra gets weeds in it just like any other grass. What do we use to get them out?

A. Dichondra is not a grass, but a plant. So to control the weeds, pull them. Banvel will help in many cases. Read the directions.

Q. We are having problems with a large bank washing away. Can we plant grass on it to hold it?

A. There are some ground covers that will hold it better, but I would refrigerate field timothy and clover, and then I would seed it during dry weather. Just sprinkle it for a few days until it is damp, not wet. This will help.

Q. We have a flying-ant problem in our yard every year. What can we use?

A. Soap and water. If this fails, try forty-four percent chlordane as directed.

2
Evergreens:
Sentinels of Beauty

Evergreens Are Forever

We have thoroughly discussed the lawn and agree, I am sure, that with a little bit of pride, mixed with a pinch of patience and blended with a dab or two of persistence, you can have a pretty good-looking lawn. But you can't stop there. Just having a lawn, a green carpet from walk to walk, drive to drive, is like having wall-to-wall carpeting in your living room and no furniture. It just doesn't look lived in. A garden, to be truly appreciated, must have the warmth and lived-in look that can only be achieved through the use of evergreens.

The common term "evergreen" means what it implies—that it will keep its foliage year-round, and in most cases the foliage is green. There are, however, many evergreens that have two faces—the summer face and the winter. Examples of this would be the conifers (the professional classification of evergreens) called Andora junipers, a spreading evergreen; and the hills Dundee, an upright grower. These two plants are both green in the summer months, but when frost comes they turn a beautiful burgundy color.

When selecting plants for your landscape, you should take this into consideration and buy plants that are as attractive in the winter as they are in the summer.

Not all evergreens, contrary to the belief of many a new gardener, have needles, as do the pine, spruce, juniper and yew. Many have large or small leaves, like any flowering shrub. These are called broad-leafed evergreens. Many in this group also have two faces, the difference being that they produce foliage in the winter and burst into flower in the spring, like rhododendrons and azaleas. So you see that you can make quite a masterpiece out of your property, be it large or small, with a little bit of planning and a lot of imagination.

Plan Before You Plant

This phrase is like beating a dead horse, becaue it is constantly used by nurserymen, writers and garden broadcasters, until it makes one sick of hearing it. But it is one of the most important steps that you will take in building a desirable and presentable landscape design to complement your home and surrounding property.

A good, workable plan doesn't have to be some sophisticated, complicated work of art by an architect, though this type of plan is desirable if one has the funds to afford it. A piece of brown paper, a grocery bag cut open, will do nicely. Now survey your property. Pace off the length and width if you do not already know them. Next, pace off the distance from your property lines. That will give your house and other building locations. Then continue by adding the walks, drive, fences and existing flower beds or other gardens. On your plan you must indicate where the downspouts are, any low spots that can or do hold water, and existing shade trees. On the paper show the size of the shadow they cast and for what period of time each day. It will be necessary that you use some sort of a scale on your paper. This will vary with the size of your paper, but try to use the largest scale possible. I have found that the use of my children's crayons makes identification much easier. I use green for tree, gray for walks, black for buildings, brown for garden and beds, chartreuse for wet spots, blue for water, ponds or streams. Be sure to code the colors in the margin for quick identification.

There are still two more things that you must indicate on your plan. Indicate all windows and doors. For windows, show their height from the ground and their width; doors, their width and which room they belong to. The last thing to do is to indicate the direction north on the plan in the lower right-hand corner with a small red "N" and an

arrow pointing to the north of your property. The end?
Not by a long shot! What next?

Shopping for Beauty

There are many things that go into the selection of evergreens, just as there are in picking the right dress, sport
coat or slacks. Does it fit your personality, does it complement your features, does it make you look taller,
shorter, fat or slim, is it the real you? Get the message?
Uh-huh, you pick evergreens to complement your home,
not hide it.

Pick colors that will not clash with the brick or siding.
Pick shapes that will not make your house look taller or
shorter, wider or narrower. Pick plants that grow low in
front of low windows, so as not to shut out the view, and
taller plants for corners to break the sharp edges. But
where do you find all this information? I suggest that you
send away for the many free nursery catalogues offered
in any of the national magazines, or refer to those that I
have included in this chapter. Some have a small charge,

but they are worth the money and are an encyclopedia of garden information and background on the guests (evergreens that is) that you are going to invite to share your little corner of the world. Pictures are included, lots and lots of them. When the catalogues arrive, look them over and decide what you want where. Then pencil them in on your plan (don't use pen or crayon for this because they are subject to change for one reason or another).

Your next move will be to visit your local nurseryman or garden center which specializes in these materials. I say this with tongue in cheek, as I have found very few garden centers or patio departments attached to department stores or discounters that have more to offer than a value. They also seem to be a little short of knowledgeable personnel, although there are exceptions. The nurseryman will gladly go over your plan, point out a change or two, offer suggestions and help you to figure out your costs.

Money Talks

It is absolutely necessary that you decide how much you can afford to spend on your total landscaping: lawns, trees and flowers, evergreens and shrubs. If you don't, you will soon find yourself in trouble, and when this happens a person finds it difficult to enjoy his garden because he must worry about money. Go slow and easy; you don't have to do it all at once, and any good nurseryman will help you decide just where to start and which plantings should be first.

Don't Over-Plant

The deadliest mistake a new gardener can make is to get carried away with his buying and planting, so that he ends up burying his home in a virtual forest of evergreens. By this I mean he can't see out and enjoy the view of his garden, and passers-by can't see in even a little bit. He also buries himself in work and can't enjoy the fruits of his labors. Never, never make your garden so busy that you are too busy to enjoy it. To avoid over-planting, make sure that you do not buy plants too large. Give them a chance to grow a little before you have to trim them for the first time. The identification tags will tell you how wide and how tall the plant will grow.

Don't Build a Back-Breaker

With the railroad-tie craze at its peak, I hear more complaints about backaches from gardeners who get carried away with terraces and walls. They have lost sight of the fact that lawn mowers and the various other machinery were not designed to go up stairs. When designing your landscape, make sure that you design turf ramps in hidden spots to allow for easy maintenance. Also, avoid sharp turns for beds. Make them with gentle, sweeping lines, wide enough that the lawn mower can lie off the edge and mow the border line. This will eliminate the necessity of hand-clipping on bent knee.

Play and Pet Areas Must Be Planned

As a rule, these two areas just happen, because we tend to overlook them in the basic plan, and by the time we discover our oversight, it's too late to work them in or screen them off without making it look obvious. Consequently, they stick out like a sore thumb. I have included a basic check-off and personal landscape survey that can be used to avoid some common oversights.

Should You Plant a Pool in Your Garden?

Whether or not to have a swimming pool is a big question with lots of homeowners these days. Many people who love their gardens hesitate to install a pool because they are afraid that the pool and its associated chemicals will kill the lawn and shrubs.

From the horticultural aspect I have no objection to a swimming pool, as long as it is well designed, placed, constructed, maintained and landscaped. Pools are highly recommended by most landscape architects and designers.

Let's start with the design. The shape of any pool should complement the home. It should become part of the landscape and lend pleasure and beauty. It shouldn't be a big round or square hole in the ground or an oversized tin can in the middle of the lawn.

A good pool builder will take into consideration the style of building and design the pool to blend gracefully. For example, a ranch house can have any size or shape pool. But, to make it fit in, one would only have to place a coping of ledge rock around the edge, and the pool would take on a rustic appearance.

Above-the-ground pools present more of a challenge. On large lots, soil can be mounded up around the exposed sides and sandstone steps added, leading up to the deck. Pines and groundcovers can be used at the base, so that the mound gives the illusion of being a natural hill.

Small lots are a bit more difficult, but I have used arborvitaes in random groups with spreading junipers in small beds between and have accomplished a very pleasant result.

Before selecting any pool, look at many pictures and books just as you would when choosing a home. Then select a reputable pool dealer.

The proper placing of the pool is very important. It is best to avoid shade as much as possible. This doesn't mean you should put it right in the middle of the lawn. For safety's sake it is recommended that you locate the pool where you can have a clear view from the house.

I need not linger on the aspect of construction quality. Common sense should tell you to be sure of a manufacturer's or a builder's reputation.

The true secret to success or failure in enjoying a swimming pool is proper maintenance. It is a never-ending job which can be assigned to the teen-age members of the family, or can be done by hiring a professional pool service, or you can always assume the responsibility yourself. Do not mix, or allow the mixing, of any pool-purifying chemicals on the grass areas or alongside evergreen and flower beds.

Have a cement slab poured with at least a three-inch curb on which to place the pumps and filters. Do not store the chemical out of doors on the ground where the containers can become damaged and leak on the turf areas.

The list of plant materials that can be used near and around the swimming pool is endless. The only restriction is your imagination. The only caution I always mention is to avoid planting deciduous trees and shrubs (ones that lose their leaves) near the pool itself, or you will always be skimming the leaves out of the water. I have found that using members of the juniper family (Hetzi, Armstrong, Greek, Andora, etc.) and combining them with a variation of ground covers can make your swimming pool a truly beautiful and scenic spot, summer or winter.

Remember, when you are talking to your pool builder or landscape designer, to inform him that you would like the plant materials to have winter character as well as summer, and the joining link will be the selection of the right ground covers. You have over thirty of these to choose from.

Plants to avoid in and around your pool are the yew family and most of the arborvitaes. Neither can stand a great deal of water. When you combine the water with the acid-salt buildup from the splashing of pool water, the plants just don't have a chance.

I have found over the years that a lawn of perennial rye, overseeded in early March, June and August, makes the most attractive and durable swimming-pool lawn available. It will take the pitter-pat of tiny feet wet with chlorine.

Pool chemicals seem to be the primary concern of most home gardeners. They kill flowers, shrubs and evergreens. This need not be the case. Plain, old-fashioned garden gypsum should be spread on the lawn areas, in the flower beds and evergreen rows, at a rate of fifty pounds over 1,000 square feet, two or three times a season. This will render the chemical reaction harmless to the plants.

Insects do not object to the pool area and will join in on the fun from time to time, living up to their reputation as pests. It is advisable to install one or two of the electric insect-destroyers. But when it becomes necessary to spray, use only the patio sprays containing dibrome (the safe replacement for DDT). Even though it is safe around people, pets and birds, it is a good idea to spray early in the morning or the last thing at night.

To summarize the discussion I need only to quote myself: "A garden is to be lived in and enjoyed, not just admired."

Don't deprive your family or yourself of the pleasure of a swimming pool if you have the room, patience and capital.

Permanently Planted

Most folks think that all there is to planting an evergreen is to dig a hole, drop it in, refill the hole with soil and watch it grow. This attitude, if not changed, can lead to death, not life. When planting any living plant, be it a tiny petunia or a large pine, you must handle the plant as delicately as you would have the movers handle your furniture. The precise location as well as the permanent angle should be as well thought out as the placement of a mirror, plaque or painting.

The planting procedure begins before you ever bring the evergreen home. By this, I mean that you must determine the soil conditions in which you are going to ask these plants to grow. Most evergreens, needled or broadleafed, are grown in light, loose soil, or growing mixes with good drainage. It is, therefore, suggested that when preparing your evergreen beds you add liberal quantities of 60-40 gravel to the existing soil if it is of a heavy consistency. Sandy soil will need no preparation.

In heavy clay soil, it is of the utmost importance that you determine your water table and the direction of the water's surface flow. Many an unsuspecting gardener placed a plant in a spot that displayed it at its best, only to find that when it rained, the water from the downspout or the surface water from the grade flowed right over the top of the evergreen he planted, the hole filled up with water and the plant died.

Evergreens come in three basic containers. The first is the traditional balled-in-burlap, the second in metal containers and the third in plantable paper-pulp pots.

Which type you purchase doesn't make much difference. However, the plantable container is fast becoming the most popular, mostly because of the fact that the average home gardener can plant it with the least amount of fuss and shock loss of plants. The metal container is rather cumbersome, and the plant must be removed from the container; that means cutting the sides of the can, which may result in a few minor cuts and scratches. Soil is often shaken loose from the roots in the process, exposing them to the air, which can cause damage to the plant.

The balled-in-burlap is an excellent container but is fast becoming extinct because of automation, increased production and a lack of ballers. This, my friends, is a true art and a good baller has the skill and speed of any good journeyman. How he handles the plant when it is dug determines whether or not it lives in your yard.

Choosing the Guards

When you go to purchase your plants, look at the container just as critically as you do the plant. If, for instance, you have picked out a tall and statuesque juniper and then you look down at the ball of soil covered with burlap and find that it is loose and sloppy and that the soil is falling out, don't buy it. Odds are it will die in your yard from root shock. If paper-pulp containers are split, don't buy them. If the plants in the metal containers are loose and wobbly, don't buy them. Use as much care in the selection and purchase of an evergreen as you would a piece of furniture. There should be no flaws, and the plant should be shiny, bright and healthy.

The size of the container has a lot to do with the future health of your plants. Make sure that you get as much soil as you can with the plants. I always pick the plants with the biggest ball or container.

The Ride Home

You have now selected and paid for your plants. Next comes the ride home. This may just be a one-way ride if it is not done right.

Plants are just like some people and pets. They get carsick if some precautions are not taken. Whenever it can be avoided, plants that are in containers should not be laid down on their sides in a trunk or back seat. This tends to crush the sides, loosen the soil and expose the roots. Balled-in-burlap plants should not be allowed to roll around and bang the sides for the same reasons. Set the plant containers upright and brace them. Block balled plants to keep them from rolling.

Do not bend tops to fit into car trunks or close the lids and tie them down on the limbs or foliage, or you can kiss your purchase good-bye. If your evergreen has a bad ride home, he may never adapt to the spot where you plant him, not to mention what he is going to tell the rest of the plants at home about you. If delivery from the nursery can't be arranged, and the plants won't be as comfortable riding home as you, rent a small trailer. Place all of the plants in an upright position and fasten their safety belts. That's right—sudden stops and starts cause soil shifts and shocks. I tie the foliage gently, but snugly, with soft strips of cloth or old nylon hosiery to prevent the tops from blowing in the breeze and drying out or snapping off. When loading or unloading evergreens, do not let anyone rough-handle them, drop or plunk them down, as this will separate the soil from the roots. Do not handle the plants by grabbing them by the trunk. Move them by picking up the container and not by dragging them around by the foliage. Remember, plants have feelings. How would you or your pet feel if you were dragged around by the hair, tail or legs? Your pet would bite or scratch, and you would yell! Evergreens can and do scream with pain, *so be gentle.*

Don't Delay

More evergreens lose their lives on a driveway or in a garage than any place else. Once you have made the plan, selected the plants, purchased the materials, take time! Take the time to plant your evergreens the day you bring them home. The worst thing I can think of is inviting someone to visit and then leaving him standing on the porch. It is rude and unkind. The plants that you are putting in your yard are invited guests. They did not ask to come to live with you, you asked them. So, be a good host or hostess and make them comfortable as quickly as possible. They will soon show you their appreciation.

Plant all plants the day you purchase them. If you are unable to plant immediately, make additional trips and purchase them a few at a time.

After All, a Hole Is Just a Hole

This caption is only true if you don't have to live in one! When you do, it is home and, since "Home is where the heart is," let's make it enjoyable. No one likes to live in cramped quarters, and it is especially true of evergreens. If the planting hole is too small and cramped, the new visitor will be uncomfortable, its growth will be stunted and it will soon become ill. I was always taught to dig a hole half again as wide as the width of the container. This is referred to as digging a five-dollar hole for a fifty-cent plant.

The new evergreen visitor should be planted only one to one-and-a-half inches deeper than it was in the nursery. If you plant it too deep you might smother the roots.

Onward and Upward

Certainly a physical phrase, but it's an important one in the life of your landscaping. A steel rigger would never be satisfied if one of his steel beams were not straight as an arrow. The reason is obvious. The rest of the building would be crooked. A home landscaper must not be satisfied with a slanted plant, because his whole garden will look crooked, and the plant will be terribly uncomfortable. After you have dug a wide hole, one-and-one-half inches deeper than the plant was planted at the nursery, set your new friend in position. Be gentle! Don't drop him or her! Now stand way back and check the stance of the plant. Is it straight? Look from all angles, just as you size up a putt in golf. If the plant appears crooked, do not bend it or pull at it. Remove it from the hole and alter the angle of the bottom of the hole to compensate for the crookedness of the plant. This same procedure goes for all of the evergreens, whether they are low spreaders or tall uprights. They should always appear straight and level.

Fill It Up Filtered

I stated earlier that almost without exception, all evergreens, broad-leafed and needled, love loose, well-drained soil. If your evergreen friends do not have these first-class living conditions, they soon will not be living. First, you should determine if you have good drainage. The hole is now dug and you are reasonably certain that the plant will sit straight and level. Get out the garden hose and fill the hole with water (but don't wash away the sides or alter the base). Watch closely. If the water has not subsided in a very few minutes, you have a drainage problem. To correct this, dig a narrow trench the depth of the hole on an angle parallel with the downward grade of the property and fill with gravel. If, on the other hand, the water runs through the hole like a sieve, you can line the five-dollar hole with a clay loam to hold some moisture.

It is now time to plant the evergreen permanently. As one of my neighbors said, "Just throw the dirt back in." That is not the way to make a friend of your evergreens.

In the case of the balled-in-burlap plant, after you have half refilled the hole, it will be necessary to cut the twine at the top of the ball and where it is bound around the trunk.

The metal container is the toughest one. In most cases, the nurseryman will cut the sides of the can before you leave and bind the sides with cord. If not, you have to cut three sides all the way down with tin snips. Once this is done, place the can next to the hole and gently pull the cut can sides away from the soil ball inside. Now gently lift out the evergreen and lower it into the hole. Do not touch the plant, only the ball. Do not drop it. I talk to the plants all the time while I am planting them. It keeps them calm and me too. It also lets them know that they are welcome friends and not just decorations.

The paper-pulp container should be placed in the hole, with the sides sliced on both sides and left to decompose.

Once the plant is in place, begin to refill the hole with a mixture of half sandy gravel and half garden soil. Fill in on all sides evenly until the hole is half full and pack the soil firmly around the ball with your foot to eliminate any air pockets or hollow spots that will later sink and cause exposure of roots or a tilt to the plant. After you have half refilled and packed down, fill the hole up with water to further settle the soil. Then continue to fill up the hole with the balance of the mix.

Cover Up Your Dirty Work

Your new friend is now almost comfortably situated in his or her new home, but not quite yet. *Do not,* I repeat, *do not* feed newly planted shrubs right away. Let them get used to the soil and their new neighbors for a couple of weeks and then give them a light snack of any one of the fish emulsion fertilizers. Then feed them again at the end of a month with a low-nitrogen, dry garden food, like 4-12-4 or 5-10-5, to stimulate root growth. In the meantime, cover up the roots with a mulch of wood chips about two inches deep all the way out to the ends of the bottom branches. This mulch holds down weeds, conserves moisture, covers up the bare soil and eliminates having to hand-clip the grass from under the branches.

You will notice that I did not put any food in the planting hole. Nothing living wants food crammed down his throat—especially not a newly moved evergreen.

Say a Few Kind Words

After you have each of your guests well planted, take a few minutes out to stand back and look them over to see if they were damaged in the move or during planting. You might tell them how pleased you are to have them come stay with you and your family, and that you hope they will be comfortable.

You might also tell them how nice they look. No, I am not crazy. I do talk to the plants. I find it both tranquilizing and rewarding. If a few of the skeptics of this world would walk out into Mother Nature's living room and communicate with the Almighty through plants, they wouldn't need uppers and downers (as the junkies refer to them), and there would be no need to blow pot to get happy. Happiness is all right here, right around us all the time, and I can get high and happy just mowing the lawn or tending the roses. I get the troubles off my chest just by talking to the friends in my garden. Try it sometime; you might be surprised and enjoy it.

Personalize Your Plants

Hey you! must be the rudest salutation anyone can use. At my house we take a small label maker and give all of the large permanent plants in the garden a name. Ours are mostly Indian names, but you can use any names you wish. I have a close friend that is looking over my shoulder most of the time I am writing this book. His name is Paul. He is a Paul's scarlet hawthorn. You will be surprised at how much interest your entire family will have in your yard and garden when you make a few new friendships this way.

Chow Time! Feeding Evergreens

Most folks who plant evergreens or move into a home with an existing landscape of evergreens just take them for granted. Soon the plants figure, "To hell with you. If you don't notice I'm around and don't care about me, I'm not

going to try to look nice." And, soon they don't. Then
you notice them, but sometimes it's too late. If you want
to get along with your garden but don't want to get personal, that's your business, but I would suggest that you
take a little time out and at least be friendly—feed them.
They need food and they aren't capable of foraging for
themselves like their ancestors who grew free in the woods
in a thick rich layer of natural organic mulch which fed
them continuously. They must now rely on you, and from
some of the conversations I hear that a lot of you "green
thumbers" are stingy and only feed a few favorites. That
southern gentleman, Kentucky Blue and his girlfriend,
Merion, get all the choice food and keep you broke. Well,
food that's good for them is good enough for the evergreens, except for those special blends with weed killers in
them. Write this on your garden calendar: Feed the
evergreens in February, coast to coast, also April and
June. But, never after August 15 if you live in snow
country. If you live in the warm areas, feed them in
August and October.

  You should feed all of your evergreens with the same
lawn food you use for your lawn, except "Weed and
Feeds" at the rate of one-half pound per foot of height.
Sprinkle the food over the top of the wood-chip mulch
underneath the evergreens, then watch the difference. The
plants have a little change for one of our songs, and they
say it is number one on the Tree Top Parade: "What a
Difference a Meal Makes."

  You can also use any of the liquid fish emulsions. As a
matter of fact, the evergreens appreciate a varied menu,
just like the lawn. Why not use dry one time and liquid
the next. The cartridge feeders will also do nicely.

In Sickness and in Health

  With a little care and kindness shown towards our evergreens, we can expect some pretty, happy and healthy results. But from time to time even the healthiest person
succumbs to a minor illness, and if it is not immediately
taken care of, it can become a very serious problem, even

resulting in a fatality. Heaven forbid this should ever happen in your garden.

Let's review the needs of our fine green friends. Like the lawn, they need plenty of fresh air, sunshine (broad-leafed evergreens don't need as much), water, a balanced diet and plenty of soap and water.

In the early spring, or late winter in the West and South (see Planting Map) begin your health-cure program for your evergreens and foliage plants. Give them a soap-and-water bath with a hose and sprayer. One ounce of liquid green Palmolive soap per ten gallons of water. Wash inside and out, over and under. Don't miss a spot. Viruses and fungus diseases are the result of poor hygiene, airborne soot, dust and various polutants that settle on the foliage and needles, and are also carried by insects. Soap and water are disinfectants of a sort which keep the plant clean and free of the viruses. It is, therefore, absolutely necessary that you bathe them once a month. In heavy smog or industrial areas, you should bathe your evergreens as often as needed. These frequent showers also keep the pores and cells open by removing the surface tension and allowing photosynthesis to take place in a normal manner. If you are in close contact with your garden, you will actually sense trouble before it really gets a start.

Fungicides are the chemical materials used to control and cure the diseases that attack your evergreens, and every manufacturer of lawn and garden products has at least one broad spectrum fungicide that will solve most problems. It is necessary that you understand that these chemicals will not restore the appearance of your evergreens after an injury caused by a virus. They only prevent the spread of the disease.

To keep your evergreens ship-shape and free from the "foliage flu," I suggest that along with a good diet and frequent baths, you keep their home clean and free of weeds and debris as these usually bear bad tidings. I have found that to provide a two-inch layer of wood chips is the best preventive step you can take in protecting your evergreens. This mulch should be from a healthy tree, never a diseased one. A good layer of mulch will hold down weeds, act as a source of food, and contain moisture. A good-looking mulch enhances the appearance of the plant itself and lets it show off. There are many to choose from. Some are better than others, because they do not attract rodents. The ones I like best are hardwood chips, redwood and pine bark. Next best is chunky peat. The ones that I do not prefer are cocoa bean shells, buckwheat hulls and straw, because these attract insects and mice. Tobacco stems are attractive but can be a source of tobacco mosaic, a virus disease that attacks vine crops.

Stone chips are an attractive mulch and do hold down weeds and contain moisture. The assortment of stone materials is limitless, from hard coal chips to pea gravel. There is on the market now a type of coated stone of bright colors that is extremely attractive. With some imagination, you can use these stones to create the most unusual effects. A clean, neat, well-trimmed and mulched garden will display healthy evergreens at their best. And remember, a clean garden is a happy one.

Pardon the Pests

I can't help but feel sorry for the poor bugs. They are going about their business doing their thing, helping to balance nature, and what thanks do they get? They get slapped, swatted, flicked, gassed, burned, sprayed, dusted and sworn at when all they are doing is what they were meant to do.

If you will just think for a minute about how we prevent ticks, fleas and lice from bothering our pets, you will suddenly discover the simplest method by which you can encourage the insects to pass your garden by.

That's right, we are right back to the bath routine. Bugs have eyes, a mouth, nose and a very delicate stomach. When you wash down the garden, the bugs that are around get soap in their eyes, up their noses and in their mouths. They soon move on. New bugs flying by stop for a snack or begin to set up housekeeping and soon discover the

food in "dis here plaze" is not very tasty and their stomach is constantly upset. So they move out.

Insects have a great communication network and they will soon pass the word along about your place. Not all bugs fly, as you know, nor do they all like the taste of foliage. Some prefer the tender young roots, just as we like bean sprouts in our chop suey. To discourage these underground visitors, poke a series of holes into the soil beneath the branches and water down this area with the soap solution. If you are wondering what happens to all of these insects that you chase away, they run into one of their natural enemies along the way. Not all of the bugs will give up quite this easily, and it may be necessary to turn to the garden chemicals. When this step becomes necessary, then use only the strength of the chemical to do the job that is recommended by the manufacturer. I have found that malathion will take pretty good care of the chewing and sucking insects and chlordane ends the problem under the ground.

I will make a brief comment at this point about using combinations, i.e. two or more chemicals mixed together to form a stronger whallop. I do not find it necessary to use these. The softer chemicals are effective, and when it becomes necessary to use any of them, I use the most effective recommended.

There has been a big push on the use of systemic garden chemicals. These products are applied to the soil and then accepted by the roots and transmitted throughout the plant's vascular system, making the plant and its products totally insecticidal. I am opposed to them because these chemical groups are far stronger than the so-called "hard pesticides" and are applied to the ground, where they can easily be caught up in the movement of surface waters and deposited in the soil near vegetable gardens, fruit trees or other food crops—thus making the fruits and vegetables very dangerous. For this reason alone I avoid them like the plague.

I have turned to the use of the safer materials for minor infestations like Cook Chemicals' "Real Kill" line. They use pyrethrum and other mild chemicals for roses and food plants alike.

Just one thing to remember. Chemicals are medicine to your plants, and they don't like taking medicine any better than you do, because it smells bad and tastes worse.

Keeping in Shape

If you properly plant, feed, mulch and care for evergreens, they are going to grow tall, wide and full. Evergreens are just like people or pets; if they are allowed to get too fat, they tend to get sloppy, lazy and weak from lack of exercise.

I am not suggesting that you walk your evergreens, but I am suggesting that once in a while you gently shake them. This is like scratching your dog's back, and it will help to shake out some of the natural needle drop that occurs in most evergreens. It also lets them know that you are thinking about them.

Needle drop seems to upset many a home gardener when he is not aware of what is occurring. Most evergreens naturally shed the older needles towards the center of the tree in the fall of the year, and this is no cause for alarm. It is when the outside needles begin to fall that you should worry.

When evergreens begin to look thin-haired, it is usually because of one of two things: insects, or poor trimming procedure. First, check for insects. If you can't see them, get a sheet of clean white paper and place it under several different branches and shake the foliage. Look closely at the paper. If bugs are the problem, you will see them scoot around on the paper. If there are no signs of insects, look over your tree carefully and ask these questions: Are all of the sides getting the full sun? Did I use dull shears and injure the foliage? Did I cut too far back and expose coarse inner branches?

When trimming any plant, it is absolutely necessary that your tools be sharp. You can trim evergreens as often as you like, and should do so periodically to contain them, in order not to have them growing over the sidewalk or covering the windows or their nearest neighbor. When trimming the yews and junipers, you cannot invert your

trim. I mean that your design can be perpendicular or flared, but not cut inward, because when you do this the upper branches cast a shadow and shut out the sun. When this occurs, the needles will begin to drop off on the ends.

Trimming can begin in the warm climates in March and as soon as the snow disappears in the rest of the country. As new growth appears, continue to trim, to keep the evergreen looking neat and natural. I find that the electric hedge-trimmers work fine and save a lot of work.

When a large branch is broken or cut it is necessary to sterilize the wound and seal it. A solution of household ammonia (three teaspoons) in a quart of water will do to sterilize the wound, then seal it with pruning paint.

Broken limbs should have a fresh clean cut made. Do not allow broken limbs to go untended for any period of time, or further damage will occur.

When it is necessary to cut into large wood, it is an excellent idea to cut just ahead of a young branch. This will then fill out and cover up the heavy stub. Pruning and trimming errors have to be lived with for a long time, so be sure before you cut.

Moving Day: Transplanting

There comes a time in every gardener's life when he finds that he must move a plant from one location to another. The reasons can be many, and they really make no difference. Before you make up your mind to move an evergreen of any size, be sure that it is absolutely necessary and not just a whim. Talk it over with the plant to be moved. If poor drainage is the reason and the plant is in danger of losing his life, you should tell him. Or, if wind scald is giving him first degree burns, or something like that, the plant will understand the necessity of the move! If his style is cramped and he is going to raise the roof if he's not moved, then go ahead. I don't recommend moving a plant just for the sake of looks and, believe me, he won't like it either.

If and when it becomes necessary to move any kind

of evergreen, broad-leafed or tropical, it is mandatory that you take some pre-surgery steps. To begin with, tie the foliage up snugly but not tightly with old nylon hose. This will allow you to work beneath it without breaking any branches. Next, water the plant to be moved the night before. Do not soak it, just get it damp enough so that when you dig, the soil will hold firmly around the roots. The next step is to dig the new hole in the same way as you would to plant a new evergreen. The quality of the tools you use can determine whether your plant will live or not, so be sure that your spade has a razor edge. I always sharpen and re-sharpen the blade of my shovel with a file to insure that when I cut through the many feeder roots, the cuts will be clean and not ragged. I prepare a stretcher to move my friend as quickly and comfortably as possible. For this I use a large heavy cardboard box broken down to resemble a flying carpet.

To dig an established plant, one must take into consideration his age and the general condition of his health. The older the plant, the longer he has been there; and this will determine the amount of soil you must move with him—much like the cherished objects of an older person who is forced to move. As a rule, I take no less than half the soil beneath the lower branches. On some plants that can be a big, big ball and you will need help.

Take your spade and begin to dig straight down in a full circle around the plant. When this is completed, move one spade-width back and begin to remove the soil in a trench form all the way around. Once this is completed, turn your spade over and dig with it backwards, again digging down the depth of the spade. You are now two spade-depths deep. On the side of the plant closest to the new location, dig a slight ramp up and away from the soil ball. Continue to dig beneath the ball until it is free and will rock a bit. Placing one end of the cardboard rug under the edge of the ball, pull the plant downward toward the cardboard. Now begin to pull the rug along the soil until you are opposite the new hole. Gently, ever so gently, work the plant into its new location. Don't drop, jerk or bump the ball. Move as slowly as you can. Once the plant is seated well, make sure it is straight and then begin to refill the hole in a normal planting procedure.

When the job is done, mulch with two inches of fresh clean mulch and water well. Feed two weeks later with a fish emulsion plant food.

The best time to transplant is in the early fall or very early spring when the evenings are cool, never during very hot weather.

There is now equipment that can dig up any size plant and reset it, so that the plant never knows it was moved. I would suggest that you call a professional tree mover for bids, if you are going to move any large evergreen or tree.

Re-Landscaping

I guess I am asked more questions about this subject than about any other phase of gardening. You will need to re-landscape if you purchase a home that has a runaway garden or a neglected landscape that's overgrown, out of proportion or insect-infested to the point where it contains too many dead plants to cover up the empty spots. The same rules apply to re-landscaping as to a brand new plan, except you don't have to start from scratch.

Begin by drawing the paper-bag plan. Put in the house, walks, buildings, trees, good shrubs and any other plantings that exist. Be sure to show on your plan shadows cast, low spots or any drainage problem. Next, check the catalogue for varieties and their uses. Then, take your plan and catalogue to your local nursery and see if the pieces to the puzzle will fit. Since your plants are all full-grown or larger, you are going to have to purchase plants of somewhat similar size, which will mean more money per plant. However, not as many plants will be needed. I would ask "the man" if he would stop by and guide you on which plants to cut back severely and which to remove. I find that most of these gentlemen are glad to assist anyone who is truly interested. Your county agent is also available for no fee in most cases, though a cup of coffee and a piece of homemade cake or pie sure works wonders. Re-landscaping is best done in the early fall when both the days and evenings are comfortable for you and the garden.

It is a lot of work, but the results are amazing. Some of your overgrown junipers need not come out, but can be trimmed and pruned into some pretty interesting and unusual shapes. A visit to your local library for a look at a book that describes in pictures topiary designs can make you the standout in the neighborhood.

Catalogues Available

ADDRESS	FEE
George W. Park Seed Co., Inc. Greenwood, South Carolina 29646	Free
Lord & Burnham Division of Burnham Corp. Department 49 Irvington, New York 10533	Free
Wayside Gardens 158 Mentor Avenue Mentor, Ohio 44060	$2.00
Gurney Seed & Nursery Co. 1020 Page Street Yankton, South Dakota 57078	$ .25
Aluminum Greenhouses, Inc. 14615 Lorain Avenue Cleveland, Ohio 44111	Free
Audubon Workshop Glenview, Illinois 60025	Free
W. Atlee Burpee Co. 3490 Burpee Building Philadelphia, Pennsylvania 19132 Clinton, Iowa 52732 Riverside, California 92502	Free
Armstrong Nurseries, Inc. 815 West Phillips Ontario, California 97164	Free
Burgess Seed & Plant Co. Department M-29 P.O. Box 2000 Galesburg, Michigan 49053	Free

ADDRESS	FEE
Ackerman Nurseries 216 Lake Street Bridgman, Michigan	Free
Wilson Bros. Roachdale, Indiana 46172	Free
Krider Nurseries, Inc. P.O. Box 309 Middlebury, Indiana	Free
Rocknoll Nursery P.O. Box 225 Morrow, Ohio 45152	Free
Savage Farm Nursery P.O. Box 125-FG McMinnville, Tennessee 37110	Free
Michigan Bulb Co. Department Z-1455 Grand Rapids, Michigan 49502	Free
Emlong's P.O. Box 106 Stevensville, Michigan 49127	Free
R. H. Shumway Seedsman Department 389 Rockford, Illinois 61101	Free
Putney Nursery, Inc. Putney, Vermont 05346	Free
Fischer Greenhouses Department FG12 Linwood, New Jersey	$ .20
Stark Bros. P.O. Box 760 Louisiana, Missouri 63353	Free
Rayner Bros., Inc. Department 40 Salisbury, Maryland 21801	Free
McComb Greenhouses New Straitsville, Ohio 43766	$. 25
Schreiner's Gardens 3620 Quinaby Road N. E. Salem, Oregon 97303	Free
Kelly Bros. Nurseries, Inc. 212 Maple Street Dansville, New York 14437	Free

ADDRESS	FEE
Western Maine Forest Nursery Co. Department F-129-A Fryeburg, Maine 04037	Free
Melvin E. Wyant 200 Johnny Cake Ridge Mentor, Ohio 44060	Free
Joseph Harris Co., Inc. 28 Moreton Farm Rochester, New York 14624	Free
Henry Field Seed & Nursery Co. 904 Oak Street Shenandoah, Iowa 51601	Free
Brittingham Plant Farms 2538-F Ocean City Road Salisbury, Maryland 21801	Free
Sunnyslope Gardens 8638 Huntington Drive Department HG San Gabriel, California 91775	Free
J. E. Miller Nurseries 907-M West Lake Road Canadaigua, New York 14424	Free
Bountiful Ridge Nurseries, Inc. Dept. 11 Princess Anne, Maryland 21853	Free
Spring Hill Nurseries Department C-1 Tipp City, Ohio 45371	Free
Thon's Garden Mums Department K 4815 Oak Street Crystal Lake, Illinois 60014	Free
Star Roses P.O. Box 216 West Grove, Pennsylvania 19390	Free
Turner Greenhouses Department HG-2 P.O. Box 1260 Goldsboro, North Carolina 27530	Free
Greenhouse Co., Inc. 2717 St. Louis Avenue Fort Worth, Texas	Free

ADDRESS	FEE
Tube Craft, Inc. 1311D West 80th Street Cleveland, Ohio	Free
Nursery Specialty Products, Inc. 410 Greenwich Avenue Greenwich, Connecticut 06830	Free

Landscape Planning Guide

ESTIMATED BUDGET? _____

Lawn	$_____
Evergreens	_____
Shade Trees	_____
Flowering Trees	_____
Flowering Shrubs	_____
Flowers	_____
(A) Annuals	_____
(B) Perennials	_____
(C) Bulbs	_____
Vegetable Garden	_____
Total	$_____

MEMBERS OF THE FAMILY   **OUTDOOR HOBBIES**

_____   _____

_____   _____

_____   _____

PLAY AREA

Pool? _____
Swing Set? _____
Tennis or Ball Court? _____
Other Game Areas? _____

ANIMAL RUN? _____

GREENHOUSE and/or POTTING SHED? _____

SEND FOR CATALOGUES _____

Questions and Answers

Q. When is the best time to plant evergreens?

A. Take a map of the United States and draw a line from the coast of Massachusetts to the top corner of the Kansas-Missouri border, draw a line from there, south to the middle of Texas and west to the middle of Arizona. Next, continue the line right up the middle of California, Oregon and Washington. Plant evergreens south and west of that line all winter, north of this line in the early spring and early fall.

Q. What's the largest evergreen that can be planted? We would like a ten to twelve foot spruce.

A. They have equipment now that will allow them to plant spruces twice that size or larger.

Q. When is the best time to take cuttings from my cedar trees? And can I grow plants from these?

A. I take them in the early spring and root them in perlite, then transfer them to peat pots to get a good start. You bet you can grow your own, and they turn out to be the best kind, because they are your babies.

Q. What can we plant in a wet spot, in the evergreen family, to make a hedge?

A. Got just the thing. Canadian hemlock. Makes a great hedge, looks rich and it's thick. The American arborvitae will take some water, but not too much.

Q. How many different types of evergreens are there, and can I grow most of them in Southern California?

A. Almost as many as there are stars in the sky and more on the way each season from the propagators. Yes, you could grow most of them in Southern California. If you would like to see most of them, take a Sunday ride up to Monrovia Nursery in Azusa, California. They are the largest nursery in the world.

Q. How do I keep dogs away from my evergreens?

A. Get a big, mean cat. You can dip pipe cleaners in Black Leaf 40 and hang them on the plant, sniff high. Also spread parabenzine moth crystals on the soil underneath. This will also control some of the soil insects that try to move in.

Q. I love rhododendrons, but I don't have a northern location in which to plant them. Am I out of luck?

A. No, not really. They like shade but will tolerate some sun. An eastern exposure, or any other, will do if you can shade the rhododendrons, say with a large tree. Azaleas, mountain laurel and *Pieris japonica* are all great friends and like the same acid soil, moist and shady.

Q. Are ground covers considered as good as a mulch under evergreens?

A. You bet. They are really great and, when possible, I do use them. If you want to be the talk of the town, use strawberries as a ground cover beneath evergreen; foliage, flowers *and fruit* . . . delicious. You can also use vinca, ajuga and pachysandra, to name a few.

Q. How do you get rid of red spiders once and for all?

A. Dig up all of your evergreens. Or you can also spray with soap and water. If that fails, use malathion.

Q. Will bag worms kill my evergreens, and how do I get rid of them?

A. They sure do make your evergreens uncomfortable. They won't destroy them, just make them itch a lot. You can use Black Leaf 40 and soap and water.

Q. The leaves on our rhododendrons look terrible in the winter, they droop so bad. What causes it?

A. At ten degrees below zero your bones would droop too. That's natural. You can help them by spraying late in the fall with Wilt Pruf; that is like putting a snow suit on them.

Q. Is poultry manure good for palm trees?

A. Do you mean the one the birds deposit on top or the one you use at the bottom? Sure, it's great. As a matter of fact, it's good for most any plant.

Q. When and how do you trim a Scotch pine?

A. In June and July. You can use a sharp knife or hedge trimmers, which should also be sharp. Cut the main leader the same height as the swirl below. That way each layer of branches is the same distance apart.

Q. How do I keep the birds from eating the new shoots off the top of our spruce tree?

A. Place a small plastic bag over it until it breaks open —the bud, that is. This takes about three weeks.

Q. What are the brown balls that appear on the ends of our spruce tree?

A. This is a gall, caused by an insect. Use soap and water and malathion.

Q. The children want to grow Christmas trees from seed. Is this possible?

A. That's what cones were put there for. Soak, pierce and plant.

Q. Is plastic good to use as a mulch under evergreens?

A. Alone it would look terrible, with stone over the top of it, it's great. Poke plenty of holes in it to let some water through.

Q. Is limestone a good ground cover?

A. If it is washed, it's okay, but I don't like it as well as mixed stone or marble chips.

Q. How much should it cost to have a set of plans drawn up for landscaping?

A. How high is high or deep is deep? It depends on what you are having done. A registered architect will charge a reasonable fee; he has earned it. A landscaper might furnish you plans free if you buy from him.

Q. We have a large upright yew on the corner of the house that never has been as dark green as the one in the back yard bought at the same time. We feed and water it. What's wrong?

A. I am just guessing from what you tell me, but I would say it is a little chlorotic, and a dose of iron will help. Four to six ounces of Green Garde micronized iron will do the trick.

Q. How often should you water evergreens?

A. In the warm, dry periods, three times a week. Let the hose run on the ground and water them deep, so that the roots stay down where it's cool. In the early spring when the drying winds are blowing, spray the foliage every day.

Q. I have a space problem, and I want to grow tomatoes between my evergreens. Will it hurt the evergreens?

A. No, but the tomatoes will be awfully strong tasting. I have seen all sorts of vegetables grown among evergreens, and they both do well. Go ahead.

Q. What good does root-pruning do?

A. Makes more feeder roots for the plant. Root pruning is a must in a nursery. This is done by pushing a sharp spade down in the ground out at the weep line (farthest branches).

Q. How do you kill scale on evergreens?

A. Spray with a para scaleicide in the spring. Make sure you read the directions.

Q. What kind of evergreens do you use in a rock garden?

A. Low-growing junipers like Armstrong and many, many others. Check the nursery catalogues.

Q. How can you prevent winter kill on evergreens?

A. There is no such thing as winter kill. It is early spring dehydration. When the early spring winds blow they dry out the moisture in the foliage, and the ground is not yet thawed out, so it can't send water up to replace the loss. You can water the foliage on days like this and prevent this from happening.

Q. Why can't we grow those soft, beautiful Japanese yews in the Southwest?
A. You can, but they never look quite as nice as they do where they get that cold weather in the winter to harden them up.

Q. Are root feeders good to use on evergreens?
A. They are excellent if you use them right. If you use them wrong you can destroy the root system of the plant. A root feeder attaches to the end of your hose and works on water pressure. If you turn it on too strong you wash away soil and leave air pockets. Slow and easy is the answer.

Q. Why do mice eat the bark off our evergreens in the winter, and what can I do to stop them?
A. They are after salt. You could give them what they are after and leave feed stations where they, the rabbits and the deer, can get food and salt and leave plants alone. I do.

Q. What good does gypsum do for evergreens?
A. It helps them to grow nice strong roots. The sulphur discourages some soil insects. Gypsum, when applied to the soil beneath evergreens in the early spring and late fall, keeps the soil loose and improves drainage. I highly recommend it.

Q. When is the best time to plant bare-root evergreens?
A. In the early spring. They are an excellent buy, and I have a great luck with them. You can generally purchase bare-root stock from catalogues. Know your company.

Q. If regular lawn food is good enough for evergreens, why do they go to the trouble to advertise evergreen food?

A. Come on! These companies are in business to make a profit, and the evergreen foods do have added trace elements for evergreens. But lawn food will do the job.

Q. Our garden club has taken on a project of financing and supervising the landscaping of a children's home. Where can we get a crash course in landscape design?

A. You can take a home study course through National Landscape Institute, 11826 San Vicente Boulevard, Los Angeles, California, 90049. The director is Norman Morris, a registered landscape architect. After this course you will probably know more than the landscape contractor.

Q. Should you tie up evergreens for the winter?

A. I tie the tall upright arborvitaes and junipers so that the ice and snow do not break them. The rest I just leave alone. After a heavy snow I suggest that you go out and sweep them off.

Q. How high should a wind screen be for evergreens?

A. High enough to protect all of them. Generally you are only worried about a west or southwest wind.

Q. We have a large colony of carpenter ants under our evergreens. Will they hurt them? I have tried drowning them.

A. If I were you, I would check the foundation of my house closely. Those nasty varmints are not in your evergreens, they are probably in your house. Use forty-four percent chlordane and call an exterminator quickly.

Q. What attracts grubs?

A. The roots of your evergreens. They make a mighty

fine meal for a hungry, growing grub. Punch plenty
of holes in the soil, spray with soap and water and
apply liquid chlordane. Check the soil in a week and
repeat, if necessary.

Q. How often should lime be added to the soil for evergreens?
A. As often as a soil test indicates it is necessary. Lime is
only added when the pH factor indicates high acidity.

Q. Are coffee grounds good for evergreens?
A. Three cups of coffee grounds a season are recommended for rhododendrons, azaleas, perris and mountain laurel.

Q. Is it okay to mulch with oak, maple and elm leaves
in the fall?
A. It was the only mulch before you and I came along.
Make sure the trees are not blighted or diseased.

Q. What is the best spray for Jack pine?
A. If you are a Christmas-tree grower, gasoline and a
match. The Jack pine is a disease and insect drawer
and grows wild in the southwest. The C. C. C. boys
planted them in the North. Spray with soap and water
and follow with malathion.

Q. When should you cut down a yucca candle?
A. As soon as it is done blooming. The yucca or lord's
candle, as it is called, is the most versatile evergreen
growing. It grows in the hot Southwest, cold North
and humid South. I design them into almost every
landscape.

Q. How can you make a pyracantha have more berries?
A. Feed it a low nitrogen and screen it from drying winds
when it is flowering.

Q. How do you dry bittersweet?
A. Hang it up, upside down in the sun. Here is a plant

that is really forgotten and yet it makes one of the best hedges I have ever run into.

Q. What makes the edges of holly leaves get black?
A. Wind scorch. Spray with Wilt Pruf in the fall and protect them from winter winds.

Q. We wanted to make an old-fashioned, formal garden. What can we use for a low formal hedge? Evergreen?
A. Boxwood grows no more than two feet high, but can be kept trimmed lower than that.

Q. Is it true that marigolds planted with evergreens keep the bugs away?
A. I have found it to be true, but only when you use the old-fashioned, bad-smelling ones.

Q. Our cedar trees are overrun with aphids every year. Are they in the soil?
A. No. They are in the foliage. Wash, spray with malathion and plant wild garlic around the cedars. This will keep the aphids away.

Q. What attracts all of the cats in our neighborhood to our evergreens?
A. Could be your girl cat. It has been said that the Hetzi juniper attracts them. I can certainly understand why, since the juice from the juniper berries attracts an awful lot of human "tom cats."

Q. When can you plant a live Christmas tree after the holidays?
A. Boy, that's a loaded question. I find that the best time is when the tree is back to normal, as far as the weather is concerned. I set it in the garage and wait until a nice sunny day comes along and then move it to a hole I have already dug. I set it in, but do not cover it up until spring. Good luck!

3
Shade Trees:
Your Monument

IN
MEMORY
—
GRANMA
PUTT

Every Man's Monument

When I was a small boy, I spent a school year with my Grandmother Putnam. I learned more about love and tenderness in that year than any other time of my childhood. You see, my grandmother truly knew the language of the flowers. I am convinced she could talk to Mother Nature and would be answered. She spent most of her days in her garden. When I would come home from school each evening, I would hustle into the house and head for the kitchen and the cookie jar and then on out into the garden. On nice days I'd find Grandma sitting in her wicker chair, with her Bible in her hand, under the shade and protection of Great Grandpa Coolidge. She would tousle my hair and kiss my cheek and want to know about the important happenings of my day.

Of course a lot of things happen in the ordinary day of a six-year-old boy. Billy Annoble caught a frog in the ditch on the way to school and put it on Maxey Smith's seat, and he sat on it. I spilled water paint on the new linoleum, and so on. Grandma Putt would take the time right then to tell me a story about Mr. Frog and all the good he does and explain that Billy shouldn't hurt frogs. We would sit there in the garden and she would tell me a story from the Bible and then get up and pat Great Grandpa Coolidge and would go inside and begin to make dinner, and I would do my chores and go to play. By the way, Great Grandpa Coolidge was her favorite maple tree.

The way the story goes in our family, Great Grandpa planted that maple tree himself as a living monument.

And to this day, whenever I pass that way, Great Grandpa Coolidge is still standing. Not too far from him stands my Grandpa Putt. His monument is a horse chestnut. Grandma Putt told me that particular kind of tree was picked for him because he raised and raced racing-trotters. My grandmother said that every man should plant a tree on a spot where he would like to be forever, and I happen to believe that is one of the most important ideas that anyone ever told me.

Could you imagine what the world would be like with no trees? To me, there is no greater beauty than the tall elegance of these masterpieces of Mother Nature's craft.

Shade trees give so much and ask so little. They shade you when you are tired, cool you when you are hot. The soft rustle of their leaves can calm you when you're uptight, and to lie on your back and look at the sunlight filtering down toward you can bring your mind and heart closer to happiness than most of us have a right to be. So why not plant a tree as your own living monument?

Trees Are Taken for Granted

Most homeowners who have trees take them for granted until it looks like they are going to lose them, and then they begin to worry. Most of the time, their concern comes too late.

After a heavy rain or a hard wind, the first thing I do is walk under and around the shade trees on my property and survey them. I look them over very closely, much in the same way as I look over my children when they come to me crying after a spill or a fight. I check first to see that nothing is broken, and then I look for cuts and bruises. I do not take anything for granted with either my children or my trees. You must understand that trees are like humans. They suffer pain. They weep and bleed. They become arthritic and feeble, anemic and even neurotic. Trees go into shock and develop ulcers. So, you can see and understand that there is really a human side to growing trees.

The Perfect Match

Selecting a shade tree should be done in the same manner in which you pick your spouse. But this is one time that I don't recommend love at first sight. You see, your home and your shade tree are probably going to be married for a lot longer than you or I, so it is important that they be compatible. The trees in your yard (since your home can have a harem) should complement your house and garden in the same way a woman complements her man. As the saying goes, for every man there's a woman; likewise, for every tree there is a garden. I have never met an ugly tree or one that I couldn't like. But, there are happy trees and sad ones, happy-go-lucky trees and selfish trees. There are trees to match every human personality, so pick the tree that matches yours.

Plan Ahead

If you have completed your evergreen landscaping, now you're ready to turn your attention to the shade trees for your property. You will find that you can use trees to screen off objectionable views, deaden the sound of street traffic, as windbreakers, to control poor drainage areas and to fit almost any bill. But first you must plan.

Let's refer back to our paper bag plan. Look it over carefully and take a sharp pencil and draw lines representing telephone or electric wires and note their heights. Now, take a felt tip pen and indicate your sewers or drain tiles and their depth, if you can find out. Get out your catalogues and begin to make a list of the trees you would like in the order of your preference. Then and only then, take your plan back to the nurseryman. Check the tags to find out how tall and broad the trees will grow. You do not want to plant too close to the house or garage and have to remove your tree in a few years because it raised the roof or tried to grow into the living room. Check to see if it is an explorer of sewers and tiles. If so, it may end up trying your patience when you have to call a plumber

a couple of times a year to drill and clean out the roots from your sewage system.

When you have finally decided on the variety of tree you want, one that is compatible to your home and garden, pick out the right spot to plant it. Never plant a tree under any wires or directly over drains. Never plant it too close to walks or driveways, or you may have to end up moving it. And, above all, plant it on your property, not the neighbors' or city property. Remember, it's a lot easier to change a mistake made with a pencil than one made with a shovel!

Forever Yours!

Shade trees, like evergreens, come in an assortment of containers: balled-in-burlap, paper pulp and tin cans. And again, you want all the soil with your tree that you can get. It is more difficult to transport shade trees than evergreens, so you must make sure that the trunk is wrapped with a large blanket or rags when it's put into your car or trailer. Also make sure that the limbs are securely tied with old nylon hose. I don't recommend that you move a shade tree in an automobile trunk. In the first place the ball or container weighs too much for one man to handle. I suggest that you pay the few dollars extra to have your tree delivered.

When the tree arrives, you should go through the same procedure I've suggested for planting your evergreens. Make sure that the hole is large enough and wide enough to plant without cramping. Shade trees are to be planted on the day they arrive, even if they have been grown in a container. All too often, they are blown over or upset in some way, and stand a chance of breaking the soil ball, which will damage the roots. It is absolutely necessary that the tree be planted straight and braced for the first six months. Too many times there is a soil shift, or a prevailing wind that causes the poor tree to grow cockeyed the rest of its life. Shade trees are best braced by the use of a guy wire attached to a heavy band of nylon hose. Nylon is extremely strong, yet it is soft and pliable enough so that it will not chafe the bark.

The tree of your choice is now in the ground, straight as an arrow. Now, mulch the ground around it and soak the soil. Do not feed it for two weeks, then feed with fish emulsion and follow with any lawn food that does not have a weed killer in it.

Now it's time to wrap it up—I mean the trunk. For this job you'll need a roll of tree wrap, a strong paper with a tar center which keeps the dry winds from *cooking* your young trees in the summer and keeps them dormant in the winter. I wrap all new trees and leave the wrapping on until it rots off. Start at the lowest main branch and wrap it all the way to the ground.

The best time to plant shade trees is in the early spring or early fall. In the snow country, you can plant or set trees in a hole and partly cover with soil and straw in the cold of winter when both the ball and the soil are frozen.

Stand back and look over your new friend. Make sure he was not bruised or broken in the move to your home. If he was, sterilize the wound and dress it with pruning paint to seal. A week after he's in the ground, give him a shower with soap and water. Make sure you do this again before the winter freeze.

Help!

I stated earlier that all too often we tree owners are not conscious of damage or disease until it is almost too late. And I find that in many cases it is because the trees are so big that we can't see what's wrong with them, or we think that they are big enough to take care of themselves. None of us, man or tree is ever quite that big. We all need attention and help once in a while. I had an elm tree where I once lived, and he moaned only when he was in trouble. Once I heard the noise and looked him over and found that the crook of the tree was split. I repaired it and the noise stopped. Next time he moaned, I found a bees' nest in a large crevice that was hidden. As soon as I removed it, he stopped moaning. So you see, trees can talk. Just listen!

I'm sure you don't let your kids stop taking showers when they get big. Well, small trees and big trees need showers too! Now this can be a big undertaking, but with a little imagination—or a community effort—you can have the trees sprayed. My neighbors and I share the cost.

If you have had a problem with insects or disease, it is necessary that you dormant-spray. This is done with a lime, sulphur and Volk oil combination. Dormant-spray in the fall after the leaves have fallen and again in the spring before the buds swell. In the West and South, you continue with the shower and spray with malathion if you have had an insect problem. Average-size trees, of fifteen to twenty feet, can be sprayed with the standard hose and equipment and should be placed on the shower list for once every three to four weeks.

This Won't Hurt

Pruning and trimming of shade trees should be approached with care and caution. An inexperienced, amateur tree surgeon can do more damage than good if he doesn't know what he is doing. If you think you have spotted a problem that requires surgery, stop right where you are, turn around three times and then look at it again! Now ask yourself, "Can I handle the saw, pruners and branches myself without damaging my own safety or the tree's good health?" If the answer is no, then ask yourself if you can do the job with the help of your neighbor. Still no? Then call a professional tree surgeon. You will save time, money and the tree. If you do decide that you are capable of doing the job, make sure you have the right tools. Makeshift surgical tools are as out of place in tree surgery as in an appendicitis operation. Make sure your saws and pruning tools are sharp and clean, and not rusty.

If a limb has been injured or broken and at least half of the bark is intact, the limb can be set much like a broken arm. First, thoroughly sterilize the break with three tablespoons of ammonia per quart of water. Next, with a sharp pair of hand pruners, cut the splintered and ragged edges away so that the limb will come back into place and fit normally. Avoid lifting more times than necessary, as it hurts. Cut two lengths of board the width of the limb.

Wrap the ends with nylon. These splints should be twice the length of the break. Now splint the break on top and bottom and tie with nylon. The last step is to seal the wound and leave splinted until a heavy adhesion has occurred.

When it is necessary to amputate a branch or limb, make your first incision below and behind the break, just deep enough to penetrate the bark. This will prevent the bark from being torn all the way down the trunk. Now complete the operation by cutting from above. Sterilize and dress. Talk to the patient. It is comforting to both of you, and, after all, nothing mixes better than tree and sympathy!

General trimming and shaping is best done when the tree is dormant, during the cold of winter. In warm weather you can do maintenance trimming at any time. However, fall still appears to be the safest time for minor surgery. Always sterilize and dress the wound. I have found that tree maintenance on a neighborhood level is much more economical for the care of large trees. Since any tree enhances the beauty and value of any neighborhood, it should be of vital interest for you and your neighbors to share the cost. Get more than one bid and appoint a treasurer. By sharing the cost and having a professional do the job, you'll save yourself a lot of hard work and sore muscles, and you'll probably get much better results.

Feed for Foliage

The toughest thing to convince a homeowner is that it is necessary to feed a great big old maple, oak or elm, or any of the other big trees. He looks at you like you are out of your mind. But, as the old saying goes: "You ain't seen nothing yet!"

The first spring that you feed a large, mature tree, it will put on a foot or more of new growth, the foliage color will deepen and the leaves will be thicker. The second year you won't recognize him as the same tree. The large older trees need a meal early in the spring when the rains stop in the West and South. In the North, you'll have to wait until you can pound a stake into the ground. Drill or poke holes two feet apart in circles under the farthest branches, ten to twelve inches deep, and fill with any lawn food that contains no weed-killing chemicals.

The old trees are fed in the spring and fall at a rate of one pound for every inch around the trunk.

Spare the Rod and Spoil the Tree

From time to time we find a lazy bones, sleeping in the sun, in our garden. He can be an old fellow or a young guy. He can be large or small. He is a lazy tree, lying down on the job, not producing enough shade because his leaves are not thick enough. What he needs is a rude but effective awakening. To wake up a sleepy tree and get him back to work, you whip him. That's right, give him a good spanking with a stick on his trunk. "Wake up!" you shout, like my ma, who used to whip me and yell all at once. Believe me, he will wake up and grow! Grandma Putt called her switch "a bearing switch." Today, the nurseryman calls this whipping act "scoring." What happens when you hit the bark is that you make it jump, and you jar the layer of tissue beneath the bark that carries the sap up to the foliage. This is just like when you go to a steam bath and get a rubdown. They pound your flesh to improve your circulation.

Spank a tree and see. I use a four-foot soft switch, not a ball bat. I want to wake him up, not break his back. Whip your tree from the crook all the way to the ground, all around the trunk. If you don't think this works, try it. I once had an old, soft maple tree, that just didn't have it anymore. Sleep, sleep, sleep. So one day I cut myself a four-foot sucker shoot off a lilac bush and as I passed ol' "sleeping branch" (that's his Indian name), I gave him one hell of a crack. I'm sure I woke him up because he really paid me back later! He dropped his maple spinner-seeds by the millions, leaves by the ton! Before, I was lucky if I got two bushels of spinners and some leaves. What really made me mad was when he spit his sap all over my new car. If your fruit trees aren't delivering the kind of harvests that you'd like to see, just get out your trusty "bearing switch"!

Doctor, I Have This Pain

From time to time, even the best-cared-for trees become ill for one reason or another. There are various and sundry diseases and insects that attach themselves to shade trees. When this happens, you'd better act at once, without delay! Call a doctor immediately. The best tree doctor are your local professional nurserymen or tree surgeons.

When you call for advice, it is necessary that you give the tree doc the same information that you would give if a loved one were ill. Your trees are loved ones; someone else would love to have them. Tell him the name of the patient and its variety. Next tell him how old the tree is. This is done by telling him how thick the trunk is. Also, describe the care you have already taken. Example: Tell him when you last dormant-sprayed and when you showered it and how often. Tell him also when you fed it, and what food you used. Now, describe the symptoms: color of foliage, shape of the leaves, color and description of the blight or insect, or the area where the disease appears. If at all possible, ask if he can make a house call. In most cases there will be no fee, but should he require one, I would gladly pay it to save my tree.

Most insect infestations of the foliage can be stopped with malathion, the safest of the chlorinated hydro-carbons, and soil bugs should be controlled with chlordane. Tree diseases can, generally, be controlled with a good washing with soap and water, followed with a spraying of broad spectrum fungicide.

Dutch elm disease presents a different problem altogether. At this time we have no known cure, though some have claimed partial control with various concoctions. The elm bark beetle carries the disease, and he will generally not stop at strong healthy trees, only weak and injured ones.

I'm Not Moving

Want to bet? Almost any tree can be moved nowadays, if you have the money. Modern day equipment can safely move virtually any tree, with the exception, of course, of the big redwoods.

I do not recomend that you, the ambitious home gardener, try to transplant any tree larger than two inches in diameter. I say this for the tree's safety and yours! When transplanting a shade tree, I suggest that you stand underneath the tree and look up. Make the soil ball half the size of the outer circle of the branches. Follow the same procedure as in moving evergreens.

A large tree or a small, weak tree should be braced to combat the wind damage that can be caused on a stormy day. Most braces should be placed by a competent tree surgeon, as a poorly placed guy wire or loop can do more damage than good.

Iron-Poor Blood

A shortage of natural iron in the soil can cause a condition known as chlorosis. It is known as anemia in humans. The leaves turn a yellowish color, with the veins remaining a deep green.

When the tree has a bad case of chlorosis, the whole leaf turns yellow and drops off. The tree stops growing, the foliage becomes sparse and, in many cases, the plant dies. This chlorotic condition can be corrected with an iron chelate much like Geritol. Iron chelates place a storage supply in the soil for the roots to absorb. I have found that the best methods for feeding trees iron is with a Ross Root Feeder. This is a hose attachment with a long spike. At the top is a chamber where water-soluble cartridges of iron are placed. Two feedings are recommended, ten days apart. Chelated iron is applied any time the chlorotic condition is noticed.

Every tree in your yard is like money in your pocket when you go to sell your home. Just ask the man who doesn't have any. If you will be firm, but friendly, you will find that the shade trees in your garden will go out of their way to please you.

Beware of Builders

I often feel that there should have been an eleventh commandment, and it should have said. "Thou shalt not deliberately kill a tree." I am sure this would have influenced an awful lot of real estate developers, bulldozer operators and builders. I have never in my life seen such willful destruction of native trees as when a builder moves into an area for construction.

A friend of mine purchased a lot not too long ago to build a home. He selected the lot because it had some twenty-eight maple trees, sixteen hawthorns, three poplars and a half-dozen other trees. When he described the lot he was so excited with his great luck in getting so many beautiful trees. I cautioned him to protect the trees closest to where the building was to be placed. "Oh," he replied, "the builder assured me that he will take special care." Construction began, and three weeks later I received a desperate call, "Come quick and look at my trees." When I got there it looked like the Battle of the Bulge had been fought on that spot. Limbs were broken, and bark was torn from the trunks. Some trees had been uprooted or bent, and many were buried in as much as ten to twelve feet of earth. By the time construction had been finished, he had less than one-third of the original trees. This can happen to you if you do not take precautions.

On Guard

I am aware that some trees must be removed for various and sundry reasons prior to or during construction. If at all possible, these trees should be moved and can be by professionals. Trees close to the house should have boards fastened to three sides and held by banding of nylon stockings to prevent gouging. Next, excess soil should be removed from root surfaces as soon as possible. No more than eight inches of new soil should cover the roots.

Holes should be bored or drilled through new soil out at the tops of the farthest branches so that the plant is able to breathe and eat. I have always recommended feeding trees before construction begins on your property.

Mother Nature's Fan

When we talk about shade trees we often forget that palm trees are shade trees too. The palms will grow up to the northern part of zone eight, and palms can be grown in pots indoors almost anywhere.

Patio Palms:

Arecastrum	Howea
Chamaedorea	Livistona
Chamaerops	Phoenix
Chrysalidocarpus	Syagrus
Hedyscepe	

Palms are divided into two types: hand-shaped and those with feather-like leaves.

Most Popular Palms

These are available in most garden centers:

PROFESSIONAL NAME	HOME GARDEN NAME
Buteia	Pindo Palm
Chamaedorea	Neanthe Bella Palm
Chamaerops excelsa	Windmill Palm
Chamaerops humilis	Mediterranean Fan Palm
Cocos	Queen Palm
Cycas	Sago Palm
Erythea armata	Mexican Blue Palm
Erythea edulis	Guadalupe Palm
Phoenix canariensis	Ornamental Date Palm
Phoenix reclinata	Senegal Date Palm
Seaforthia	King Palm
Trachycarpus	Takie Windmill Palm
Washingtonia	Mexican Fan Palm

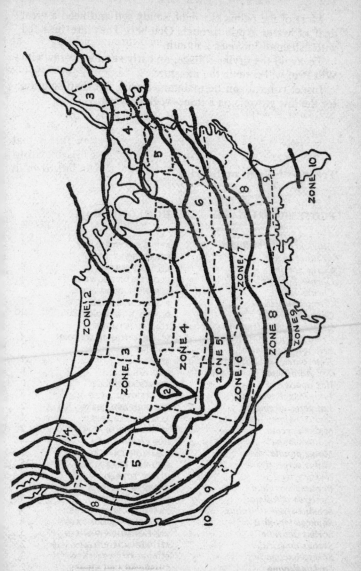

Most of the palms like light, sandy soil and need a great deal of water April through October. They are best fed with fish emulsion once a month.

To avoid the drying foliage, an early summer spray with Wilt Pruf will contain the moisture.

Insect control can be maintained with the soap solution for the low growers on a three-week program.

Trees with Fruit or Berries

PROFESSIONAL NAME	HOMEOWNER NAME	ZONE
Amelanchier grandiflora	APPLE SERVICEBERRY	4
Arbutus unedo	STRAWBERRY TREE	8
Citrus species	CITRUS FRUITS	9
Cornus floridus	FLOWERING DOGWOOD	4
Cornus kousa	JAPANESE DOGWOOD	5
Cornus nuttalli	PACIFIC DOGWOOD	7
Crataegus mellis	DOWNY HAWTHORN	4
Crataegus merdenensis "Toba"	TOBA HAWTHORN	3
Crataegus phaenopyrum	WASHINGTON HAWTHORN	4
Eriobotrya japonica	LOQUAT	7
Heteromeles arbutifolia	TOYON	7
Ilex Aquifolium	ENGLISH HOLLY	6
Ilex opaca	AMERICAN HOLLY	5
Juniperus scopulorum	WESTERN RED-CEDAR	4
Juniperus virginiana	EASTERN RED-CEDAR	2
Malus "Almey"	ALMEY CRAB APPLE	4
Malus baccata	SIBERIAN CRAB APPLE	2
Malus "Hopa"	HOPA CRAB APPLE	4
Malus pumila	COMMON CRAB APPLE	3
Malus sargenti	SARGENT CRAB APPLE	5
Nyssa sylvatica	BLACK TUPELO	4
Photinia serrulata	CHINESE PHOTINIA	7
Poncirus trifoliata	HARDY ORANGE	5
Schinus terebinthifolius	BRAZILIAN PEPPER TREE	9
Sophora japonica	JAPANESE PAGODA TREE	4
Sorbus alnifolia	KOREAN MOUNTAIN-ASH	5
Sorbus americana	AMERICAN MOUNTAIN-ASH	2
Sorbus aucuparia	EUROPEAN MOUNTAIN-ASH	3
Sorbus decora	SHOWY MOUNTAIN-ASH	2

Trees with Flowers

PROFESSIONAL NAME	HOMEOWNER NAME	COLOR OF FLOWER	ZONE
Acacia baileyana	COOTAMUNDRA WATTLE	yellow	10
Acacia decurrens dealbata	SILVER WATTLE	yellow	9
Acer platanoides columnare	COLUMNAR NORWAY MAPLE	yellow	3
Acer platanoides "Crimson King"	CRIMSON KING MAPLE	yellow	4
Acer platanoides "Emerald Queen"	EMERALD QUEEN MAPLE	yellow	3
Acer platanoides schwedleri	SCHWEDLER MAPLE	yellow	3
Acer platanoides "Summershade"	SUMMERSHADE MAPLE	yellow	3
Albizzia julibrissin	SILK TREE	purple	6
Albizzia julibrissin "Charlotte"	CHARLOTTE SILK TREE	purple	6
Albizzia julibrissin rosea	HARDY SILK TREE	purple	5
Albizzia julibrissin "Tryon"	TRYON SILK TREE	purple	6
Amelanchier canadensis	SHADBLOW SERVICEBERRY	white	4
Amelanchier grandiflora	APPLE SERVICEBERRY	white	4
Arbutus unedo	STRAWBERRY TREE	white	8
Bauhinia variegata	PURPLE ORCHID TREE	lavender	10
Bauhinia variegata candida	WHITE ORCHID TREE	white	10
Castanea mollissima	CHINESE CHESTNUT	white	5
Ceratonia siliqua	CAROB	red	10
Cercis canadensis alba	WHITEBUD	white	5
Cercis canadensis "Withers Pink Charm"	WITHERS PINK REDBUD	purple	5
Citrus species	CITRUS FRUITS	white	9
Cladastris lute	YELLOW-WOOD	white	4
Cornus floridus	FLOWERING DOGWOOD	white	4
Cornus kousa	JAPANESE DOGWOOD	white	5
Cornus nuttalli	PACIFIC DOGWOOD	white	7
Crataegus mollis	DOWNY HAWTHORN	white	4
Crataegus phaenopyrum	WASHINGTON HAWTHORN	white	4

PROFESSIONAL NAME	HOMEOWNER NAME	COLOR OF FLOWER	ZONE
Eucalyptus ficifolia	CRIMSON EUCALYPTUS	red	9
Halesia carolina	CAROLINA SILVERBELL	white	4
Heteromeles arbutifolia	TOYON	white	7
Jacaranda acutifolia	SHARPLEAF JACARANDA	lavender	10
Köelreuteria paniculata	GOLDEN RAIN TREE	yellow	5
Laburnum vossi	VOSSI LABURNUM	yellow	5
Lagerstroemia indica "Ingleside Pink"	INGLESIDE CRAPE MYRTLE	purple	7
Lagerstroemia indica "Wm. Toovey"	RED CRAPE MYRTLE	red	7
Ligustrum lucidum	GLOSSY PRIVET	white	7
Liriodendron tulipifera	TULIP TREE	yellow	4
Magnolia denudata	YULAN MAGNOLIA	white	5
Magnolia grandiflora	SOUTHERN MAGNOLIA	white	7
Magnolia stellata	STAR MAGNOLIA	white	5
Magnolia virginiana	SWEET BAY	white	5
Malus "Almey"	ALMEY CRAB APPLE	red	4
Malus arnoldiana	ARNOLD CRAB APPLE	white	4
Malus atrosanguinea	CARMINE CRAB APPLE	red	4
Malus baccata	SIBERIAN CRAB APPLE	white	2
Malus floribunda	JAPANESE FLOWERING CRAB APPLE	white	4
Malus "Hopa"	HOPA CRAB APPLE	red	4
Malus hupehensis	TEA CRAB APPLE	white	4
Malus "Katherine"	KATHERINE CRAB APPLE	purple	4
Malus "Prince George"	PRINCE GEORGES CRAB APPLE	purple	4
Malus pumila	COMMON CRAB APPLE	white	3
Malus sargenti	SARGENT CRAB APPLE	white	5
Oxydendrum arboreum	SORREL TREE	white	4
Photinia serrulata	CHINESE PHOTINIA	white	7
Poncirus trifoliata	HARDY ORANGE	white	5
Prunus cerasifera nigra "Thundercloud"	THUNDERCLOUD PLUM	white	4
Prunus persica	PEACH	purple	5
Prunus sargenti	SARGENT CHERRY	purple	4
Prunus serrulata "Amanogawa"	AMANOGAWA CHERRY	purple	6
Prunus serrulata "Kwanzan"	KWANZAN CHERRY	purple	5
Prunus serrulata "Shirofugen"	SHIROFUGEN CHERRY	white	6
Prunus serrulata "Shirotae"	MOUNT FUJI CHERRY	white	6

PROFESSIONAL NAME	HOMEOWNER NAME	COLOR OF FLOWER	ZONE
Prunus subhirtella autumnalis	AUTUMN CHERRY	purple	5
Prunus subhirtella pendula	WEEPING HIGAN CHERRY	purple	5
Prunus yedoensis	YOSHINO CHERRY	white	5
Pyrus calleryana "Bradford"	BRADFORD CALLERY PEAR	white	5
Pyrus communis	COMMON PEAR	white	5
Sophora japonica	JAPANESE PAGODA TREE	white	4
Sorbus alnifolia	KOREAN MOUNTAIN-ASH	white	5
Sorbus americana	AMERICAN MOUNTAIN-ASH	white	2
Sorbus aucuparia	EUROPEAN MOUNTAIN-ASH	white	3
Sorbus decora	SHOWY MOUNTAIN-ASH	white	2
Stewartia pseudocamellia	JAPANESE STEWARTIA	white	5
Styrax japonica	JAPANESE SNOWBELL	white	5
Syringa amurensis japonica	JAPANESE TREE LILAC	white	4
Tilia cordata	LITTLE-LEAF LINDEN	yellow	3
Tilia cordata "Greenspire"	GREENSPIRE LINDEN	yellow	3
Tilia euchlora	CRIMEAN LINDEN	yellow	5
Tilia tomentosa	SILVER LINDEN	yellow	4
Tilia tomentosa "Princeton"	PRINCETON SILVER LINDEN	yellow	4

Standard Shade Trees with Attractive Foliage

PROFESSIONAL NAME	HOMEOWNER NAME	ZONE
Acer ginnale	AMUR MAPLE	2
Acer palmatum	JAPANESE MAPLE	5
Acer palmatum atropurpureum	BLOODLEAF JAPANESE MAPLE	5
Acer palmatum atropurpureum "Bloodgood"	BLOODGOOD JAPANESE MAPLE	5
Acer palmatum dissectum	THREADLEAF JAPANESE MAPLE	5
Acer pseudoplatanus	SYCAMORE MAPLE	5
Acer saccharinum pyramidale	PYRAMIDAL SUGAR MAPLE	3
Acer saccharum	SUGAR MAPLE	3
Acer saccharum columnare	COLUMNAR SUGAR MAPLE	3
Acer saccharum monumentale	SENTRY MAPLE	3
Acer saccharum "Green Mountain"	GREEN MOUNTAIN MAPLE	3

PROFESSIONAL NAME	HOMEOWNER NAME	ZONE
Betula papyrifera	CANOE BIRCH	2
Betula pendula	EUROPEAN BIRCH	2
Betula pendula laciniata	CUTLEAF EUROPEAN BIRCH	2
Betula populifolia	GRAY BIRCH	4
Butia capitata	SO. AMERICAN JELLY PALM (PINDE PALM)	9
Cedrus atlantica	ATLAS CEDAR	6
Cedrus atlantica glauca	BLUE ATLAS CEDAR	5
Cedrus deodara	DEODAR CEDAR	7
Cercidiphyllum japonicum	KATSURA TREE	4
Cercis canadensis	EASTERN REDBUD	4
Cinnamomum camphora	CAMPHOR TREE	9
Cocos nucifera	COCONUT PALM	10
Eucalyptus globulosus	TASMANIAN EUCALYPTUS	9
Fagus sylvatica	EUROPEAN BEECH	4
Fagus sylvatica atropurpurea riverse	RIVER'S PURPLE BEECH	4
Fagus sylvatica pendula	WEEPING BEECH	4
Ficus retusa	INDIAN LAUREL FIG	10
Fraxinus americana	WHITE ASH	3
Fraxinus pennsylvanica "Marshall's Seedless"	MARSHALL'S SEEDLESS ASH	2
Fraxinus velutina "Modeste"	MODESTE ASH	5
Ginkgo biloba	GINKGO	4
Ginkgo biloba fastigiata	SENTRY GINKGO	4
Gleditsia triancanthos inermis	THORNLESS HONEY-LOCUST	4
Gleditsia triancanthos inermis "Moraine"	MORAINE LOCUST	4
Gleditsia triancanthos inermis "Rubylace"	RUBYLACE LOCUST	4
Gleditsia triancanthos inermis "Shademaster"	SHADEMASTER LOCUST	4
Gleditsia triancanthos inermis "Skyline"	SKYLINE LOCUST	4
Gleditsia triancanthos inermis "Sunburst"	SUNBURST LOCUST	4
Gymnocladus dioicus	KENTUCKY COFFEE TREE	4
Lagerstroemia indica	CRAPE MYRTLE	7
Liquidambar styraciflua	SWEET-GUM	4
Metasequoia glyptostroboides	DAWN REDWOOD	5
Olea europaea	COMMON OLIVE	9
Phellodendron amurense	AMUR CORK TREE	3
Phoenix canariensis	CANARY ISLAND DATE PALM	10
Phoenix reclinata	SENEGAL DATE PALM	10
Picea abies	NORWAY SPRUCE	2
Pinus canariensis	CANARY PINE	8

PROFESSIONAL NAME	HOMEOWNER NAME	ZONE
Pinus strobus	EASTERN WHITE PINE	3
Pistacia chinensis	CHINESE PISTACHIO	9
Platanus acerifolia	LONDON PLANE TREE	5
Platanus occidentalis	AMERICAN SYCAMORE	4
Populus nigra italica	LOMBARDY POPLAR	2
Prunus avium	SWEET CHERRY	3
Prunus cerasus	SOUR CHERRY	3
Pseudotsuga taxifolia	DOUGLAS FIR (ROCKY MOUNTAIN STRAIN)	4
Quercus agrifolia	CALIFORNIA LIVE OAK	9
Quercus alba	WHITE OAK	4
Quercus borealis	RED OAK	4
Quercus coccinea	SCARLET OAK	4
Quercus palustris	PIN OAK	4
Quercus phellos	WILLOW OAK	5
Quercus virginiana	LIVE OAK	7
Reystonea regia	ROYAL PALM	10
Salix alba tristis	GOLDEN WEEPING WILLOW	2
Salix babylonica	BABYLON WEEPING WILLOW	6
Salix elegantissima	THURLOW WEEPING WILLOW	4
Sophora japonica "Regent"	REGENT PAGODA TREE	4
Thuja occidentalis nigra	DARK GREEN AMERICAN ARBORVITAE	2
Trachycarpus fortunei	CHINESE WINDMILL PALM	8
Tsuga canadensis	CANADA HEMLOCK	3
Ulmus americana	AMERICAN ELM	2
Ulmus americana "Princeton"	PRINCETON ELM	2
Ulmus carpinifolia "Christine Buisman"	CHRISTINE BUISMAN ELM	4
Ulmus parvifolia	CHINESE ELM	5
Washington filifera	WASHINGTON FAN PALM	10
Washington robusta	MEXICAN FAN PALM	10
Zelkova serrata	JAPANESE ZELKOVA	5
Zelkova serrata "Village Green"	VILLAGE GREEN ZELKOVA	5

Questions and Answers

Q. What is the white cotton-like substance that covers branches of a maple every year?

A. It is called cottony maple scale, and it can be controlled with the use of a dormant spray in the fall and again in the early spring, followed by regular soap and water showers.

Q. What causes bark to split when no one has hit the tree?

A. This is called southwest bark-split and is caused by temperature changes on winter days when the sun warms the bark on one side of the tree and there is no room for expansion, so it splits. To avoid this I have wrapped the trunks of large trees subjected to the severe southwest winds with laminated tree wrap.

Q. What is the fastest growing tree I can plant as a living fence?

A. There are quite a few, but I doubt that you would care to have them around because they are called weed trees. I would suggest a silver maple or the male box elder tree.

Q. We live on a new lake development. It is sandy soil, hot and dry most of the time. What do you suggest we use as shade trees? I would like four.

A. Silver or white poplar, quaking aspen, black locust, European white birch. I suggest that you send for the nursery catalogues and check for a few more.

Q. The rabbits have ruined several trees by eating the bark in the winter. What can we do?

A. Set out feed stations for the rabbits and give them salt blocks. Set chicken wire or heavy screen wire collars around the trunks.

Q. Our son was in such a hurry to mow the lawn that he ran into several trees and tore the bark. Two of them are losing leaves on the side he hit. What can we do?

A. You can cut through the bark with a sharp knife to streamline the damage. By this I mean to make the top and bottom of the damaged bark come to a point. Sterilize and dress the wound. Do not let grass grow that close to the tree. It's not good for the tree or the grass.

Q. What can we do to stop these awful tent worms from making these awful webs in our fruit trees?

A. You can spray with soap and water, dormant-spray, and also spray with malathion when foliage is out. The worm feeds during the day on foliage close by and returns to the tent at night. I was taught not to burn the tent but to douse it with old dirty auto oil at night when it is at home asleep.

Q. What are the funny but dirty-looking reddish-brown bumps on the leaves of maples, and will they kill the tree?

A. Maple bladder gall is what they are called, and they are caused by a small mite. If they are not controlled, the tree will eventually be destroyed through sheer exhaustion and irritation, much like a person who has an itchy rash for months on end. Wash early and spray with malathion.

Q. The edges of our sycamore turn brown, and then all of the leaves fall off in the middle of summer. What's wrong?

A. Anthracnoses is the cause of your trouble. It's a fungus disease brought on by lots of rain and hot weather. Spray with bordeaux mix as soon as foliage appears. Dormant-spray in fall and spring.

Q. Do trees like ground cover to grow beneath them?

A. They much prefer ground cover to grass. Ground covers are good friends of trees and share some of the same likes. Do not plant climbers under trees—only spreading ground covers. When you feed the tree, you are also feeding the ground cover.

Q. Is it true that you should not use a weed killer under a tree?

A. You bet it's true. Don't ever use a weed killer under a tree, or you might just as well kiss it good-bye.

Q. Is it necessary to trim shade trees every year, as you do fruit trees?

A. I go out of my way to trim shade trees, no matter what

kind they are. When you do any cutting on a tree of any kind you signal the food factory far below to send the juices up to heal the wound. This means good blood circulation. Trees are very proud of their appearance; they love to look good.

Q. How close do you cut a branch when you remove it?
A. As close to the tree as possible without tearing or scarring any more bark than is necessary.

Q. Is cow manure good for trees, and how often should you apply it?
A. You just can't beat barnyard gold to feed any and everything. But, I doubt that your neighbors would appreciate this. You can use the compost manure two or three times a year—the same as lawn food.

Q. When do you recommend that I plant packaged shade trees?
A. These are considered bare root and are best planted in early spring in snow country and in the fall in the rest of the country.

Q. What is meant by root-pruning?
A. Root-pruning is the cutting of the feeder roots with a sharp blade or shovel to force the roots to branch and concentrate them in a smaller location. Root-pruning is best done in late August.

Q. Is peat moss a good top dressing for trees?
A. Peat moss is a soil conditioner which loosens soil and improves drainage. I do not recommend it as a top dressing.

Q. Why must I cut back half of my new tree when I transplant it, or plant a bare root?
A. The top is cut back to equalize the moisture loss, which is a result of root reduction. Spray trees to be moved with Wilt Pruf before moving them.

Q. We would like a palm for our vestibule. What do you suggest?

A. *Neanthe bella* palms make excellent indoor plants for large tubs or pots. Give it plenty of humidity.

Q. We irrigate every other night because of a field crop, so I have a wet area on the irrigation line. What kind of a palm can I plant?

A. I would suggest that you plant a queen palm. It's a fast grower and needs water.

Q. Is there such a thing as palm wine, and can it be made from the sap of any palm tree?

A. Yes, there is a palm wine and it is extremely potent. It is generally made from the sugar palms of Asia. The sugar palm can be grown in the warmest parts of this country, but has a short life span.

Q. How do you remove a tree stump without breaking your back or your pocketbook?

A. Go to the drug store and buy about four ounces of saltpeter, or go to the garden center and buy a can of Stump Nott. Drill lots of holes in the stump five or six inches deep and fill half of it with the saltpeter or Stump Nott. Then plug the holes for one year. Pull the plugs, fill with kerosene and light. The stump will smoulder away to nothing.

Q. Is it true that you cannot keep the wood from trees you have cut down to burn? I was told that there is a law against it.

A. In many states you cannot keep and burn elm trees that have been infected with Dutch elm disease. I would suggest that you know the fragrance of the wood you want to burn, as some of them smell so bad you can't stay in the same room.

Q. How do you kill borers?

A. The hard way! You can get a coat hanger and poke them to death, or you can get a tube of Borgo and squirt them to death. You can also paint the bark with parabenzine paint or sprinkle moth crystals containing parabenzine on the soil beneath. Another remedy is to spray the soil in late fall with chlordane.

Q. Does it do any good to paint trees?
A. I guess it does, but for what little good it does it looks terrible. A much better idea is to place a three-inch band of tree tangle foot, a sticky substance, around the trunk about four or five feet above the ground to catch insects climbing up to their dining room.

4
Flowering Trees: The Candy Store

Cotton Candy

I think the reason I communicate so well with the garden group (plants) is because I can experience the same feelings as they do at the same time, even if not always for the same reason! One good example of how human activity can parallel plant activity is the ferocious appetite I get in the spring of the year. Spring is the time of the year when your whole garden gets hungry. This is especially true of your flowering plants, including the small flowering shade trees. They are hungry because of the long sleep, and because of all the early chores they are called on to perform, almost before their eyes are open. My appetite increases with their efforts. When I was a small boy, I went to Washington, D. C., in the spring of the year when the Kwanzan cherry was in full bloom. The more I looked at them and admired their beauty, the hungrier I got. They looked like cotton candy to me. They were so bright, pink, fluffy and mouth-watering that my father had to take me a mile away to a carnival to satisfy my appetite.

In the spring of the year, when the small flowering trees are beginning to bloom, our grocery bill soars sky high! You'd be surprised at some of the unusual foods that my appetite associates with those trees and their blooms. We have a Paul's scarlet hawthorn that gives me a yen for pumpkin pie, an ornamental purple leaf plum that turns me on for plum pudding, and so on. I have found that most flowering trees are extremely conceited, self-centered and selfish, and they will do best if set away from most of the other plants. I guess I am suggesting that you flatter and spoil your flowering trees for best results.

The ornamental flowering tree, because of its early elegant blooms and fine delicate foliage, makes an extremely versatile addition to any landscape. An exception to this is the dogwood tree. This should be showcased as a specimen tree, one that stands alone. Here's an idea for you ladies. If you have a lovely flowering tree in your yard, have a name tag with your first name made for it and watch all of the special attention your husband will suddenly give it.

The Many Faces of Eve

Flowering trees can be made to fit into many situations. I have mentioned earlier that they are great to use as a specimen tree but can also be used to divide lot lines, shade the patio, frame a gate or other opening, accent a corner and add privacy from the street. You can also use them as shrubbery borders. You must learn a great deal about the trees you wish to plant, because they have many different likes and dislikes. You can learn all of these idiosyncracies from the nursery catalogues that we have talked about earlier. Refer to that list.

Handle with Kid Gloves

The flowering trees are available in balled-in-burlap, paper-pulp containers and tin cans. However, there are more bare-root flowering trees sold than any other bare-root stock, with the exception of the rose. These small and colorful trees are planted in the same way as any shade tree. Since many of you have purchased your flowering tree from a garden center, department store or some other type of retailer, because it is much less expensive, I will explain planting procedure step by step to insure your success.

Make sure the plant you buy is alive. Since it is dormant when you purchase it, it is going to take a little detective work on your part to find out. First, look for definite signs of new growth, like small bud breaks. If there are none of these visible, then gently peel a small piece of bark back in two or three places up the trunk to see if it is moist and green underneath. If it passes these tests, you can go ahead and purchase it. It is now your responsibility to keep it alive. When you arrive home, fill a bucket with two gallons of tepid water and throw in a tea bag. Next, remove the package from the roots very carefully. You will notice, in most cases, that wood shavings have been used to protect the roots and retain moisture. This packing should also be removed. When the roots are free and loose, look them over to make sure that none of them is broken. If you find any, cut them off above the break, and also cut any real long straggly roots. Now, soak the roots in the bucket of tea water overnight. When you are digging a hole for a bare-root plant, you must make sure that it is wide enough to spread out the roots, but don't make it more than one inch deeper than it was in the nursery. To help you determine the depth, you will find a telltale "bath tub ring" around the trunk.

It is now time to plant your very young flowering tree. Remove the plant from the bucket and bring it to the hole site. Laying it aside for just a moment, put enough soil back into the hole to make a pointed mound in the center, high enough that when the roots straddle it they will be comfortable, but not cramped. Cut off any that want to wind around. Now begin to recover the roots, packing the soil down as you go. Leave no air pockets. When you have returned half of the soil, fill the rest of the hole with water and wait until it settles down. Then continue to replace the rest of the soil. Make sure that the tree is straight and true. When you have completed the job of planting, add a half-pound of any garden food to the soil and three pounds of garden gypsum. Just sprinkle this on the soil beneath your trees. Bare-root plants have no root support to keep the wind from blowing them over, so it is now necessary to drive a stake into the ground alongside, and to tie the young tree to the stake with a couple of ties made from old nylon hose. These will stretch and not cut into the bark. When you have finished planting and bracing the new tree, it is time to cut the new growth back one third. This is to control the evaporation that results from the short root supply.

Spoiled Rotten

You can't plant a flowering tree and just forget it, or it will pout, be stubborn and refuse to bloom. These little ladies insist on special and undivided attention—much like any other woman. The flowering trees must be fed on a regular basis in early spring with any good garden food, and then once a month until September. To feed these trees I suggest that you cast the food beneath the tree from just beyond the weep line, back to halfway from the trunk. The amount of food at each meal will vary with the size of the tree. Five pounds for a fullgrown, two-and-one-half pounds for a seven or eight-foot tree, and a pound for the younger trees. The average flowering shade tree will not exceed fifteen feet in height.

Something for Everyone

There is a colorful flowering tree to fit everyone's taste. The most popular are: the dogwoods (red and white), the purple leaf plum (this beauty has a lovely pink flower and purple leaves), the red-bud tree, goldenchain and its sister, the goldenrain tree, magnolia (one of the most widely used), Paul's scarlet hawthorn (this is a favorite of some of the older folks because of its long blooming season), the flowering cherries (always in demand), the Kwanzan and the Hisakura. Right behind the flowering cherries come the flowering crabs—Hoppa, Almey, the pink Semcoe, Van Essentine, Sisipuk, Dolgo and Amisk, Geneva and on and on.

Keeping in Shape

Like most women, the flowering trees worry about their figures, so it is essential that you trim them each winter when they are asleep. Only trim the branches that are out of proportion. When you trim these lovely ladies, be sure to sterilize the wounds or cuts and seal them. Nothing looks worse than a flowering tree that's out of proportion, fat and sloppy, or one that is ill. Remember to shower these trees at least twice a month. All of the deciduous flowering trees must be dormant-sprayed in the colder climate to destroy the wintering insects before they can interrupt the flowering process in spring. A cupful of parabenzine moth crystals beneath the trees in the fall, and again the early spring, will keep the trees free from boring insects. Many folks who own these trees love the flower colorama, but find the fruit a nuisance. To cut down this nuisance, you can spray a chemical called Amid-Thin when the flowers appear. Sometimes a tomato veg spray containing sevin will do the trick. I have found that most of these trees grow better when they have a little company to talk to, so I always plant a flowering friend beneath each of my flowering trees. Petunias in contrasting colors seem to satisfy both the tree and me. If you don't want to use flowers, then let your tree be lonely and surround the base with wood-chip mulch.

Beware of the Underground

Since these flowering beauties are so gracious and tender, they are fair game for the grubs. A light spray of forty-four percent chlordane, applied to the soil at the first hint of irritation, can curb a catastrophe. When it is necessary to spray the foliage for insects, I use a regular fruit-tree spray as recommended. If you will poke holes beneath the trees from time to time through the season, you will find that you will cut down on your trees' problems with these bugs.

Questions and Answers

Q. When we lived in Kokomo, Indiana, we had a beautiful red-bud tree. We have just moved to Sacramento, California, where it is cold. Can we plant one here?
A. You sure can. They are in the same temperate zone. Check the map on page 111.

Q. Can I grow a strawberry tree in Virginia, the kind they grow in California?
A. If you live in the southern part of Virginia you are in luck.

Q. What makes the leaves of a dogwood turn red and fall off in the summer?
A. Odds are your dogwood tree is calling for help for the third time. He is drowning! Check the drainage quick!

Q. Why can't I just use some black enamel to seal tree cuts?
A. Because when the freeze comes the paint will also freeze and crack, and then it won't act as a seal any more. Commercial tree paints are flexible and will expand and contract with weather changes.

Q. Is there an "animal-free" tree? One that the rabbits and mice won't bother?
A. About the only one that comes to mind is a Paul's scarlet hawthorn.

Q. Will wild morning-glory hurt a flowering crab tree? It grows up the trunk and all through the branches.
A. Obviously it has not destroyed it yet, but you can be

sure your crab tree is not happy with its piggyback rider. You can stop this by pulling the plants off and hoeing them out of the soil below. Next, apply a product called Garden Preen, by Greenfield; then cover with a good wood-chip mulch.

Q. Is it okay to place stone chips underneath a weeping cherry tree?
A. I love the appearance of large stone chips, either #10 or #12, beneath all of the small weeping trees. They just seem to go together.

Q. How do you stop borers in dogwood?
A. Apply a cup or two of parabenzine moth crystals on soil beneath the tree in early spring and late fall.

Q. We have a fig tree that gets overrun with red spider mites. How can I stop them?
A. Soap and water first. Malathion if that doesn't stop them.

Q. Our flowering cherry gets about every tree disease that is in the neighborhood. What kind of spray should we use?
A. The same spray that is used on fruit cherry trees. Use any home orchard spray as recommended by the manufacturer.

Q. Should you wrap the trunk of a flowering tree for the winter?
A. I wrap all trees, and I do it when I plant in summer, winter, spring or fall. I help my friends fight sun scald with tree wrap.

Q. How much do you prune off a weeping cherry tree when you plant it bare root?
A. About one-third, just like any other packaged shade tree or shrub.

Q. What is an espaliered tree really used for?
A. According to an old story, the monks wanted to have fresh fruit in their monastery, but there was not enough

room to plant the trees. These monks were sworn never to leave the monastery, so they could not grow trees outside the walls. Then, one of the monks planted the fruit trees against the sides of all of the buildings and trained them to grow up wires. He would not let them grow out. I have heard other stories about the espaliered tree, but I like this one best.

Q. How big does an orchid tree grow?

A. I sure hope you didn't waste your money and buy one expecting it to grow in Sandusky, Ohio, where your letter is postmarked. The orchid tree (*Bauhinia variegata*) will only grow in Zone 10 (see map). It gets up to, and sometimes past, twenty feet.

Q. We have a magnolia tree that has never bloomed, but the foliage is thick, green and healthy. What's wrong?

A. Nothing. You have a seed tree, and I have known them to take ten years to produce flowers.

Q. Which of the flowering trees will grow in clay soil?

A. I have found the purple leaf plum or thunder cloud to be a great clay fighter. I guess the reason for that is that it was developed in clay country.

Q. When is the best time to prune a purple leaf plum tree that is growing up into the overhang of our home?

A. Ordinarily we do not recommend that you do much pruning of the stone fruits. In your case, when it is growing will do the trick.

Q. We have a tree wisteria that has very few clusters. What can I do to increase the blooms?

A. Odds are the soil is too dry. The wisteria will grow in almost any kind of soil as long as you keep it damp. I have always planted an evergreen ground cover under the wisteria.

Q. What is the tree that has foliage that looks like mountain ash but has a flower like wisteria, only yellow?

A. This is called a goldenchain tree by us common folks,

Laburnum vossi by the professionals. It grows very well in Zone 5, but will do pretty good in Zone 4 if protected by other trees.

Q. When I was a small girl in Germany, we had a tree called halesia. I saw one that resembled it in Pennsylvania; could this be it? If so, where can I get one?

A. It can be. It's called a *Halesia carolina* or by the common American name of Carolina silverbell. I don't know why more designers don't use them. They are virtually insect and disease-free, as well as being one of the cleanest, neatest and most beautiful trees I have seen. You can get one from Cottage Gardens, Inc., in Lansing, Michigan.

Q. We have a Kentucky coffee tree in our back yard. Can we roast the beans and make coffee?

A. I was taught that in the Revolutionary War days they did brew these beans; however, I have never tried it. This is another good-looking tree that is often overlooked.

Q. What can we do to a flowering crab tree that has sap oozing out of it?

A. Inspect the tree to see if it is broken or damaged where it is bleeding. If it is, sterilize and dress. Wash often.

Q. Should weeping trees be braced at any time?

A. I brace all of the main stems in the winter and gently tie the streamers before snow so the heart won't break.

Q. We have a small Japanese maple that keeps turning green. What's wrong?

A. Soil is not acid enough. Feed the tree in the spring with azalea food and mulch with wood chips.

Q. How can I keep grubs from killing all of my flowering peach trees?

A. Poke holes beneath and apply soap and water, followed with forty-four percent chlordane.

5
Fruit Trees:
Two for the Money

An Apple a Day

Every garden should have at least one fruit tree, if for no reason than for the gardener to experience the joy of biting into a shiny red, delicious apple, and know that he and Mother Nature worked together, against all odds, to produce this object of man's heritage. Remember, all gardening began in an orchard. Most nutritionists say that fresh, home-grown fruit is the most health-giving food that we can possibly eat. With fruit being the basic diet food, I'd like to begin this chapter by suggesting that all people who are, or think they are, overweight, plant a fruit tree or two; that all people with children plant a fruit tree, and that all the nation's beer drinkers plant a nut tree. By the time we get this far, we have included about ninety percent of the nation's homeowners. When you stop and think about it, the fruit tree, with just a little care, returns more for the time and effort expended than any other friend in the Plant Kingdom. Along with the fruit they produce, we must consider the enjoyment we get from branches we bring inside in the winter. They will bloom in a vase of water and fill the room with their fragrance of spring. Also, consider the weeks in the spring when we enjoy the splendid variety of pinks, reds, whites and lavenders of the fruit-tree blossoms. Then, when the flowers are gone, we become fascinated watching the day-by-day formation of the fruit. And then comes the harvest . . . what a delight! After harvest time, we have those cider and donut times in the fall that create warm and happy memories of our youth. There are other traditional factors to consider, and they are: the use of the cherry tree to remind us always to tell the truth, or the apple switch to teach obedience. So, you see, fruit trees mean a great deal to each of us and should be included in any master plan of gardening.

Buyer Beware

When a home gardener decides to buy a fruit tree or two, the first thing he does is shop for the lowest price. This almost always turns out to be his first mistake. The difference between the top-grade tree and the bargain seller is usually a few cents, but their vigor and quality are miles apart. When you buy a fruit tree, buy it from a nurseryman who can answer some questions and who knows what he is talking about. It is always a good idea to remember that what you pay for is what you get, and that a fruit tree that cost you a few cents more in the beginning doesn't have to produce too much to pay for the difference. Many gardeners purchase new fruit and nut trees from catalogues. This is fine if you stick to the old-line, reputable nurseries. The ones listed in this book have been in business for a good number of years and are proud of their reputation. They will stand behind the vigor and quality of their stock.

First Come, First Served

Most bare-root stock is dug in the fall and stored in cellars for early spring shipment. Those who order first are sure to get the best selection of plants. If you wait until later, then they must go into the fields and dig additional stock to fill orders. By then the sap has begun to flow, and there is a greater chance of a problem arising with the tree. Canned and potted stock is planted in the fall and some in the early spring. Balled-in-burlap is dug in the fall, as a rule. It is a good idea to plant new trees as soon as the frost has left the ground, to insure a strong root growth and heavy foliage the first year.

Quality First

All nursery stock is graded by how tall it is and how thick or dense its foliage is. Fruit trees are no exception. Fruit trees are usually graded as number 1's, 2's and 3's. The taller and thicker they are, the more expensive. They are also called one and two-year-old trees. As a rule of thumb we suggest that you buy the one-year-old apples, peaches and cherries and two-year-old plums and pears. Whichever you select, make sure you buy the first or top grade.

On Your Mark, Go!

Fruit and nut trees can be planted in either the fall or spring. If there is a possibility of the location you have selected being too wet to plant next spring, then by all means plant this fall and mulch. If it is not necessary to fall plant, then I suggest that you wait until spring, for several reasons. The first is that field mice and rabbits are elated when you serve them such a tender and delicious meal to tide them over the winter. Next, the new plant could make too much new soft growth and be frozen out by severe weather. Soil is generally healthier and more fertile after the winter snows. So, all in all, it is best to plan your orchard for spring if you live in the snow country and for the first of February in the warmer climates.

Green Side Up

Fruit trees are planted like any other normal tree, with the one exception that you don't return the old soil to the hole. It is highly recommended that you discard the soil you removed and use a commercial mix. I have found the Cornell University mix, called Redi-Earth, to be about the best. When planting bare-root trees, dig the hole thirty inches wide and eighteen inches deep, then build the soil mound in the center and follow general planting rules. It is always recommended that you stake new fruit trees to keep them from getting a crooked start, and mulch the soil beneath with oak-leaf mulch to discourage grubs.

When planting more than one fruit tree, plant them fifteen feet apart and keep them separated, or else they will fight and break each other's limbs.

Fruit trees need food even more than shade and flowering trees, because of the great effort it takes to produce a bumper crop. Feed flowering trees as follows: new young trees, five pounds, spring and fall; middle-aged trees, ten pounds; and mature old trees, fifteen pounds. Spread any garden food—4-12-4 or 5-10-5—on the soil beneath and water in slightly.

Help the Birds and Bees

Fruit trees need to be cross-pollinated to bear fruit, and the failure of a tree to set blossoms is usually caused by a light-pollinating variety grown nearby. The birds and bees do their best, but it just isn't enough, so we must help. Cut a great big bunch of flowers from a similar variety of fruit tree with lots of pollen. Hang them up in the top of the non-blossoming tree in a bucket of water to make them last. Now, if there are lots of bees and other bugs flying around, you will get fruit.

Trees to Fit Any Yard

Dwarf fruit trees have become America's favorite fruit trees, because they seldom ever grow taller than eight feet, and you can grow several varieties in the same space that it takes to grow one of regular size. I have found the following varieties to be the most rewarding bearers for beginners. Dwarf apples: red delicious, yellow transparent, red McIntosh and yellow delicious. Dwarf peaches: Elberta, redhaven, halehaven and champion.

The best-bearing pear tree is the dwarf Bartlett, and the best-bearing plum is the dwarf Stanley. Dwarf north-star cherry is the best pie cherry, and last, but not least, dwarf Hungary is the best apricot.

For a real experience, order one of the five-in-one dwarf apple trees. This super-bloomer produces five different varieties from one tree. It is a great gift tree for a house-warming present.

If you have the room, then by all means plant regular-sized fruit trees. Here are my favorites: for a quick-bearing apple you can't beat Anoka, or "old folks apple"; next in order come yellow transparent, double red delicious, yellow delicious, McIntosh, Grimes golden, Jonathan and double red Staymen winesap. In a pear, I am old-fashioned and enjoy the Bartlett, while a Stanley plum pleases my children. Peaches are good no matter which variety you choose: halehaven, Elberta, golden jubilee, redhaven, Burbank early Elberta and champion improved. The largest peach you can grow is Rio Oso gem, and you will be delighted with the new free stone called reliance. It is hardy all the way up into Zone 3 (see map). Black tartarian and the Royal Ann cherry complete your home orchard.

My wife, Ilene, has suggested an addition to my list, and that is the dolgo crab apple. The reason is because this is my favorite breakfast jelly. Dolgo crab is about the heaviest producer of the crab apples and these, in my opinion, make the best jelly ever.

Nuts to You

If you fancy a nut tree, let me make a few suggestions. Remember, the nut trees are as beautiful for their foliage as they are for their fruit. Let's begin with the American hazelnut and hardy mission almond. Check your map. They will grow in Zone 5 and southern Zone 4, if protected. Thin-shelled hardy pecans will grow in lower Zone 4 and south. For more northerly regions, we go to the American butternut, mammoth hickory and black walnut. I like the hardy Carpathian walnut. Another one of my favorites is the Chinese chestnut. The foliage is superb, and the roasted nuts are a true delight.

To grow a nut tree, you need the same type of soil as you need in your vegetable garden. Nut trees need very little care; however, they need to be fed in the same manner and as frequently as fruit trees.

Beware of Intruders

You are not the only admirer of the beauty and tastefulness of your orchard. The bugs of the world have their eye on it too. But don't be disturbed; a little foresight will ward off the intruders. Grandma Putt would plant nasturtiums beneath each of her fruit trees and mulch them with shredded oak leaves. That was bio-dynamic gardening long before it was named or popularized.

In the days of Grandma Putt, the only thing gardeners had with which to control insect onslaught was the insects' natural enemies. For instance, those old timers knew that the grubs did not, as a rule, bother the oak, so they would use the foliage of this tree against them. The red spider mite would run from sour milk on a table, so they fought him with sour milk, which has since been adopted as a control. Use two cups of wheat flour and one cup of buttermilk to five gallons of water. Coddling moths on pears can be controlled by planting spearmint plants beneath. The only chemical control that these gardeners used was nicotine sulphate and Fels Naptha soap which is still used to this day.

I have found that a dormant spray with lime sulphur solution and Volk oil combined, used in the late fall when the foliage has dropped and again in the spring before the buds swell, followed with regular soap-and-water sprays at three to four-week intervals, takes care of almost all problems. When I spot a new problem, I use a home orchard spray and apply it at fourteen-day intervals up to two weeks before harvest. However, I seldom have needed it.

Pucker Up for Pleasure

For some unknown reason, most garden writers seem to forget about the citrus trees when they write about the home orchard. I find that most of my south and west

acquaintances have a large number of trees, and I suggest
that one or more be made a regular part of your warm-
climate landscape.

Lemons, limes, oranges, mandarins, and avocados should
be planted in the early spring or fall. I find that the con-
tainer-grown citrus trees are easiest to plant.

Insect control should not be too difficult if these trees
are given a shower from time to time.

They should be fed lightly each month from February
through September with a low nitrogen fertilizer.

Citrus Varieties Available at Garden Centers

PROFESSIONAL NAME	HOMEOWNER NAME
Citrus Chimotto Orange	CHIMOTTO ORANGE
Citrus Frost Nucellar Navel Orange	NAVEL ORANGE
Citrus Frost Nucellar Valencia Orange	VALENCIA ORANGE
Citrus Kara-Kara Mandarin Orange	MANDARIN ORANGE
Citrus Kumquat Nagami Fortunella Margarita	KUMQUAT
Citrus Limequat	COMMON LIME
Citrus Limonia Eureka Lemon	EUREKA LEMON
Citrus Limonia Dwarf Meyer Lemon	DWARF MEYER LEMON
Citrus Limonia Rough Lemon	ROUGH LEMON
Citrus Reliculata Calamondin	CALAMONDIN LEMON
Citrus Tangerine Dancy	TANGERINE

Avocado

This has become a very popular salad fruit and is becoming a highly desired hobby tree by many home gardeners, including my friend, actor Ed Nelson, who has
more avocado trees than children. Or is it the other way
around? There are two varieties that Ed prefers over most
others because one is a late and one is an early bearer. We
both recommend that two compatible varieties be planted
together to avoid sex reversal of the flower, which would
result in non-setting.

Avocado-bacon is a medium-size tree. It has wide
branches with heavy foliage. This variety has medium-size
green fruit in the winter.

Avocado-Haas, a large tree with spreading branches, bears black fruit which ripen in the summer.

To grow avocados properly, mulch heavily with bark chips and feed with an organic food at drip line. Wash with a mild soap for insect control.

Questions and Answers

Q. We moved into an old house with an orchard of twelve trees. Some of the branches are dead, the bark is split, limbs are broken and there are holes all up and down the trunk. Can we save any of them? There are four peach trees and eight apple trees, and no one knows the variety.

A. I would sure give it a go. To begin, cut down and remove all of the weeds in the orchard and burn them. Next, feed each tree with fifteen pounds of low-nitrogen garden food, apply half a pound of parabenzine crystals to the soil beneath within three feet of the trunk, to control borers. Poke holes three feet apart and eight inches deep in a circle below the farthest branches. Spray the tree seven days apart with soap and water, followed by a dormant spraying in the late fall and early spring. Before the dormant spraying, apply the ammonia-spray solution to the trunks. Prune out all dead, broken or weak branches in February and keep the center of the tree open to avoid heavy shade. It will be necessary to spray during the first year with a home orchard spray every seven days up to fourteen days before harvest. Wash the tree before every third spray.

Q. How do you protect fall plant peach trees from rabbit damage?

A. Feed the rabbits and get one of those plastic tubes that you can put into your golf bag to separate clubs. Split it and place it around the trunk, about an inch into the ground. Tape the cut shut.

Q. What is the best variety of nectarine?

A. As an amateur in this line, I must agree with the professionals who say "Sure Crop Hunter" is the best. There are others, but this will perform best for you.

Q. How much water does a young fruit tree require?
A. I would suggest eight to ten gallons a week in dry periods and four to five in the average.

Q. How do you keep mice out of the mulch you put under the new apple trees?
A. I have always felt that if I could keep the mice from chewing at my trees, then I wouldn't bother them. In wintertime, I place small feeders on the ground near each tree. This has worked for Grandma and me for years.

Q. Is it true that the twigs of a cherry tree are poisonous?
A. You can bet your life it's true! No one should chew on any non-edible parts of a plant unless it is known to be palatable and non-toxic.

Q. Can an adult apple tree be moved by mechanical means and still bear fruit?
A. If the tree was moved in the winter, severely pruned, and mulched heavily right after it was moved, it might.

Q. Is it true that garden lighting will affect the health of fruit trees?
A. Only if the heat of the lamp is coming in contact with the tree itself. I am all for special lighting effects in any and all gardens.

Q. What would you suggest as the best cooking apple for sauce?
A. You just can't beat Rhode Island greening. Some say it's also a good eating apple, but I suggest you use them for applesauce.

Q. We are weekend farmers. How many trees can we take care of by ourselves without a whole lot of work?

A. I think four will keep you busy enough and give you and your friends all the fruit you can handle.

Q. How heavy do you apply mulch to an old tree? Or don't you advise mulching old trees?
A. Yes, I suggest you mulch old trees with a four to six-inch layer of oak leaf mulch or other hardwood, two feet to three feet wide in a band under the farthest branches.

Q. Is it true the colder the weather, the better the fruit?
A. That's what they say. Cold weather is supposed to form stronger buds and firmer fruit (apples and pears).

Q. Is it true that if you plant an avocado seed upside down it won't sprout and grow?
A. That's nonsense! You should plant them pointed end up for speed. The shoots will find their way to the top any way you plant them, but the stem will be weak if the seed is planted upside down and the shoot has to grow around the seed to find its way to the surface.

Q. We have a bee hive in our peach tree, and we can't go near it. What can we do?
A. Clap your hands and shout with joy because you are going to have a bumper crop! The pollen should be so thick around your tree that the limbs will bend. Buy a hive and have a bee man move them for you and learn how to take care of them. Honey is great, especially when it's free!

6
Flowering Shrubs: The Kindergarten

More for Your Money

With the cost of living in recent years at its peak, many young home-buyers are too strapped to finance any kind of landscaping. Flowering shrubs offer gardeners in the limited income bracket an opportunity for beauty, color and fragrance, at a very low cost. I by no means am implying that flowering shrubs are a second-class landscape. On the contrary, I personally prefer them to the evergreens because they have so much more to offer, not only from a cost factor, but from a beauty standpoint. Flowering shrubs are fast growers and spread out rapidly to cover a much larger area in a shorter time. These versatile plants can be used to deaden noise, hide a work or play area, or for dog runs. They can also provide privacy to patios and pool areas. The flowering shrubs can be used as living fences or as formal plantings, or they can be planted alone as specimen plants. If you will take a little time in selecting the right shrubs, you can have flowers of all colors of the rainbow, gorgeous foliage all summer, edible fruits throughout the season and colorful and interesting wood all winter when the foliage has dropped off. All in all, you get more for your money with flowering shrubs than with any other garden group in the Plant Kingdom.

Never Turn Your Back on a Shrub

I have cautioned you throughout this book to plan before you plant, to know all there is to know about each plant in your garden. I have referred to some groups and varieties as males and others as females. I have said some are temperamental, and now I am going to discuss the children. Flowering shrubs are like playful children. Every time you turn around they have grown inches, or they are doing something they shouldn't be doing, or they are growing into some place they shouldn't be. I find that I have very good luck with all of my shrubs when I treat them like my children. I am firm but affectionate. I scold them when I find them doing something they shouldn't be doing and praise them when they bloom extra heavily. I reward them with an extra ration of food when they are good. I baby them when they are ill, and I have to scold them when they get sagging posture and their foliage lies in the dirt, because I have to give them an extra bath. I give this group of plants childrens' names like Patty, Susie, Tommy, Bobby and so on. I keep my eye on them all the time because, if I don't, they will grow right out of their home and right into some other plant's—or into mine! So, be sure to know all of the children in your garden and any you intend to plant. They'll need extra care.

Flowering Shrubs Are for the Birds

All too often we are selfish when it comes to planting. We think only of our pleasure and enjoyment when we select newcomers for our garden. If you really want Mama Nature to smile on your garden, plant something for the birds. Grandma Putnam used to say, "There are three things that make a good garden, and that is a bird, a bee and thee!"

Almost any plant that has a berry or fruit will attract birds, so plan a few spots to place these plants and don't be too upset that the birds eat a few seeds or some of your small fruit, because when our feathered friends are around, the bugs move out. Along with planting some favorite shrubs for them, add a shallow birdbath or a small fountain. The splashing water will call to the birds, and the bubbling and babbling of the fountain will please both you and the rest of your garden friends. To discourage the birds from eating more than their share of the food on your fruit-bearing trees and bushes, put up a bird feeder or two and keep them full all year around. In the spring, I hang out two or three birdhouses for the mama birds to turn into happy chirping nurseries, much to the delight of my family! We watch the new babies learn to fly and fend for themselves. To see the antics they perform for us all winter is better than having front row seats at the circus.

Any Bed Will Do

"Nothing fancy." That's the word from the shrub family when it comes to living requirements. They can live pretty comfortably in any soil if it is well drained and mulched, and if they don't have to compete with weeds. All of the foliage and flowering shrubs come in the standard selections: bare-root, balled-in-burlap, potted in tin cans and the paper-pulp pots. They should all be planted in the same manner as deciduous and evergreen friends. One suggestion I have is to discard the soil you remove from the new hole and replace it with the Cornell University mixture (Redi-Earth, as it is called commercially). It has a little added punch for the shrub kids and gets them off to a good start. I have never found it necessary to stake shrubs when I plant them; some of my colleagues do, however, for no real purpose that I can see. It is necessary to cut back the bare-root shrubs at least a third of the way when they are newly planted, to encourage branching. I also do the same with the potted and balled-in-burlap shrubs, just to let them know what I expect from them. The best time to plant shrubs is any time you can get a shovel in the ground. I add one pound of bone meal to the hole if the Cornell mix is not available, then add one pound of low-nitrogen garden food on top of the soil after planting.

Don't Be Too Hasty

The worst enemy a flowering shrub can have, is a pair of pruning shears in the hands of a novice. You can destroy everything you and your shrub have worked for if you prune at the wrong time. Flowering shrubs make the

following spring's flowers on this year's wood. The best time to give them a haircut is when they are in full bloom or just after they are finished blooming. The year I lived with Grandma Putt was the year I received my best grades in school. Not because of my academic ability alone I am sure, but partly because I would take a bouquet to class each day from March to May. The reason for the bouquet was twofold—to share the fragrance and beauty with others, and to have bigger flowers and more of them the following year. You should never let the blooms die on the vine. A dying bloom takes too much from the rest of the plant. To improve your plant's production and your youngsters' grades, cut bouquets all spring. By the way, little girls can carry the bouquets out in the open. Little boys prefer them in plain brown paper bags, for obvious reasons.

Don't Bug Me Now

Since many shrubs resemble the present generation of hippies in their bedraggled appearance, they tend to talk that way too. I was talking to a rather sad-looking spiraea bush not too long ago, and he was complaining about the aphids on his new growth. "Hey man, can you help me out and flick the fleas from the flesh? They're bugging me." I suggested a good shower, which was not quite what he had in mind, but it did the job and we parted friends, I happy, he still looking sad, but healthy. As with most children, I do not mention the word bath until the last minute, but to keep these shrubs healthy and happy, they too must be clean Showers should be given at least once every three weeks to control most of the insects that crawl, fly and chew or suck, and oak-leaf mulch should be used on the soil. If trouble comes to the tops of the shrubs, spray with malathion. Soil insects can be eliminated with chlordane.

Dig Them Crazy Roots

The roots of most of the shrubs are as unpredictable as their tops. They go every which way. Root pruning in the spring will help build a stronger body for the wayward children of your garden. This is done by forcing a sharp spade straight into the ground in a circle at the weep line once a year. This root-pruning operation stimulates more feeder roots and gives the plant an appetite.

Always Hungry

Like all children, the flowering shrubs are always on the go; consequently, they are always hungry. I feed them 4-12-4 or 5-10-5 garden food from February to August. I give three-foot shrubs half a pound per month, three to six-foot shrubs one-and-one-half pounds, and six feet and up two-and-one-half to three pounds. Spread the food on the soil beneath. What a difference a meal makes to your shrubs!

You Can Hedge on This One

Fifty feet of chain-link fence can cost you somewhere in the neighborhood of $150.00. Fifty feet of privet hedge, a living fence, will run about $15.00. I have never seen a flower on a chain-link fence. At least not one that the fence itself grew. Here are a few suggestions for hedge fences: red spiraea, boxwood (short), *Multiflora rosa,* forsythia, privet, burning-bush and spiraea. There are many others.

Money Can Grow on Shrubs

It has always fascinated my neighbors to watch me take hard and softwood cuttings from my shrubs and pass them out at no cost. I can do this because they cost me nothing. You too can make new plants from your existing shrubs with just a little "know-how." It's easy. There are two basic types of cuttings: the softwood and the hardwood.

Softwood cuttings are slips of plants taken from the adult plant's soft growth. Most all of your perennials and your flowering shrubs will yield these cuttings. Take your cuttings in May and early June from new growth. Make them three to six inches long, and remove the bottom three layers of leaves. Dip first into water, then about a half-inch into a product called Rootone. Shake off the excess and place in a pre-poked, pencil-sized hole in your rooting material (sharp sand), covering at least one or two of the nodes (leaf breaks). The best temperature for rooting is sixty to seventy degrees, while the soil should be five degrees warmer. Keep the soil shaded and always damp, but not soaked the first few days. Sprinkle the foliage often to control humidity.

Move the cuttings into the light as they progress in rooting. When roots are well established, pot them up and move them into the garden. I plant pots and all into soil to protect them. Following is a list of softwood cuttings you can take:

Softwood Cuttings

HOMEOWNER NAME	PROFESSIONAL NAME
AZALEA	
BARBERRY	*Berberis*

HOMEOWNER NAME	PROFESSIONAL NAME
BEAUTY-BUSH	*Kolkwitzia*
BITTERSWEET	*Celastrus*
BOXWOOD	*Buxus*
BROOM	*Cytisus*
BUSH ARBUTUS	*Abelia*
BUTTERFLY BUSH	*Buddleia*
CAMELLIA	
CRAPE-MYRTLE	
DOGWOOD	*Cornus*
FIRETHORN	*Pyracantha*
FRINGE-TREE	*Chionanthus*
GOLDEN BELLS	*Forsythia*
HEATHER	*Erica*
HEMLOCK	*Tsuga*
HOLLY	*Ilex*
HONEYSUCKLE	*Lonicera*
HYDRANGEA	
JASMINE	*Jasminum*
JUNIPER	*Juniperus*
LAGERSTROEMIA	
LEUCOTHOE	
LILAC	*Syringa*
MOCKORANGE	*Philadelphus*
OLEANDER	*Nerium*
PACHYSANDRA	
PRIVET	*Ligustrum*
RHODODENDRON	
ROSE	*Rosa*
ROSE-OF-SHARON	*Hibiscus syriacus*
SENECIO	
SEQUOIA	
SILVER VINE	*Actinidia*
SPIRAEA	
SPRUCE	
VIBURNUM	*Picea*
WEIGELA	
WINTER CREEPER	*Euonymus*
YEW	*Taxus*

Hardwood cuttings are collected in the late fall or winter. Cut them six to eight inches long, tie in bundles, and store in a box of peat moss in the basement until spring. After the frost has gone, remove them and dip in Rootone and then place the slip into the soil in your garden, leaving about half of the stem above the ground. Here are the hardwood cuttings that you can take:

Hardwood Cuttings

HOMEOWNER NAME	PROFESSIONAL NAME
BARBERRY	*Berberis*
BURNING-BUSH	*Euonymus*
CATALPA	
CHAENOMELES	
CRAPE-MYRTLE	
DEUTZIA	
DOGWOOD	*Cornus*
ELDER	*Sambucus*
FIRETHORN	*Pyracantha*
FLOWERING QUINCE	
GOLDEN BELLS	*Forsythia*
HAZEL	*Corylus*
HONEYSUCKLE	*Lonicera*
LAGERSTROEMIA	
NINE BARK	*Physocarpus*
OLEANDER	*Nerium*
POPLAR	*Populus*
PRIVET	*Ligustrum*
RUSSIAN OLIVE	*Fleagnus*
VIBURNUM	
WEIGELA	
WILLOW	*Salix*
WISTERIA	

Following is a list of flowering shrubs for home use.

Flowering Shrubs for Home Use

KEY:

Zone hardiness indicates the coldest climate area plants can survive.
COLOR

Y	Yellow	L	Lavender
R	Red	B	Blue
W	White	G	Green
P	Pink		

HOME GARDEN NAME	ZONE	COLOR FLOWER	FRUIT
ANDROMEDA	5	W	
AZALEA	5	Many	
BARBERRY, STANDARD AND DWARF	3	Y	*
BEACH PLUM	4	W	*
BEAUTY-BUSH	5	P	*
BLUEBERRY	4	W	*
BLUE-SPIREA	5	B	*
BOTTLE-BRUSH BUCKEYE	5	W	
BROOM	6	Y,R,B	
BUTTERFLY-BUSH	6	L	
CALIFORNIA LILAC	4-8	B	
CAMELLIA	7	P,R,W	
CHERRY-LAUREL	6	W	
CHINESE REDBUD	6	L	
COTONEASTER	4	P	*
CRAPE-MYRTLE	7	P,R,L,W	
DAPHNE	5	R,P,L,W	
DEUTZIA	5	W,P	
FIRETHORN	6	W	*
FLOWERING ALMOND	5	P,W	
FLOWERING PLUM	6	P	
FLOWERING QUINCE	5	R	
FORSYTHIA	5	Y	
GARDENIA	8	W	
GENISTA	2	Y	
GLOSSY ABELIA	5	P	
HARDY ORANGE	6	W	*
HEATH	6	R,W,L	
HEATHER	5	R,L,W	
HOLLY OLIVE	7	G	*
HONEYSUCKLE	3	P	*
HYDRANGEA	3	W,P,B	
JAPANESE SNOWBELL	6	W	
JETBEAD	6	W	
KERRIA	6	Y	
KOREAN ABELIA-LEAF	5	W	
KONSA DOGWOOD	5	W	
LEATHERWOOD	6	W	
LEUCOTHOE	5	W	
LILAC	3	P,L,W,R	
MAHONIA	5	Y	*
MOCKORANGE	4	W	
MOUNTAIN LAUREL	4	P,W	
OCEAN SPRAY	5	W	

* Shrubs bearing fruit or berries.

HOME GARDEN NAME	ZONE	COLOR FLOWER	FRUIT
PARROTIA	6	R	
PEARL-BUSH	5	W	
PHOTINIA	7	W	*
PRIVET	4	W	*
PUSSY WILLOW	5	Gray	
RHODODENDRON	5	R,L,P,Y,W	
ROCK-ROSE	8	P	
ROSE	5	Y,W,P,R	
ROSE-ACACIA	6	P	
ST. JOHNSWORT	6	Y	
SAND-MYRTLE	6	W	
SAPPHIREBERRY	6	W	*
SHADBLOW	4	W	*
SKIMMIA	7	Y,W	*
SMOKE-TREE	5	G	
SNOW-WREATH	6	W,G	
SPICEBUSH	4	Y	*
SPIKE-HEATH	6	P,W	
SPIRAEA	4	W,P,R	
STAR MAGNOLIA	5	W	*
STEWARTIA	7	W	
STRAWBERRY SHRUB	5	Y	*
SUMMER-SWEET	4	W	
SUN-ROSE	6	Y,R,W	
SWEET SPIRE	6	W	
TAMARISK	5	P,R	
TRAILING ARBUTUS	3	W,P	
TREE PEONY	5	W,P,Y	
VIBURNUM	5	W,P	*
VITEX	5	L	
WEIGELA	4	P,R,W	
WINTER-HAZEL	6	Y	
WINTER JASMINE	6	Y	
WITCH-HAZEL	4	Y	

Questions and Answers

Q. What flowering shrub would you suggest for long-lasting fragrance and a white flower?

A. Double mockorange blooms almost all summer and smells great. I like them near a patio. This plant grows five to six feet.

Q. Can I use raw fish for my hydrangea?

A. The plant will love it, but so will all the cats in the neighborhood.

Q. When and how do you prune azaleas?
A. You don't, if you can avoid it! If it's absolutely necessary, prune them when they're in bloom. Use a sharp pair of pruning shears, mulch beneath azaleas, and never cultivate.

Q. Can I prune a rhododendron?
A. Not in my garden! If you must, cut above a foliage branch, sterilize and seal. Don't cultivate, but do mulch.

Q. What is a lavender shrub?
A. The professional name is *Vitex,* and it has blue flowers with a great smell. The foliage is star-shaped and has real character.

Q. What kind of a shrub can we plant in wet soil?
A. You can plant my favorite, the red twig dogwood, or the speckled alder.

Q. How far north can we grow bottle-brush shrub?
A. This can be used as a tree or shrub, and you can grow it as far north as Zone 7.

Q. Which flowering shrub is the first to bloom?
A. Most folks say the forsythia, but the pussy willow beats it by a long shot.

Q. Which of the flowering shrubs can you take wood from and force to bloom in water in the house?
A. My grandma made just about all of them bloom inside.

Q. What would keep a hydrangea from blooming?
A. It could be any number of things: poor soil, too much shade, or too much nitrogen fertilizer. The most common reason is pruning at the wrong time. You only prune when the plant is through blooming.

Q. We haven't had a bloom on our lilac in three years. What would make it stop?

A. More likely than not, you have mostly sucker shoots. These are straight shafts from below the soil that will never flower.

Q. Can I take cuttings from my flowering shrubs? If so, when and how?

A. You sure can—almost any of them. One way is air-layering. The other is to take cuttings in the fall and root them in sand.

Q. Are there any heavier varieties of flowering almond?

A. If you are talking about wood, not that I know of; that's what makes it so desirable.

Q. I have heard that sumac is a bad shrub for beekeepers to have around.

A. If you are a beekeeper, you would not care to have this honey in the frames, for no other reason than the fact that it is a bright green. But it is still good pure honey.

Q. Can we use regular fruit-berry shrubs in our landscape plan?

A. That's what it's all about. Use the land to the best ends for you and the plants. I suggest blueberry, currant, gooseberry.

7
Roses:
The Royal Court

Long Live the Queen

The rose is the most popular flower in the world today, as it has been for thousands and thousands of years. According to the geologists, rose fossils have been found that were growing thousands of years before Christ. The rose has played a big part in man's life. It has influenced our religion, health, romance, war and peace, and is often regarded as a living tranquilizer. In the United States alone, there are from forty to fifty million roses sold a year, in a color range that virtually spans the rainbow. Rose flowers range from very delicate thumb size blooms to giant hybrid teas, with a wide variety of fragrances.

Most home gardeners take the rose at face value. Little do they realize the versatility of this glorious lady. Her petals can provide tasty food for party snacks, and can be fermented into one of the finest wines you'll ever savor. Her dried petals can add scent to silks and linens. Her bright and fragrant flowers can flood a room with the sight and smell of spring love. They will lift the spirit of the sick of heart and body.

A Rose for Every Garden

I have yet to see a garden where I couldn't find a place for at least one rose, and, since she is the grand lady of the Plant Kingdom, it is only right that we find a proper place. There are certain classifications that roses fall into, and one must first understand these classifications before one can begin his selection. All roses are named after a person, place or characteristic.

Roses are classified by their structure of growth. Thus, we get hybrid tea, floribunda, grandiflora, hybrid polyantha, polyantha, hybrid perpetual, tree and, in common circles, climbers.

The hybrid tea . . . is the most popular, because of its straight stems, large buds and giant blooms. This type will grow three feet high and four feet across in a single season. Use as a specimen.

Floribunda . . . is a cross between the polyantha and hybrid tea and produces a good, full, healthy bush, loaded with stems of single and double flowers. It's best used for borders and group plantings.

Grandiflora . . . as a group of roses is not very old. It has large clusters of flowers on long stems. The easiest rose to take care of is the grandiflora. This is a rose that can be planted by itself as a property divider or in a formal bed.

Hybrid polyantha . . . is really the same rose classification as the floribunda but, because of a technicality, the Rose Society would not officially adopt the name floribunda. If you see either of these names on a package, they are the same.

Hybrid perpetual . . . is one of our oldest types of roses, of which the American beauty was the most popular. The perpetuals are often called the "June bloomers." They grow a tall bush not generally seen anymore.

Miniature roses . . . is a group of roses too often overlooked. They begin to bloom in May and continue 'til Jack Frost paints them out. Miniatures grow between twelve and eighteen inches and are an excellent border rose.

Climbers . . . are the roses that most of us remember when you mention the rose. Cottage walls, trellises and garden fences are the home for these active young ladies.

Tree Roses . . . are one of my favorite groups because they stand above all of the other small evergreens and shrubs to show off color and character, like the true queens they are.

Any bush-type rose—including some climbers—can be made into a tree rose.

The ordinary commercial rose is budded onto a wild understock. The tree rose can also be budded onto a wild understock, but only after the cane is three to four feet tall. A great deal more work goes into the tree roses you buy than into other roses. This accounts for the additional cost.

My favorites are: the dark red Chrysler Imperial, the orange Sutter's gold, the yellow Diamond Jubilee and the deep pink Charlotte Armstrong. If you want a couple of really beautiful weeping rose trees, try cherry chase, a dark red. Rose trees have one bad feature in the colder parts of the country: the whole tree must be buried beneath the ground.

When you are planning your landscape, make sure that you plan a front row seat for your roses, because they love to see what's going on and love to be seen. After all, they are royalty, and royalty always gets the favored spot. Dinah Shore, the lovely songstress, says roses are her favorite flowers. When I visited her garden recently, I was delighted by the many different rose varieties I saw there. Too many gardeners concentrate on one type and miss out on the beautiful blendings that come from mixing varieties when planting.

Let the Sun Shine In

I am so sick and tired of the so-called rose experts telling everybody how difficult it is to grow roses when, in reality, the rose is one of the easiest plants to care for. The real secret is sunshine. Roses must have a half-dozen hours of sunshine in the early part of the day and shade from the hot afternoon sun. If you pick a spot where you would be comfortable sitting out all day and plant a rose there, you will have the best bloomers on the block!

Keep 'em Loose

The rose works so hard producing those great big, beautiful, fragrant flowers and that green rich waxy foliage, that it just can't take time out to play ground hog or mole and have to burrow through heavy soil. So it's up to you to give it a helping hand. The queen would like you to prepare her court in loose, fertile, well-drained soil. Not heavy, wet, clay soil.

When preparing a rose bed, add five pounds of rose or garden food to the soil surface, fifty pounds of peat, twenty-five pounds of gypsum and three bushels of 60-40 gravel. All of this on a hundred-square-foot area. Now, spade it all in. It is important to make sure that all of the soil builders are mixed in well.

Spare Time

The best time to plant a rose is when you can get a spade in the ground. If you plant your roses in the fall in the zones below freezing, then do not bother to cut the wood back. Remember what I said. You plant them the day you bring them home. Don't go off and leave them in the trunk of the car or the garage and expect them to be bright-eyed and bushy-tailed two or three days later. If they are worth buying, then they are worth the time to plant them.

Not Too Deep

I think all too often the home gardener takes the term "bury" too seriously. These plants are alive and we intend to keep them this way. All I want you to do is plant the bush.

Dig the hole just as we have been discussing for bare-root trees and shrubs. Place the mound of soil in the bottom and spread out the roots. Next, begin to refill, pushing the soil down firmly as you go. All have one rule about the large bump or bulge above the roots; make sure it is two inches below the soil. Then, if die-back occurs in the early spring, some of the grafted stock will survive. When the rose is planted and tamped down, build a small dirt wall around the outside to hold water. For both fall and spring-planted roses, I suggest that the plant be covered completely with a light soil mixture and left for ten days on spring roses, and all winter on fall roses. When the threat of frost has passed, I suggest that you mulch

with wood chips or buckwheat hulls. Another important thing you can do is add a half-cup of epsom salt to the soil surface. This promotes richer color, thicker petals and stronger roots. To plant balled-in-burlap, potted or canned stock, you follow shrub and tree directions, but cover the plant as described above.

The Way to a Gal's Heart Is through a Rose's Stomach!

If you don't feed roses, then you can't expect many flowers. Roses are to be fed a handful of any rose food once a month. An excellent method to feed and water roses at the same time is to cut both ends out of a large fruit-juice can and bury it between each rose. Then fill it half full of pea pebbles and, from time to time, add a small amount of food to the can, for deep-penetration feeding.

Don't Get My Head Wet

Roses do not like regular sprinkling. They prefer deep watering from the end of an open hose about twice a week. The reason deep watering is so necessary is that a healthy rose, during a hot July or August, can take three to five gallons of moisture from the soil a day. This does not mean that you shouldn't use the soap solution to wash her pretty face.

Bugs Are No Bother

If the roses are healthy and happy, that is to say, well fed, bathed regularly with soap and wild garlic planted, you won't have to worry about insects. If you should run into a hardhead, a bug that just won't go away, refer to the chart at the end of this chapter.

Keep Her Fancy

Since a rose is a woman, it is a good idea to keep her sharp. All her flowers are to be gathered and placed in the home or given to friends. Do not let them die on the vine, as this is bad for the plant. Whenever you cut a rose, always cut just above a five-leaf cluster of leaves. This is where the next break will come from. Always keep

the center open and free for sunlight. Cut out this foliage. Roses like to be covered up in the winter with a light mix of leaves, soil and peat moss. Pile it as high as it can go without falling off. Then, cut the tops just to make them look neat. In May, in snow country, remove the mulch and cut back to just above an outside eye—that is, a foliage bud that points to the outside. All in all, it is not much work to tend them. If you do, you'll have blooms all summer long.

Climbers Need Control

Climbers are a hardy variety and do not need mulch. However, they do require that suckers and dead wood be removed at once. Suckers are growth that is coming from below the graft and will not bloom.

The Queen in Her Kerchief Settled Down for a Long Winter's Nap

It is important to understand that a great majority of the commercial roses are grown in Texas and California and are shipped all over the United States to gardens where the climates are much different. When the foliage has dropped off in the late fall, dormant-spray, then pile a mixture of peat, leaves and soil two to two-and-a-half feet high over your roses. Do not remove until May flowers replace those April showers. Then you will avoid "spring kill" (mistakenly called "winter kill").

For Your Viewing Pleasure

I have included a partial list of some of my favorite roses. There are hundreds and hundreds more, but this will give you a good start. A self-addressed stamped envelope and a dime will get you the American Rose Society "Rose Buying Guide," with the ratings of most of the roses on the market today. Send to The American Rose Society, 4048 Roselea Place, Columbus, Ohio 43214.

HYBRID TEAS

ALLEGRO *Fragrant Geranium-red*

AMERICANA *Brilliant red*

AMERICAN HERITAGE *Cream-yellow with scarlet and vermillion*

ARLENE FRANCIS *Golden yellow*

AUTUMN *Burnt-orange, streaked red*

BEWITCHED *Rose-pink, lighter reverse*

BIG RED *Large, vibrant, dusky red*

BOB HOPE *Brilliant red, vigorous*

CARLA *Large double-pink, fragrant*

CHARLOTTE ARMSTRONG *Blood-red buds, flowers spectrum-red to cerise*

CHICAGO PEACE *Rich pink blend*

CHRISTIAN DIOR *Crimson-red*

CHRYSLER IMPERIAL *Crimson*

CONDESA DE SASTAGO *Oriental red, yellow reverse*

COUNTESS VANDAL *Salmon-pink with coppery-pink reverse*

CRIMSON DUKE *Pure, rich red*

CRIMSON GLORY *Deep, velvety crimson, purple shadings*

DIAMOND JUBILEE *Large buff-yellow, fragrant*

ECLIPSE *Golden yellow*

ETOILE DE HOLLAND *Bright red, very fragrant*

FIRST PRIZE *Deep rose-light red blend*

F. K. DRUSCHKI *Snow white*

FLAMING PEACE *Blood red and gold bicolor*

FRAGRANT CLOUD *Bright coral-red*

GARDEN PARTY *Pale ivory with pink*

GOLDEN MASTERPIECE *Golden yellow*

GOLDEN SCEPTER *Fragrant, deep yellow*

GOOD NEWS *Large silvery pink-apricot fragrant*

GRANADA *Scarlet red to lemon yellow*

GRAND SLAM *Large cherry-red*

HELEN TRAUBEL *Large pink-apricot*

INDIANA *Brilliant, vivid red, fully double large flowers*

JOHN F. KENNEDY *Pure white, fragrant*

KARL HERBST *Dark scarlet, very fragrant*

K. A. VIKTORIA *Snowy-white, center tinted lemon, very fragrant*

KING'S RANSOM *Rich chrome yellow, glossy dark green foliage*

K. T. MARSHALL *Deep rose-pink flushed yellow*

KORDES PERFECTA *Bicolor, cream-white pink-to-carmine edges*

LADY ELGIN *Huge apricot-orange blooms*

LADY X *Soft, cool, pink-lavender*

LOWELL THOMAS *Rich yellow*

MEXICANA *Red, reverse white, fragrant*

MIRANDY *Garnet-red, very fragrant*

MISS ALL-AMERICAN BEAUTY *Vibrant pink*

MISTER LINCOLN *Deep, velvety red, fragrant*

MOJAVE *Orange*

NEW YORKER *Velvety bright scarlet*

NOCTURNE *Cardinal-red shaded crimson*

OKLAHOMA *Very dark red, fragrant*

HYBRID TEAS

ORANGE FLAME *Smoky orange-scarlet*

PASCALI *Pure white, bright green foliage*

PEACE *Golden yellow, edged rose-pink*

PHARAOH *Brilliant red*

PICTURE *Velvety-clear rose-pink*

PINK PEACE *Pink*

PINK RADIANCE *Rose with lighter reverse*

POLYNESIAN SUNSET *Double coral-orange*

PRESIDENT HOOVER *Orange, rose and gold, lighter reverse*

RED RADIANCE *Light crimson sport of radiance*

ROYAL HIGHNESS *Clear, light pink*

RUBAIYAT *Rose-red, lighter reverse*

SAN FERNANDO *Scarlet, very fragrant*

SOUTH SEAS *Warm coral-pink*

STERLING SILVER *Silver-lavender, fragrant*

SUMMER RAINBOW *Pink, yellow*

SUMMER SUNSHINE *Brilliant, yellow*

SUTTER'S GOLD *Very fragrant golden orange*

TANYA *True orange*

TALISMAN *Golden yellow and copper*

TIFFANY *Pink yellow base*

THE DOCTOR *Satiny-pink, very fragrant*

TROPICANA *Fluorescent orange-red*

VALENCIA *Intense apricot-orange*

VIKING *Large crimson, dark foliage*

WHITE QUEEN *Sparkling white*

GRANDIFLORAS

BUCCANEER *Sunshine yellow*

CAMELOT *Luminous coral-pink*

CARROUSEL *Deep, rich red*

COMANCHE *Brilliant, scarlet, tall vigorous*

JOHN S. ARMSTRONG *Glowing, dark red*

LUCKY LADY *Light pink with deeper pink reverse*

MONTEZUMA *Scarlet-orange*

QUEEN ELIZABETH *Delicate pink*

SCARLET KNIGHT *Velvety scarlet-red*

FLORIBUNDAS

ANGEL FACE *Rich, deep lavender spicy fragrance*

APRICOT NECTAR *Large-flowered apricot*

BETTY PRIOR *Carmine-pink, single*

CIRCUS *Bicolor red and yellow*

CIRCUS PARADE *Fragrant multi-color, redder than circus*

ELIZABETH OF GLAMIS *Clusters of flame-colored blooms, fragrant*

EUTIN *Glowing carmine—red double*

EUROPEANA *Large clusters of satiny-red blooms*

FASHION *Double coral-peach*

FIRE KING *Fiery red*

FLORADORA *Double cinnabar-red*

FRENSHAM *Semi-double deep scarlet*

FLORIBUNDAS
(continued)

GARNETTE *Double garnet-red with light lemon-yellow base*

GAY PRINCESS *soft shell, pink flowers*

GENE BEERNER *Free-blooming, deep clear pink*

GOLDILOCKS *Double deep yellow, fading to cream*

GOLD CUP *Yellow*

PINOCCHIO *Double pink*

suffused salmon, deeper edge

RED PINOCCHIO *Carmine-red, fragrant*

ROMAN HOLIDAY *Yellow shading to orange red*

SARATOGA *Buds cream, open to pure white 4-in. flowers*

SPARTAN *Reddish coral*

SUMMER SNOW *Large, clear white, slightly fragrant*

CLIMBERS

CL. ALOHA *Fragrant rose-pink*

CL. BLOSSOMTIME *Two-tone pink, fragrant*

CL. CORAL SATIN *Double-coral, fragrant*

CL. CRIMSON GLORY *Double, deep velvety crimson*

CL. DON JUAN *Velvety red*

CL. DR. J. H. NICOLAS *Double rose—pink*

CL. GOLD RUSH *Double gold, fragrant*

CL. GOLDEN SHOWERS *Yellow*

CL. HIGH NOON *Upright, lemon-yellow tinted red*

CL. IMPERIAL BLAZE *Free-blooming, semi-double bright scarlet*

CL. NEW DAWN *Double blush—pink*

CL. PAUL'S SCARLET *Semi-double, vivid scarlet*

CL. PEACE *Yellow, edged pink*

CL. TALISMAN *Double golden yellow and copper*

CL. WHITE DAWN *Double white, fragrant*

The rose is not just a favorite of ours, she is a tasty and delicate feast for the insect world.

If you use soap and water, feed well, mulch and water, you will discourage most of the winged warriors. But, should one or two penetrate your defenses, here are the chemical controls recommended:

Enemies of the Rose and What to Do About Them

THRIPS—Tiny, slender pests, $\frac{1}{16}$ inch long. Puncture buds, cause discoloration and failure to open. Dust often with rose dust, malathion or isotox. Regular spraying from time buds are very small is important.

LEAF ROLLERS—Also called rose-leaf tiers. Small, green caterpil-

lars. Feed on, roll, and tie upper leaves together, thus
distorting growth. Hand-pick, or crush leaves to kill hidden
caterpillars. Spray with malathion.

APHIDS—Greenish-yellow, black, or red plant lice. Cluster on bud
stems and suck juices. Secrete a sticky substance often called
honeydew. Multiply rapidly. Use nicotine dust or nicotine
sulfate spray if temperature is above sixty-five degrees.
Controls must actually touch aphids. Soapy water is fair
control. Sure-Nox-Em, malathion, isotox or any other good
insecticide will control aphids well. Plant wild garlic between
roses.

TARNISHED PLANT BUGS—Brassy, flat, ¼ inch long. Puncture new
growth and distort surrounding plant tissues. Cultivate soil
cleanly. Dust with rose dust.

ROSE CHAFERS—Appear in great numbers. Prevalent in sandy soil.
Iridescent beetles ⅜ inch long. Feed on buds, open flowers,
and foliage. Show preference for light-colored flowers. Hand-
pick, or dust every third day with rose dust during usual
month-long onslaught. Parabenzene on soil when breeding is
also a fair control.

ROSE SLUGS—Small green caterpillar-like pests. Bore into new
shoots and pith of pruned canes. Mutilate foliage rapidly.
Seal newly cut ends of canes. Cut below wilted portions of
others. Spray leaves with malathion.

FULLERS ROSE BEETLES—Crawling, gray beetles, ⅜ inch long.
Feed at night, leave unsightly black excrement. Repel them
with lead arsenate, or jar into water and oil to suffocate.
Dust plants with sevin.

ROSE SCALE—Dirty white, scale-like sucking insects. Often encrust
stems. Use dormant oil spray in spring, and soap and water
after leaves drop. Burn dead stems.

RED SPIDER MITES—Very tiny mites, hide on undersides of leaves.
Prevalent when weather is dry and hot. Suck juices, turn
leaves yellow, and stunt plants. Coat leaves with fine dusting
sulfur or wash off with water or good miticide such as
Tedion or Aramite. Malathion is fair control.

CANE BORERS—Enter stems, and cause death of shoots by hollow-
ing out pith. Cut off infested shoots; kill borers. Spray foliage
from June to July with isotox; seal ends after pruning.

RUST—Protect foliage subject to moist air. Wash with soap and
water. Use a dust or spray containing sulfur, or use captan,
Manzate, Phaltan. Pick off infected leaves.

ROSE CANKER—In spring, showy brown patches above which no
growth starts. Prune out all visible cankers, taking a 1-inch
margin for safety. If seriously infected, dispose of plant.

BLACK SPOT—Spots show first on leaves in early summer, grow
progressively worse. Keep foliage coated with nationally ad-
vertised brands of fungicidal spray or dust such as captan or
Phaltan or Manzate. Apply before rains. Feed to promote ac-

tive growth of bushes. Pick off black-spotted leaves promptly and burn.

HARLEQUIN BUGS—Brilliantly marked, ⅜ inch long. Bad pests in the South from California to Virginia, but not too much in the North. Branches attacked turn brown as if scalded. Handpick bugs and egg masses.

MILDEW—Whitish fungus growth, covers leaves and young flower buds and stems. Prevalent coast to coast. Use fungicides such as Acti-Dione PM, or use Natriphene sparingly and coat both sides of leaves.

LEAF-CUTTING BEES—Disfigure foliage, but main damage is by larvae that bore into ends of pruned stems. Wax stem ends with a crayon. Prune stunted stem tips and use good insecticide.

TWELVE-SPOTTED CUCUMBER BEETLES—Yellow-green, ¼ inch long, twelve black spots on his back. Eat blooms late in season. Dust with sevin every ten days.

JAPANESE BEETLES—If plants are kept clean, these won't be too big a problem. Dust on sight with sevin and spray bush with malathion.

ROSE MIDGES—Minute pests attack buds, cause necks to crook at right angles and buds to blight. If you have had rose midges in the past, dust with rose dust before growth is six inches tall. After buds show, apply rose dust at seven-day intervals.

Questions and Answers

Q. When is the best time to mulch roses for winter?

A. Right after the first killing frost. I have also found that the job is still enjoyable at that time, because I don't freeze my whatcha-ma-jigger doing it.

Q. Can I protect my roses for the winter with plastic garbage bags?

A. That's a no-no. Do not cover anything with plastic in the winter. If a rose were in the bag and the sun came out, it could very possibly start growth because of the condensation inside. Then the sun goes down, and the moisture freezes and kills the growth.

Q. Do you recommend these new weed killers for rose beds?

A. I sure do. I call them kneeless weeders. However, they are not weed killers, they are weed preventers. Any of the ones on the market will do. Don't ever use a weed killer in the roses or on any bed of flowers, shrubs or evergreens.

Q. How often do you water roses?
A. Depends on where you live and what the soil conditions are. In well-drained soil or sand, twice a week. In heavy soil, once a week. And, in clay soil, extra heavy composition, water very lightly once a week.

Q. Our roses grow tall, but have small blooms and not too much foliage. Why?
A. Not enough sun or too much nitrogen. Roses must have five or six hours of sun. Morning sun is the best. Feed roses with a low-nitrogen garden food to promote blooms, not growth.

Q. Can you tell me which mulches are best?
A. I can give you my choice, but others may prefer a totally different assortment. Oak-leaf mulch, wood chips, pine bark and redwood do the job for me.

Q. Is it okay to use my root feeder on my roses?
A. If you are careful, yes. But, too many times folks get carried away and wash the soil away from the roots and let air in to dry them out.

Q. How can I stop black spots on roses?
A. Stop watering them from the top and wash them with soap and water.

Q. How much iron do you give a rose that seems to be chlorotic?
A. About four ounces of Green Garde micronized iron per bush will do nicely.

Q. What is your opinion of foliar feeding?
A. Mother Nature teams up with Jupiter Fluvius for the only real foliar (leaf) feeding. The rest I have always considered to be hogwash.

Q. How large should a rose bed be?
A. I prefer a bed five feet wide. Floribundas and hybrid tea roses need three to four feet to spread out in, so in a five-foot bed you can stagger them.

Q. What do you think of ground covers on rose beds?

A. Not much. This is one queen who won't be happy with someone kneeling in front of her all the time.

Q. I would like a mass planting of roses in both rear corners of our yard. How far apart should I plant them?

A. Wide enough for you to get into the farthest one to work. Stagger each row and do not let them touch.

Q. I would like the name of a good fence rose.

A. I think you will be satisfied with county fair. Consult the rose catalogues for some others.

Q. Do you buy roses from catalogues?

A. Sure I do, just to see if the firms are good and the roses are true to name. I have been burned on occasion.

Q. I have heard that there is a right time to cut roses.

A. I would say that just before your evening meal, and just the ones whose petals are unfolding.

Q. Are these rose collars any good?

A. Not too bad if you can find one that is at least two feet high. Most of the commercial collars are too shallow for my liking.

Q. Is it necessary to seal every cane you prune on a rose?

A. If you want your roses to live, it is. There are several boring insects that go into those stubs.

Q. When is the best time to prune a climber?

A. Right after it blooms. First cut out any suckers. Next, take off any dead wood. Last, remove droopers that won't stay on the trellis.

Q. Which is the best kind of trellis?

A. I like redwood for effect and longevity. The aluminum fan shape and the wire are nice, but they just don't fit in my garden.

Q. I still have some DDT on hand. Can I still use it on my roses?

A. Shame on you! I'm not scolding for wanting to use DDT, but because you keep any pesticide around that you don't need at the moment. Sure you can use it if it's necessary.

Q. What grade rose will give me the best luck?
A. Grade one, two years old, with three to four canes the size of a pencil. Most home gardeners mistakenly buy those great big thick canes. Do not purchase package roses that have soft, white or light yellow-green growth on the stems.

Q. Can I put stone around my roses?
A. I prefer something that will do them some good. Stone is for our viewing benefit, and since the rose is already working overtime to give you beauty, why not give her a break?

Q. I have trouble keeping my roses blooming late in the season. Can I give them a hand?
A. Your postmark is from Oakland, California, so I would say that you should leave your roses alone after the first of October. Cut down on the water and let them rest until the first of the year; then prune and begin again. January through June is also the best time to plant roses in Southern California.

Q. Can I take cuttings from my roses?
A. You certainly can, and you will get more pride and enjoyment from these than from ones you buy. Take the cutting in late May from a flower stem, about four inches long, with at least two breaks. Take your cuttings from the middle of the branch. Dip in water, then into Rootone and place upright into damp, sharp sand, and keep shaded for a few days. When well rooted, remove and plant in soil.

Q. Is there any place in this country that roses won't grow?
A. Not if they can get sunshine, water, food and plenty of love and affection.

8
Annuals:
Magic Land

Paint with Posies

This is an area where you can let your imagination run wild. An annual is a plant species that lives its full lifespan in one season. They have only one purpose in life, and that is to give beauty and enjoyment to the world around them. These beauties are the elves of the flowering nation. Happy-go-lucky, carefree ramblers, they complement and help accent all of the other plants in your garden. The annuals keep the rest of your garden in stitches most of the summer with their antics. They crawl under the pines and tickle the limbs, they snore beneath the maple and dance with the birch. They are truly the lovable jesters of the queen's court and will try anything once. For instance, they'll try growing in the shade just because you want them to. Anyone can grow annuals if he will just relax and plan to have fun. There are only a few things that one need know to have a beautiful and successful garden full of annuals, so pay close attention and follow me down the garden path. Call out to the little ones along the way—by name, of course: Rumplestiltskin, Thumbelina and any leprechaun name you can remember.

So Much for So Little

I don't have to caution you, but I will. With annuals, as with anything else, we must stick with our brown-paper-bag master plan to make sure that we get the best possible results from the flowers we select. We must make certain

that we have a place for everyone. It's embarrassing to invite a plant over to spend the summer only to find that you don't have a spare bed for him, and then have to rush around and find a makeshift spot where he will be uncomfortable all season. His discomfort will be reflected in his performance, and you will have no one to blame but yourself. All it takes to have success is a little foresight, and that only costs a few minutes of your time.

Begin with the Best

Once you have decided which guest is going to share which spot with whom, you are ready to deliver the invitations. To avoid hurting anyone's feelings, I suggest that if you are going to have the younger generation of annuals spend the season (that is, the ones that come to us pregrown from the greenhouse), then make sure they have had all of their shots and are healthy. Invite only the fresh, strong, good-looking ones. No discrimination intended, but, for their own health, the weak ones are safer in the greenhouse! If you are going to have the babies (from seed), then I would suggest that you check the birth records to make sure that they were recently born. The package will indicate when they arrived. Only current-year seeds will do.

Preparing the Guest Room

No matter how good your plants look when they arrive, or how fresh the seed you purchase, their success depends upon how well you prepare the soil in their future bed. The best soil condition you can give the plants is one that will hold moisture, but let the extra water run off. On each hundred-square-foot surface of the annual beds and borders, add one hundred pounds of peat moss, twenty-five pounds of garden food and fifty pounds of gypsum, along with six bushels of compost, if available, and then blend and mix well, rake and level. Leave no buried stones, glass, wood or cans to plague you or your flowers later. When the blend job is done, the plants can move in.

Plant to Add, Not Cover Up

Flowers are like their cousins, the flowering trees, shrubs, evergreens and shade trees. They are just part of the big picture you call your garden. They are not supposed to dominate the whole scene. Therefore, it is necessary to make sure that the colors you use and the beds, patches or borders are wide enough and long enough to stay in proportion or in contrast to your home and lot. Remember this and you should have no problems. Flower beds are for display and should stand alone, while a border is a guideline or facing for other plants. As a rule, neither should be used as a cut flower garden. Cut flower beds should be placed next to a fence and should never be so wide that you can't cut the tallest and farthest row with ease. If you plant the tallest to the rear and the tiniest in front, no plant in these beds will ever be in another plant's shadow.

Keeping in Shape

Avoid laying out flower beds with sharp corners or 360-degree circles because of the possibility of damage to your plants and for your own comfort. Soft flowing lines give the appearance of naturalism to your garden and allow the lawn mower to follow the contours much easier, leaving smooth cutting lines behind, instead of tire tracks all over the flower bed and turf. Be sure that border flowers are planted far enough back that they will not be damaged by the lawn mower wheels. If you allow three to four inches, you can trim the edge with the mower, saving you the problem of trimming on bended knees. Also, by setting your planting back far enough, you will eliminate the happily growing plants from tubling out of their bed and onto the lawn where they will smother Leonard the Lawn.

The Wonder of the Kneeless Weeder

Science has come up with a real winner in the form of a pre-emerge weed killer for gardens. It eliminates the job of weeding on bended knees, which has never been one of my favorite pastimes. All the major garden product manufacturers have a pre-emerge garden weeder. They contain a chemical that will not interfere with any plant that is above the ground, but will prevent any other new growth from coming through—namely the weeds. By applying one of these garden weeders as soon as you have planted your flowers, or as soon as your new seed has sprouted, and after you have removed any existing weeds, you will not be plagued the rest of the summer (provided you do not disturb the surface of the soil). This scientific breakthrough has saved me many hours that I now spend on more enjoyable projects.

Planning the Menu

Your annual guests play so hard that they burn up a great deal of energy and need to eat hearty to continue their games. I have found that a hand-feeding of garden food once every three weeks, and a little side order of fish emulsion in between, keeps them in tip-top condition.

Panting for Breath

Since the flowers grow so fast and run even faster, they get rather thirsty and require a drink from time to time, except during the rainy season. To avoid letting them catch cold, it is a good idea to give them a soaking, like the queen-mother rose. Aim at their toes rather than the tip of their noses! Don't sprinkle their clothes!

Beware of the Bugs

Annuals are prone to attack from the wiggling and winged warriors, so it is important that they get the soap and water shower, and that you keep your eyes open for insects. At the first sign, use malathion or sevin. If it's something nibbling at their feet, use chlordane. From time to time a little rash or mildew will appear on the foliage, especially on the zinnia. A soap shower and an after bath powdering with rose dust will help.

This Pinch Won't Get a Face Slap

Your little annual friends are climbers, creepers and crawlers, and it becomes necessary, from time to time, to pinch them to keep them alert and in their own back yard. I let them bloom the first time and then I cut some of them back with grass shears to encourage more blooms. I do this again just before I go on vacation, since I won't be around to miss the flowers. Petunias need this trimming the most.

You Need a Score Card to Know the Players

Here is a helpful list to show you which position each flower child plays:

Annuals

FOR BORDERS
AGERATUM
ALYSSUM
BALSAM
BELLS OF IRELAND
MARIGOLD
NICOTIANA
PETUNIA
SALVIA FARINACEA AND
  SPLENDENS
CENTAUREA
CLEOME
COSMOS
CYNOGLOSSUM
LARKSPUR
SNAPDRAGON
STATICE
ZINNIA

FOR FOLIAGE
AMARANTHUS
BASIL
CANNA
CASTOR BEAN
COLEUS
DUSTY MILLER
KOCHIA
PERILLA

FOR PARTIAL SHADE
BALSAM
BEGONIA
BROWALLIA
CALENDULA
COLEUS
IMPATIENS
LOBELIA
MYOSOTIS
NICOTIANA
PANSY
SALVIA
TORENIA

FOR THE SEASIDE
ALYSSUM
DUSTY MILLER
HOLLYHOCK
STATICE
LUPINE
PETUNIA

FOR WINDOW BOXES
ALYSSUM
BEGONIA SEMPERFLORENS
COLEUS
LOBELIA
NIEREMBERGIA
CASCADE PETUNIAS
THUNBERGIA

FOR CUTTING
ASTERS
BELLS OF IRELAND
CARNATION
CELOSIA
CENTAUREA (BACHELOR
    BUTTONS)
COSMOS
CYNOGLOSSUM
DAHLIA
DAISY, TAHOKA
GAILLARDIA
GERBERA
GOMPHRENA
LARKSPUR
MARIGOLD
NASTURTIUM
PETUNIAS
RUDBECKIA
SALPIGLOSSIS
SALVIA
SCABIOSA
SNAPDRAGONS
STATICE
VERBENA
ZINNIA

MEDIUM GROWERS
BALSAM 15"
BASIL 15"
BELLS OF IRELAND 24"
CARNATION 15-20"
CELOSIA (MEDIUM CRISTATA
    TYPES SUCH AS FIREGLOW)
    20-24"
CYNOGLOSSUM 18"
DAHLIA (SUCH AS UNWIN'S
    DWARF MIX) 20-24"

DUSTY MILLER 12-24"
    (*Centaurea Gymnocarpa*)
    24"
GAILLARDIA 24-30"
GOMPHRENA 18"
HELICHRYSUM 24-30"
IMPATIENS 15-18"
NICOTIANA 15-24"
PETUNIAS 12-15"
RUDBECKIA 16-18"
SALPIGLOSSIS 20-30"
SALVIA 18-30"
SNAPDRAGONS 15-24"
    (VACATIONLAND) (HIT
    PARADE) (SPRITES) 12-15"
    (KNEE HIGH) 12-15"
VERBENA 12-24"
ZINNIA 18-30"

TALL GROWERS
AMARANTHUS 3-4'
ASTERS 36"
CELOSIA (TALL *Plumosa* SORTS
    SUCH AS FOREST FIRE)
    30-48"
CENTAUREA (BACHELOR
    BUTTONS) 30"
CLEOME 3-4'
COSMOS 3'
DAHLIA (SUCH AS CACTUS AND
    GIANT FLOWERED TYPES)
    30-48"
HOLLYHOCK 4-5'
LARKSPUR 2-3'
MARIGOLDS 30-36"
RICINUS (CASTOR BEAN) 8-10'
SCABIOSA 2-3'
STATICE 30"
SNAPDRAGONS (ROCKETS)
    30-36"
ZINNIA 30-36"

GROUND COVERS
COBAEA
CREEPING ZINNIA (*Sanvitalia
    Procumbens*)
LOBELIA

MESEMBRYANTHEMUM
MORNING-GLORY
MYOSOTIS
NASTURTIUM
NIEREMBERGIA
PORTULACA
SWEET ALYSSUM
SWEET PEAS
THUNBERGIA
VERBENA
VINCA

IN ROCK GARDEN
ALYSSUM
CANDYTUFT
GAZANIA
MESEMBRYANTHEMUM
PANSY
VERBENA
PLUS GROUND COVERS

FOR EDGING 3-18"
AGERATUM 6-12"
ALYSSUM 4-6"
BEGONIA 4-12"
CALENDULA 12"
CANDYTUFT 8"

CENTAUREA (DWARF BACHELOR
 BUTTONS) 10-12"
CELOSIA (DWARF SUCH AS FIERY
 FEATHER OR JEWEL BOX)
 4-12"
COLEUS 12-15"
DIANTHUS 12"
DUSTY MILLER (SUCH AS
 Centaurea Candidissima
 AND *Cineraria Maritima*
 DIAMOND) 6-10"
GAZANIA 8"
GOMPHRENA 9"
HELIOTROPE 12-15"
IMPATIENS 6-8"
LOBELIA 8"
MESEMBRYANTHEMUM 6"
MYOSOTIS 12"
NIEREMBERGIA 6"
PHLOX 7-15"
PANSY 6-8"
PETUNIA 12-15"
PORTULACA 4-6"
SNAPDRAGON (FLORAL CARPET)
 6-8"
TORENIA 8-12"
VERBENA 8-12"
VINCA 10"
ZINNIA-DWARF 6-12"

Questions and Answers

Q. What is meant by a hardy annual?

A. This is a tough little fellow that is planted in the fall
to come up and bloom the following spring.

Q. If I want a big, big, splashy flower bed for a shop-
ping center mall, what would I plant? We are a garden
club that has undertaken a beautification project.

A. First let me congratulate your club. I think more clubs
should undertake these projects for schools and drab
civic buildings. You can select one of the following:
ageratum, alyssum, asters, labelia, marigolds, petunias,
phlox, verbena or zinnias.

Q. What is your suggestion for a hot, dry location around Phoenix, Arizona? We just bought a retirement home there.
A. You will have luck with portulaca, aster and zinnias.

Q. I love bouquets on the table at mealtime. Any suggestions?
A. I always have a suggestion. We have a fenceful of sweet peas, with a backup of zinnias, asters, cosmos, stock, larkspur and snapdragons (tall and dwarfs).

Q. Can I collect seed from this year's annuals?
A. You can, but the hybrids won't give you a good flower, and that is what most of today's annuals are.

Q. Is rose dust good for insect control on annuals?
A. If a chemical control is necessary, rose dust will do nicely. I also use a safe flower and vegetable spray from Cook Chemical called Real Kill.

Q. I have been told that when you buy pre-grown flowers for the garden, you want short green ones with no color showing. True or False?
A. True. If you buy long, tall plants, they can soon grow out of proportion. Short, fat plants can be more easily controlled.

Q. How do you force petunias to flower?
A. Hold back on the water and run them a bit dry.

Q. What annual flower variety is the most popular?
A. Petunias are by far the number one favorite by both amateur and professional growers. They are followed closely by marigolds.

Q. Why can't I mix annuals with perennial flowers?
A. I don't know why you can't. I have done it for years and Grandma Putt did for many years before that. You can mix and match annuals, perennials, bulbs and biennials. That's the real secret!

Q. How much sun is necessary for lots of blooms?
A. I have my best luck with five to six hours of morning sun, but the afternoon sun won't hurt.

Q. When is the best time to preserve flowers?
A. Right when they are at their peak. Cut them in the morning, never after a rain. To preserve or dry annuals, cover them with silica gel, available at most garden centers.

Q. I have heard that marigolds will keep mosquitos away, but I tried and had no luck.
A. If you plant the giant, old-fashioned marigolds in pots and place on patios at night, you will have luck. Even I can't stand the smell. The newer varieties don't work so well . . . no odor.

Q. When do you start seed indoors in Illinois?
A. The first part of January or early February. Germinate the seeds in a sandy soil mix, then thin and plant in individual pots.

Q. Why do they recommend that you burn the dead floral foliage in the fall?
A. I did not know that they did. I think you will find they are referring only to sick or diseased plants. The rest go into the compost pile to make next year's garden food.

Q. We are moving to Alaska. Can we have the enjoyment of a flower garden?
A. By all means. Your time of enjoyment will be somewhat short, but you can have quite a selection. Here are a few: calendula, sweet pea, sunflower, cornflower, larkspur, zinnia, aster, lupine, marigold, forget-me-not, snapdragon, balsam, mignonette, candytuft, stock, petunia, verbena, sweet alyssum, flax, phlox and baby's breath. And, these are just a few!

Q. Which annuals will live in damp soil?

A. Begonia, impatiens and nicotina. Coleus will also tolerate some dampness.

Q. I love hanging baskets, but they are so messy to water. Are there any plants that would make it neater?
A. Stick with the same plants you have enjoyed; just change the method of watering. Drop four or five ice cubes into them every couple of days.

Q. Can you give me the name of a good flower to cascade down a wall, but not be a nuisance the rest of our lives?
A. Try trailing nasturtiums for something different.

Q. Should I mulch my annual flower bed?
A. Yes, by all means. After you have removed the weeds and applied one of the garden weeders, cover the surface with one of the organic mulches, like bark.

9
Perennials and Biennials: Top Management

The Steward of the Garden

The perennials, by virtue of their longevity, have come to be known as the supervisors or managers of affairs. They are the neat, prim, straight-laced, no-nonsense members of the Garden Kingdom. Since they are with us year in and year out, I suggest that you counsel with them before adding any more work or guests to your garden. After all, they are the mainstays, who keep things neat and tidy. The delphinium is the head man, and his assistant is the chrysanthemum. The peony is the chambermaid, the iris is the butler guiding the way through the garden, and the artemisia (silver mound) is the doorman, who is seen but seldom heard. So you see, you are not out there alone. You have plenty of assistance in management, as do most business and property owners, whether they like it or not.

Practically Problemless

The perennials live up to Webster's definition: "Persistent for several years." They continue to return year in, year out, multiplying and paying their way as they go. They seldom complain, and their general health is usually excellent. Once you plant them, you don't have to keep your eye on them too much. The biennials, which are half-brothers to the perennials, only stay around for a couple of years. They tend to be a little restless, and make good plants for spots where you haven't quite decided what you want permanently.

Don't Be Too Hasty

Let's go back to the master plan for a moment. You must remember, before you make your final selection of perennials, that they are going to be around in the same spot for years to come, just like their neighboring trees, shrubs and evergreens, so you must determine if you wish to employ them for a long period of time. After all, it isn't a pleasure to tell any employee that you don't need his help any longer. I suggest that you ask your nurseryman for some references, and check out his credentials thoroughly, before finally selecting and placing your perennials in their permanent positions.

Permanently Employed

Plants are just like people. They relax and feel more secure when their name is painted on the door and not just pencilled in, and when they have their own desk and don't have to share one with a couple of others. Plant your perennials for permanence and give each individual plant some working space of his own.

Perennials can be purchased in small soil bags in the spring, or in tar-paper pots in early summer, or full grown in boxes or baskets in mid-summer or sometimes late spring. I had to retire an old delphinium recently, and it left a big gap in my organization. So I replaced it with a big strapping new blue. Well I am sure, from the action around the garden, that the others were going kind of easy until they found out what kind of a boss he was going to be! By the way, he is working out fine.

When planting any of the perennials, dig a hole wider than the plant and only as deep as the soil line from the nursery. This group of plants likes the same soil and food conditions as annuals, and so the soil preparation is the same. When you have completed the installation, apply the garden weeder and mulch.

Since your perennials are heavy bloomers, it is necessary

to feed them on a regular basis. Give them a handful of
garden food a month, and, in between, give them the same
dessert as you give the annuals—fish emulsion.

Don't Crowd

Many of the perennials, such as iris, peonies and mums,
can be divided. Dividing is done in the early spring, either
to start new plants or to give new vigor to the older
ones. Dig and divide carefully.

When dividing mums, you simply dig out the whole
clump and gently pull off each new plant individually.
Replant each one of these separate plants wherever you
wish, but keep in mind that each will grow as large as a
bushel basket, so leave room for expansion. One clump
of mums should yield at least thirty to fifty plants.

Peonies are cut in half or into thirds with a sharp spade
and replanted in new and sunny spots.

Iris are dug up as a clump. Remove the soil and then

cut off each corm with a sharp knife. You will be able to recognize these even if you are a beginner, because each corm, or root section, will have a foliage shoot at the top.

They Can Be Pestered

Insects and disease can bother these "flower folk" from time to time. So it is necessary to wash them down with soap and water and dust them with rose dust when the problem arises. Not only insects and disease plague the perennials, but poor watering practices can prevent them from doing their best. A deep soaking once a week will do wonders.

Pick your management team carefully. Harmony results in excellent production and quality control.

Following is a list to help you make a wise selection of perennials for your garden:

Perennials

TALL

Anchusa (italica)
DELPHINIUM
Digitalis (FOX-GLOVE)
Eremurus (GIANT DESERT-CANDLE)
HELENIUM
HOLLYHOCKS (DOUBLE AND SINGLE)
IRIS (JAPANESE IRIS)
LILIES (VARIOUS VARIETIES)
LYTHRUM
PENSTEMON
RUDBECKIA
YUCCA

MEDIUM

Aquilegia (COLUMBINE)
CHRYSANTHEMUM
Coreopsis (grandiflora)
Gaillardia (grandiflora)

Gypsophila (BABY'S BREATH)
IRIS (BEARDED)
LUPINE (RUSSEL)
Lychnis (chalcedonica)
POPPY (ORIENTAL)
PEONY
PHLOX (PERENNIAL)
Platycodon (MONK'S HOOD)
Pyrethrum (PAINTED DAISY)
Veronica (longifolia)

SHORT

Alyssum (saxatile compactum)
Arabis alpina
Armeria (SEA PINK)
Aster alpinus
AUBRIETIA
Campanula carpatica
Dianthus (PERENNIAL PINKS)
Phlox subulata (CARPET)

Questions and Answers

Q. We have a large assortment of evergreens, mostly junipers. Which perennial do you suggest I use in the open spots?

A. I love the different colored painted daisies.

Q. When is the best time to plant perennials?

A. I was taught that fall is one of the best times for iris, peonies and mums, and early spring for the rest.

Q. Will perennials do okay in acid soil in Pennsylvania?

A. I would add lime every three years, but, as a rule, they will do well in soil that's somewhat on the acid side.

Q. When is the best time to sow seed for perennials?

A. I sow perennial seed in the fall and then cover it over with straw for protection. Biennials like pansies and hollyhocks must be planted in the fall.

Q. Will peonies survive in clay?

A. Not as a rule. They prefer loose, fertile soil. But then who knows, they may really like you and do the impossible.

Q. I have heard there is a poppy that is short and stout.

A. Iceland is the name, and they are great as cut flowers.

Q. What can I feed peonies to keep them from drooping?

A. Large sticks. You will have to stake many of the tall, fast growers and tie them with pieces of old nylon hose. Get your wife to save old stockings for you.

Q. How do you make delphiniums bloom a second time?

A. Cut the bloom off when it is just about done and feed. This same advice goes for the other perennials. Do not let the flowers die on the vine.

Q. When is the best time to transplant perennials that must be moved?

A. I have found that early spring is the best time.

Q. What is speedwell?
A. A very bushy, beautiful perennial, also called Veronica. It grows about six to eight inches high.

Q. How close should I plant mums?
A. That depends on what purpose you have in mind. I do not let them touch, if I can help it.

Q. Is the aster an annual or a perennial?
A. It's both. Depends on which you want to buy. The perennial is the Italian aster.

Q. How do you save Chinese lanterns?
A. That's an easy one. Cut them off and hang them upside down.

Q. What is statice used for?
A. It is a great flower to cut and dry. It grows eighteen inches high and eighteen inches across and is also called "sea lavender."

Q. How tall do lupines grow?
A. Three to five feet. They should be planted in the back row.

10
Bulbs:
The Golden Nuggets

Nature's Nuggets

I guess we have all heard the saying many times that the best gifts come in small packages. Well, it really applies to the bulb stock! I have never been able to understand why God hid such a beautiful thing as a tulip, crocus or daffodil in such ugly shells, but then some of the most beautiful people I know are not the best looking physically. I also remember another saying, that "Beauty is more than skin deep." When we plan and plant the Dutch bulbs, it's just like burying a treasure. Once a bulb is in the ground, it is there to stay until we decide to move it. And it never really loses its value. As a matter of fact, the longer bulbs remain in the ground, the more valuable they become. When properly planted, they can bring spring beauty from February to June. In snow country they break through the ice and snow with the early varieties called snow drops. In the warm climates they bring the early spring color after the dismal rains. When you plant the bulbs and your friends ask what's in that mound of soil, you can truthfully say, "There's gold in them thar hills!"

X Marks the Spot

As with any buried treasure, you must make a map so you don't forget where the bulbs are buried. You already have the map; it's the paper bag plan you used to start your garden. All you have to do now is mark on it where you planted which bulbs, so that you do not accidentally dig them up before they pop up their heads. I also put a

landmark over my bulb treasure, with the variety's name
and when I can expect it to bloom. I use long thin bamboo
stakes with aluminum flags on which I write the name and
expected bloom time.

Pick Precious Jewels

I have never heard a complaint from any gardener that
there weren't enough colors, sizes or shapes to choose
from in Mother Nature's jewel box of bulbs. She has
something inside there to satisfy everyone's taste. If you
take just a few moments of your time to look over the
blooming time of each kind of bulb, you can scatter a few
different varieties here and there throughout your entire
landscape. Plan to fill in the voids until the perennials and
annuals appear or your borders begin to smile.

In the last few years, the popularity of imported Dutch
bulbs has dwindled to a trickle of what it used to be.
That's a pity! For you younger gardeners, I will suggest
that you haven't seen anything until you see snow drops,
winter aconite or Siberian squill poke their noses through
the snow in late February to smile at the world and say,
"Spring is just around the corner!" And to you more experienced green thumbs, shame on you—look at all of
the extra beauty you are letting pass by your garden. Boy,
oh boy, I am prouder of my garden in the early spring
than at any other time of the season, when my portrait of
posies is in full swing and other folks in the neighborhood
still have a sleepy landscape to look at.

Here are a few suggestions to get you back in the
treasure hunt and make you button-poppin', suspender-
snappin' proud of your early spring garden. In the order
of their blooming, here is a bulb-planter's timetable:
snowdrop, winter aconite, crocus, Siberian squill, *Iris
reticulata,* Chronodoxa, *Puschkinia libanotica,* early tulips
(kaufmanniana), fosteriana followed by grape hyacinths,
trumpet daffodils, the single and double early tulips, regular hyacinths, medium daffodils, Darwin and triumph
tulips, short daffodils, poet's narcissus and jonquils. The
late tulips, parrot, cottage, lily-flowered, double lates,

Darwin, and breeder. Now ask yourself, what more could I ask of Mother Nature than this garden gallery of glorious colors, from the last weeks of snow to the fullness of spring.

Plant in Advance

Spring-flowering bulbs are planted in the fall and winter, from coast to coast. I do not know of anyplace where these beauties won't grow. It is simply a matter of planting at the right time. The "little bulbs," such as crocus, scilla and snowdrops should be planted as soon as they are available in snow country, and in the early December in the South and West. Tulips should be planted as soon as the weather cools and on through the fall and early winter until the ground freezes. In the South and West, bulbs can be placed in the refrigerator at forty-five degrees from five to six weeks, and then planted in January.

The Problem Solvers

The biggest problem most gardeners have is what to plant in damp, shady spots. The bulbs solve this problem, because that's where they grow the best. And, once planted, they need to be kept damp. I mulch my bulbs with leaves and let them lie until they began to poke their noses through. Then I move the mulch just enough to let them finish their climb to the sunshine but keep their feet cool.

Don't Bury Your Treasure Too Deep

Your buried treasures do not like to be too deep nor too crowded. Plant the little bulbs three inches deep and three inches apart. Hyacinths and tulips, as well as daffodils, are to be planted six inches deep and six inches apart. There is a top and bottom to each bulb, and they sure would appreciate it if you would not plant them standing on their heads. Plant the bulb with the point up. They will grow either way, but it seems to weaken the stem when they have to turn that first corner underground in order to come out right side up.

Don't Double-Deck

If you are planning on planting a large bed of bulbs, or several different kinds in the same bed to bloom one after the other, I suggest that you dig a hole the width and length of the bed you intend to plant, eight inches deep. With the soil removed, mix ample bone meal, two pounds per bushel of soil, as well as five pounds of gypsum per bushel of soil: then mix in fifty pounds of peat moss for each four bushels of soil and use this to refill the bulb bed. Plant the deepest bulbs on the bottom and then cover them up. Lay the next bulb layer in, but not so that it is directly over the one below, and place a layer of soil mix over it, continuing until all of the bulbs are planted and covered. Now mulch the top with leaves or light bark chips, pine or redwood.

Don't Forget Dinner

A bulb has a built-in lunch bucket, but there is not enough lunch in it to carry it all the way through the season. As the bulbs begin to show through the soil, scatter a half handful of garden food, 4-12-4 or 5-10-5, over the top of the soil. Make sure you do this early, before they bloom, so that they can eat and digest the food. This will keep them blooming longer and stronger. It will also help them to produce more bulbs.

Insect Intuition

The insects that wake up early will be delighted with your foresight in supplying them with such a pleasant dinner table. To discourage them, I suggest that you give the young plants a shower with soap and water before the blooms appear, and dust the soil with six or ten percent chlordane if there are any signs of insect damage. Apart

from that, you shouldn't have too much trouble with the insect world.

Clip the Wings

After the tulips have bloomed to their fullest, cut off the stems and let the foliage alone until it has turned yellow and begun to dry; then cut it off just above the ground. To hide the fading foliage, I turn it down and place a small rubber band around it to screen it from the rest of the world.

Sneak Preview

Bulbs can be grown indoors for beauty and fragrance, since they need very little effort to burst into bloom in January and February. Tulips, hyacinths, daffodils and narcissi, as well as crocuses, can be planted in the fall in pots, to be brought into the house to bloom. To begin, purchase a commercial planting mix—the type used for house plants—at your local garden center. Also, purchase a number of five or six-inch clay pots. Place a piece of

broken crock or a flat beer-cap over the drain hole in the
bottom of the pot. Begin to fill the pot with soil until the
tulip or daffodil or narcissus tops are just above the soil
line. Make sure they do not touch. Now, continue to fill
the pot but let their noses stay above the soil. Hyacinths
are planted singly with their noses one-fourth to one-half
inch above the soil. Crocuses are planted like tulips and
daffodils.

After you have planted all of your bulbs, water them
thoroughly, wrap the entire pot in newspaper and bury six
to eight inches deep in your garden. The newspaper is
placed around the pots to keep them clean for bringing
into the house. Leave the pots in the ground for eight
to ten weeks. Next, bring them into the basement where
they get some light, but have a temperature range of sixty
to sixty-five degrees. Keep them there until the foliage is
two to three inches high. At this point, bring them into
the living room and into full light. Keep them damp and
warm and watch the magic that follows. There is no room
deodorizer that can compare with the real fragrance of hyacinths in full bloom. This is an excellent experience for
both children and adults. It is not necessary to bury the
pots, you can keep them in a garage where the temperature
will be forty to fifty degrees, but you must keep them
dark and damp.

Can I Bring My Cousin?

When we think of bulbs we forget there are other bulb
types, like the tubers and corms, dahlias, glads and lilies.
A little study on your part with the seed catalogues, will
help you learn how to fit in a few of each.

Questions and Answers

Q. Do I have to dig up my bulbs each year?
A. Not as long as they continue to bloom and the flowers
   are an acceptable size.

Q. I am totally confused about which are bulbs and which

are corms or tubers, or whatever they call them. How do you tell?

A. Why bother? They are either bulbs or bulb types. The way I mulch and the way I recommend you do, you can plant any of them in the fall and let the chips fall where they may.

Q. How do you treat new bulbs before you plant them?
A. I drop them in a mild solution of two gallons of soap and water with a tablespoon of forty-four percent chlordane. Then, I plant them.

Q. I have seen crocuses planted in the lawn. How do you take care of them?
A. You don't. Just plant them and they will look out for themselves. When they have finished blooming, mow them off. They will return the following year almost without fail.

Q. What makes tulips stop blooming?
A. They are probably too crowded. Dig them up and separate them.

Q. Should you cut the mushy, gray spots out of bulbs before you plant them?
A. No, you should take them back and get new ones or your money back. They are sick.

Q. Can I plant my Easter lilies when they are done blooming?
A. You bet your boots, and odds are they will bloom again the same year and years to come. I go around to the flower shops after the holiday and collect the bulbs (cheap).

Q. What is the best mulch for bulbs and corms?
A. Oak-leaf mulch makes the best, because it acts as a natural preventative insect barrier.

Q. When should you plant gladiolus bulbs?

A. In the early spring and then two weeks apart through July first.

Q. Can I leave glad bulbs in the ground all winter?
A. Not as a rule. Glads freeze and should be dug up and stored. However, I have left them in the ground with four inches of mulch and had three good years out of them.

Q. Should you cut tulips for bouquets?
A. What kind of a question is that? Certainly you should. It makes lots of folks happy, and that's what Mother Nature has in mind.

Q. What is the difference between Dutch and Japanese bulbs?
A. Several thousand miles and competition. The Dutch bulbs are still tops in my garden. They seem to produce larger, longer and stronger.

Q. Does the size of the bulb have any effect on the size of the flowers?
A. Bulbs are graded by size. The bigger the better.

Q. What do you do to bulbs after they have bloomed?
A. Remember where they are planted and feed them once in a while. In the fall, begin to water where the bulbs are planted, and add new mulch.

Q. Will bulbs interfere with the roots of trees?
A. I have never heard a tree in my garden complain. As a matter of fact, they are the best of friends.

11
The Vegetable Garden: Your Team

Carl

The Epitome of Pleasure

You would think that as long as I have been gardening, I would take the results for granted. But I never cease to become excited when I'm able to pull my first radish from the ground, or pick my first bush bean from the vine, or bite into the first tomato taken from my garden. At that moment, I feel a true sense of accomplishment. Vegetable gardening is almost like playing baseball. Everyone on the team must work together to win the game, and if just one player fumbles along the way, or makes an error, you could well lose the ball game. It takes real teamwork to have an appetite-filling garden, and you must understand that you are just one of the team members. As a matter of fact, you call all the shots because you are the manager. Before every season you must hand in a roster, and the vegetable garden team has quite a list of stars and superstars. The captain is Mother Nature, water boy is Jupiter Fluvius, the coach is nourishment and the players are the vegetables. To put together a winning organization, the manager must know his players and their dispositions, as well as their limitations. From time to time, it is necessary to make a trade to strengthen the team so that it works together as one unit. There is no room for individualism if you want to win. Your team must learn to play hard, but fair, even though the other team has a reputation for foul play. After all, look at who's on the other team, Bennie the Bug, Willie the Worm, Windy the Blowhard, Danny Dirty Itch, Weedy the Wonder-Fielder and Nick Neglect. You have to respect a team like that. You don't have to like them, but you sure have to respect them. Always remember, the real pleasure is in eating the fruits of victory!

When the Whistle Blows

The excitement before the season is good for the whole team. Everybody is up for the coming competition. As the manager, you must select the starting team and plan the strategy. This is called having a game plan. You must lay it out on paper, and so it is with the garden. Plan every step, from your starting lineup to final out, including replacement possibilities that might occur as your garden players tire. During the off-season find out the background For your team's health and safety, I suggest that you refer to one of the many catalogues I have suggested. Once you have decided, and acquired your starting team, you are ready for the umpire's call, "Play ball!"

Check the Playing Surface

The gardening game should never be made into work; it should remain fun even when you have to play hard. For your team's health and safety, I suggest that you first walk out onto the area where you are going to play. Remove all broken objects, such as tree stumps, rocks, cans, glass or wood. We don't want to lose a star player as the result of his stumbling over a hidden object. Look for soggy spots that can cause a vegetable player to slip. The garden surface should have a slight crown at the top and taper off on all four sides, like a ball field. This will let excess water from unexpected storms run off during the growing game. Otherwise, a downpour could bog down the whole team.

Give Credit Where Credit Is Due

When I was playing baseball, I would always give the groundskeeper a Christmas gift each year to inspire him to take a little better care of my position on the field, so that I had better traction for quick starts. Now that I look back, I can see how I wasted my money, because he took pride in his work and made sure that the entire field was in top shape. You must also make sure that your vegetable garden is in top shape, so all the members can get off to a good, fast start. Let's begin from scratch. A good garden is begun in the late fall by applying fifty pounds of cow manure, twenty-five pounds of garden food and fifty pounds of gypsum, per hundred square feet, topped off with one hundred pounds of peat moss or composted leaves and cuttings. This concoction is left to lie all winter. In the spring, when the soil is just dry enough to crumble in your hand, all of your fall additions are spaded in and graded out to look just like an area prepared for grass seed, keeping in mind the crown effect, for runoff of surface water.

Exhibition Season

Early in the playing season, exhibition games are scheduled to test players' strength and condition. Oftentimes a player is injured in these exhibition games because he is not in shape. This is what happens to many home gardeners who attempt a vegetable garden. They put their ball club on the field too early, before they are in shape. Check the roster at the end of this chapter for vegetables that are qualified to start the growing game early.

Laying Out the Boundaries

Most books, articles and instructions available for the home gardener seem to assume that everybody who wants a vegetable garden has an acres or more. They give recommendations for one-hundred-foot rows. My friends, in my eyes, that's playing professional gardening, and if you don't know what you are doing, you can lose lots of players without scoring a lot of vegetable victories. I suggest that we bring that playing field down to a maximum of twenty-five feet for the semi-pro gardeners and ten-foot rows for the amateur gardeners. You must determine how much time you will have to practice vegetable gardening, before you can lay out your final guidelines.

Esprit de Corps

In order ot have a winning team, in any sport, you must have *esprit de corps*. That's a common spirit existing between members of a group. Vegetables can help each other, even though they have nothing in common. This method of helping each other is called symbiosis, that is, the growing together of two unlike organisms, to the mutual benefit of both. This is to say that one gives off as a surplus, or waste, what the other plant needs as nourishment, or as a health balance or protective control. By planting certain vegetables with others who make good companions, you will end up with an almost unbeatable vegetable garden team. The Bio-Dynamic Farming & Gardening Association has issued a list of companion plants. Their research was done by Richard B. Gregg, who later wrote a book called *Companion Plants and How to Use Them.* His co-author was Helen Philbrick. Here are some of the vegetables that make excellent teammates:

Asparagus and tomatoes.

Beans and carrots, cauliflower, beets, cabbage and cucumbers.

Beans and potatoes also do very well together.

Wax beans do well with celery if the celery is planted six to one.

Beets and beans, onions or kohlrabi.

Cabbage and potatoes, dill, camomile, sage, vermouth, rosemary and the mint family.

Carrots and lettuce and chives.

Cauliflower and celery.

Celery and leeks, tomatoes.

Corn and potatoes, beans and peas, as well as melons, squash, pumpkins and cucumbers.

Cucumbers and potatoes, cabbage, radishes.

Kohlrabi and lettuce.

Egg plant and green beans.

Kohlrabi and beets and onions.

Leeks and celery.

Lettuce and strawberries, carrots and radishes.

Onions and beets.

Peas and radishes, carrots, cucumbers, corn, beans and turnips.

Potatoes and beans, cabbage and peas.

Pumpkins and corn.

Radishes and peas, lettuce, chervil.

Spinach and strawberries.

Tomatoes and asparagus, parsley, cabbage. I have found that they also do very well with potatoes and cucumbers.

If you will take a little time out to check over your list of players, you will soon discover a winning combination.

Sick Call for the Injured

From time to time, one or two of your players could become lame or ill. It is absolutely essential that you recognize the symptoms and treat immediately. As a general rule, two or three showers a season will ward off injuries to foliage above the ground, and if pests appear, dust with Sevin vegetable dust.

I make sure my team keeps cool by mulching everything with wood chips and black plastic. The plastic is stretched from one end of the row to the other and anchored with soil. I then cut small holes in the plastic to plant through. As the plants grow, they are protected by the plastic from weeds and many pests.

Brace the Weak

You will find that you have a few tall players who, like many growing boys, get to a clumsy stage and fall all over. To prevent this from happening and their injuring themselves when they fall, you must stake your tomatoes. Place chicken wire down the rows of beans and peas, and place broken branches under bush beans. This will protect the plants and make picking easier for you.

Too Much Water Gives Cramps

When the team is hot and dry, the worst thing in the world you can do is let it drink too much too fast or throw ice water in their faces. The vegetable team should be given a good soaking at the feet. Do not water the foliage, especially not the tomato or melon crops. Rain water is the only good and accepted moisture for your vegetable garden. Soak deep once a week.

Too Many Players Cause Penalties

In order for a good team to function properly, it is necessary to have room to work. Don't crowd your vegetable team. Make sure that you thin out the weak players early. Don't let them burden the stronger players like the radishes, carrots, beets, parsnips, etc. When you plant cabbage, celery, tomatoes, melons, squash, pumpkin or cucumber, plant them with plenty of room to spread out. If you cramp them, they can't give you top performance.

Always Have Cheerleaders

Any team will perform better with a cheering section, so I suggest that you let the children plant some of the team members. You will be surprised at how close they will follow the team when they have a favorite player in the game.

Give the Reserves a Chance

Some managers make a mistake in not trying out new players. They leave some potential stars sitting on the bench, simply because they have relied on the regulars for so long that when it's time for a replacement they don't know who can fill the bill. Plant a new or different vegetable each year. You will be surprised at the number of future starters that you will discover.

Keep the Game Moving

No matter how strong a player is, he can't play the whole game. It therefore becomes necessary to send in relievers. Here is the order of replacement:

Early peas, followed by early corn, then late snap beans. Late peas are replaced by corn and then by radishes and lettuce with spinach.

Onion sets are followed by tomatoes.
Cabbage is the starter and is replaced by lima beans.
Spinach is followed by wax beans.
White radishes start and snap beans finish.
Beets are followed by peppers or parsnips.

If you keep your eyes on the game and handle your players accordingly, you can really make the game interesting.

Vegetable Team Starters

BEANS
60 days

BEETS
Dark Red Detroit   60 days

BRUSSELS SPROUTS
Long Island Imp.   90 days

F1 HYBRID CABBAGE
Emerald Cross   67 days
Swellhead   95 days
Stone Head   50 days
Jersey Queen   63 days
Golden Acre Resistant
        65 days
Marion Market   80 days
Wisconsin All-Season   90 days
Copenhagen Market   67 days
Early Dwarf Flat Dutch
        85 days
Late Flat Dutch   100 days
Danish Ballhead   105 days

RED CABBAGE
Mammoth Rock Red   100 days
CAULIFLOWER
Early Snowball "A"   55 days
Snowball "X"   65 days
Snow King   45 days
CELERY
Summer Pascal   110 days

CORN
100 days

CUCUMBER
Ball Early Hybrid   58 days
Hiyield   62 days
Pioneer   55 days
Spartan Valor   60 days
Triple Purpose   54 days
Triumph   60 days
EGGPLANT
Mission Bell   70 days
LETTUCE
Salad Bowl   45 days

MELON
Honey Rock   85 days
Mainerock   75 days
Samson   85-90 days
Saticoy Hybrid   90 days
Super Market   85 days
Watermelon:
Dixie Queen Hybrid   82 days
Sweetmeat   83 days

PEAS
Freezonian   62 days

PEPPER
Bell Boy   70 days
Canape   62 days

Aconcagua   65 days

California Wonder Select
    72 days

Delaware Belle   75 days

Hungarian Yellow Wax
    80 days

Long Red Cayenne   74 days

Mercury   80 days

Merrimack Wonder   68 days

Midway   70 days

Pimento Perfection   75 days

Red Chili   84 days

Sweet Bull Nose   65 days

Titan   75 days

Vinedale   62 days

Yolo Wonder   70 days

RADISH
Cherry Belle   23 days

SPINACH
60 days

SQUASH
Chefini   48 days

TOMATO
Beefsteak   96 days

Bonny Best   70 days

Break O'Day   70 days

Campbell   75 days

Earliana   66 days

Fireball   60 days

Firesteel   68 days

Floradel   82 days

Giant Tree   88 days

Glamour   74 days

Gulf State Market   80 days

Heinz 1350   75 days

Heinz 1370   77 days

Heinz 1439   77 days

Jubilee (TA)   80 days

Manalucie   82 days

Marglobe Supreme (TA)
    77 days

New Yorker   62 days

Oxheart   90 days

Ponderosa   95 days

Roma VF   76 days

Rutgers (TA)   82 days

Sunray   83 days

Super Sioux   70 days

Valiant   70 days

Wisconsin Chief   72 days

Gardener's Delight   50 days

Small Fry (TA/JC)   65 days

Tiny Tim (TA)   46 days

Avalanche   77 days

Ball Extra Early (TA)
    55 days

Ball Giant Hybrid   65 days

Bonny Best Hybrid   65 days

Bonus   75 days

Burpee Big Boy Hybrid
    (TA/JC)   78 days

Burpee Big Early (TA)
    62 days

Burpee Hybrid   70 days

Early Salad   45 days

Golden Boy   80 days

Mocross Supreme   70-75 days

Mocross Surprise   60-70 days

Patio (TA)   70 days

Rushmore   66 days

Rutgers Hybrid   85 days

Spring Set VF   65 days

Terrific VFN   73 days

Vineripe   80 days

Wonder Boy (TA)   80 days

Ohio-Indiana   74 days

Questions and Answers

Q. Everytime we put pepper or tomato plants in the
  ground, something breaks them off at the soil line.

A. Those are cut worms. Place aluminum-foil collars two

inches high around the stems, making sure that one inch is below the soil. Mulch with oak-leaf mulch.

Q. Is it necessary to use lime every year in my table garden?
A. It's not necessary, unless the soil has become acid. It is never advisable to use anything that is not necessary.

Q. Can you suggest a tomato that I can grow in a small area?
A. You will be delighted with F_1 hybrid patio tomato. I grow them between my evergreens with great results.

Q. How do I keep rabbits out of my garden?
A. Plant old-fashioned marigolds around the vegetable garden.

Q. Is it true that you should not cultivate around tomatoes?
A. It is a good idea not to disturb the roots if at all possible. A two-inch layer of mulch will eliminate the necessity of having to use a hoe.

Q. When I was a youngster, my uncle grew giant pumpkins. What were they?
A. I would say it was the variety called Jack-o-lantern. Make sure you give this roamer plenty of room.

Q. How much sun is necessary for a good vegetable garden?
A. If you want any kind of results at all, you had better find a spot where your garden will get six to eight hours of good sunshine.

Q. We have trouble with grubs in the garden soil. Our carrots and radishes are lost each season. Is there any control?
A. The problem sounds like root maggots. These pests can

be controlled by using forty-four percent chlordane as
directed.

Q. What causes tomatoes to turn gray or black on the top
just before they ripen?
A. This is called blossom-end rot and is the result of hot,
humid weather. Not enough water gets to the fruit.
Well-mulched plants with a sound irrigation program
are seldom bothered.

Q. Which vegetables grow the fastest?
A. For those of you who want to have two or three different gardens a season, try these few selections for
speed: leaf lettuce, radishes, bush beans, onion sets,
mustard and turnip greens, beets and peas.

Q. How important is crop rotation in a small garden?
A. A lot more important than in a large garden. I always
recommend that crops be rotated, with the exception
of tomatoes. They can stay in one spot for three years.

Q. How do you keep cabbage worms from eating more
cabbage than we get?
A. You can sprinkle the heads with ordinary table salt a
couple of times a season.

Q. Which vegetable can we grow on a patio (porch) of
our apartment? We live in the Central Park district of
New York.
A. It doesn't matter if you live in an apartment in Oregon,
Texas, Florida, Maine or Michigan, you can grow a
garden on a porch and be the talk of the building.
Start with a bag of Redi-Earth planter mix and a redwood tub or two. In one tub plant a seed potato and
a patio tomato. Results: seven pounds of potatoes and
and a half bushel of tomatoes. In another, plant pole
beans and leaf lettuce, and in another cucumbers and
radishes. You will need a pole for support in the center
of each.

Q. Our cucumbers get all eaten up and I am too old to dust every week. Any green-thumb magic?

A. There is no magic, lotion, motion or potion in gardening, but inter-planting sure resembles it. Plant a few radishes in each cucumber mound.

Q. I have heard that you can pinch tomatoes to make them climb, instead of spread out. Where do you pinch?

A. If you are going to train your tomatoes to grow up a stake, you should pinch out the side shoots that grow out of the crook of the main side stems.

Q. What variety of cucumber won't give you gas?

A. If you like cucumbers, but they don't like you, try the ones they call lemon cucumbers.

12
Ground Covers: Something to Hide

Real Cover-Up

In this day and age we all seem to strive for privacy. To block out the action around us, we seem to be cultivating the "mind-our-own-business," "don't-get-involved" culture. This is wrong. We were created to mix and mingle, talk and listen, love and be loved and help one another. I am sure that Mother Nature did not intend the beautiful vines and ivies to shut others out or us in. She is in hopes that we will use them to enhance the beauty of our homes or gardens. These climbing beauties can cover up an object or work location that might detract from the overall beauty of our garden. The ground covers were created for the purpose of cooling the toes of our trees and shrubs, or to grow in a spot where other plants don't dare to wander.

The variety of both the climbing vines and creeping ground covers is virtually unlimited in color, texture and fragrance. Both vines and covers are nearly maintenance-free, with a few exceptions. Both tend to reproduce new plants without much effort.

If you find it necessary to screen a dog pen or children's play area, control dust or muffle street noise, or if security is needed for children's safety, then by all means screen or cover up with these members of the Plant Kingdom. But never use them to block out the wonderful world around you. As the younger generation says, "Let the sun shine in" and "Let it all hang out!"

Fe-Fi-Fo-Fum

I guess the first climbing vine any of us learn about as children, is Jack's famous "beanstalk," which is still being used by some of the wiser and more imaginative home gardeners. Whenever anyone thinks of a climbing vine, he naturally thinks of a flowering vine, but since we are all concerned about space in today's day and age, we should first consider a plant that will return food and flowers. When I find it necessary to disguise an object or location, I always look at my fruit and vegetable list first. There are many vinelike crops like pole beans, peas, grape vines, etc. that can do the job, but pay their way at the same time. If it is a ground cover I need, I always check to see if strawberries will fill the bill, or cucumbers and squash. Don't waste space if you can fill your table and eye at the same time.

What's the Purpose?

When you select a vine for flowers and/or foliage, it should serve some purpose. The plant in question can be used to detract from an objectionable surface, perhaps a crumbling or stained stone wall. In this case, the plant selected should be one trained to grow on wires to form a design.

To form an arbor you should use a dense foliage vine with delicate flowers. If you wish to divide your yard into recreational areas, you can use medium foliage vines with large flowers, etc. Entryways can be enhanced with the use of cascading vines like the wisteria, to give the effect of elegance and size. Before you select a vine, decide what its purpose in life is going to be.

No Man's Land

The ground covers are a different story altogether. In the garden, we consider them lifesavers, plant lifesavers. Anyone who attempts to grow grass under trees, or in heavily shaded areas, is taking on a losing battle for both himself and the grass. Ground covers are the answer to your grass's prayers and your problem. These hardy boys can manage almost any situation. In shade, partial shade, damp, wet or soggy soil, they forge ahead! The ground cover crowd lives up to the old popular saying, "When the going gets tough, the 'tough' get going!"

Permanent Residency

Both the vines and ground covers are tough customers, but only after they have established themselves in their new homes. Spade leaf mulch, peat moss and garden food into the soil where you are going to plant your climber or crawler. Make sure that the soil is in the same shape as suggested for the vegetable garden, level and fine. I'm a little on the impatient side when it comes to ground covers, so I plant them rather close together, in staggered rows. Top-dress the soil with a regular lawn food at least twice a year.

Kin to Crab Grass

Most ground covers are virtually indestructible, just like quack grass and crab grass, and since they seem to resemble these same weeds in growing habits, I plant my ground covers in May when the weeds are growing their best. This is a good time any place in the country.

Keep Moths out of the Carpet

You will find that you are not the only one that appreciates a thick cover of green foliage. Almost every creepy, crawly bug in the garden will, at one time or another, stop by to rest beneath it. Mice and moles will occasionally take a breather or build a winter nest there. To discourage the insects, wash with soap once or twice a month. Bury a wine bottle or two to keep the moles moving, and rattle the brush to move the mice. To control the soil bugs, if they appear, use six percent chlordane. Fungus diseases will appear from time to time if you do not use a soap shower. If the itchy diseases do appear, use one of the rose dusts in liquid solution.

Weeds Are No Bother

I will, very briefly, mention this subject because it is no longer a problem if you use the kneeless weeders early in the spring. I do not cultivate ground covers, but I do mulch after I have spread my garden weeder.

Need Support

Vines are much heavier than one imagines. Primarily, because of their total mass, they hold back the winds, putting a strain on the wires, poles or arbors supporting them. Make sure that the supporting pole or post is well anchored and the wires are thick and tough. The vines can usually hold tightly to whatever you supply them to climb. Oh yes, some have fine roots like fingers, especially the ivies, while grapes wrap their fingers around anything in sight. Some twist their whole body around a wire or pole, like bittersweet. And others have sticky fingers to help them hold on. However, since there is nothing worse than trying to stand a vine back up that has tumbled down with a broken support, be sure your supports are strong enough to support the ultimate weight of a full-grown vine when you first put them in.

Best of the Bunch

Here are the names of a few good climbers and ground creepers:

CLIMBERS

WISTERIA
CLEMATIS (PRINCESS OF THE GARDEN)
STAR JASMINE
TRUMPET VINE
BOSTON IVY
WINTER CREEPER (SCALE'S DELIGHT)
PASSION FLOWER
FATSHEDERA
ENGLISH IVY
PYRACANTHA (LIVING BARBED WIRE)
SILVER LACE VINE
CLIMBING HYDRANGEA
WAXY BITTERSWEET (LOOKS GREAT IN A VASE)
FLAME HONEYSUCKLE
BOUGAINVILLEA
VINE LILAC
MADEIRAVINE

DUTCHMANSPIPE (MOST FOR
    YOUR MONEY)

GROUND CREEPERS
CROWNVETCH
SEDUM
WINTER CREEPER (COLORATA)
HARDY BALTIC IVY
MYRTLE
PACHYSANDRA

DRAGON'S BLOOD (SEDUM)
HALLS HONEYSUCKLE
CREEPING PHLOX
LILY OF THE VALLEY (NOT
    MY FAVORITE)
STRAWBERRIES
AJUGA
ENGLISH IVY
WILDGINGER

Questions and Answers

Q. Which evergreens can I use as a ground cover?
A. Any of the low-growing junipers like Armstrong, and
   many of the compactas.

Q. Which is the most fragrant of the ground covers?
A. You might enjoy fragrant sumac or peppermint. It depends on your smeller!

Q. Is there some special care for clematis vines?
A. The only special care is to plant the roots in the shade
   and keep the top growing in the sun.

Q. Is there a red clematis?
A. Sure is, crimson star. Best-looking clematis I have ever
   seen.

Q. They are going to build a new home next to us. What
   can I use as a temporary screen?
A. How about sweet peas, morning-glory or balsam-apple?
   These are annuals, and so you won't have a great deal
   of money tied up.

Q. Can I plant ground covers through plastic for weed
   control?
A. Sure you can, but I don't advise it. Plastic is a pain in
   the you-know-what when it begins to tear. Mulch and
   a garden weeder are just as good in the beginning and
   better in the long run.

Q. Will all ground covers grow in the shade?
A. No! Most of them will tolerate some shade, some full

shade, and some only full sun. Here are a few of the sun-only covers: basket-of-gold, lavender, moss pink, the sedums, snow-in-summer, ice plant and ivy geraniums.

Q. What do you recommend for a bank that keeps washing away?

A. I have had some great luck with the crown-vetch called penngift, which has lovely pink flowers. Plant in the fall or spring, three feet apart.

Q. When do you prune wisteria?

A. Prune the top twice—in the spring and early summer. Feed well, after trimming, with a garden food.

Q. What kind of wire do you use to train vines?

A. I use a galvanized twist if possible. Otherwise aluminum will pass.

Q. How do you put a vine back on the wall after the house has been painted?

A. Most garden centers have vine supports that you can cement or screw into the wall. These will hold until the clingers catch hold.

Q. How often do you trim ground covers?

A. Whenever they get out of hand. Use a sharp pair of trimmers.

Q. Do you feed all vines and ground covers with the same food?

A. If it flowers I use a garden food, and if it's all foliage. I use lawn food.

Q. Does it hurt to plant bulbs in ground cover?

A. On the contrary, it's a great idea and excellent for the bulbs.

Q. When is the best time to transplant a clematis?

A. In the early spring is about the best time in snow country and early fall in the South and West.

13
Small Fruit
Are the Berries

The Pick of the Patch

No matter how much you look or how far you travel, you will never taste a berry of any kind that tastes better than the ones you pick from your own berry patch. No matter how small or large your garden may be, you can always find room for a few strawberry plants, or raspberry, or maybe a blueberry or boysenberry bush, and maybe you will even have some room left over for a plant or two of rhubarb. You owe it to yourself, your garden and the birds, to plant at least a small berry patch. You will never regret it.

No Such Word as "Can't"

Strawberries are about the easiest crop in the world to grow, and can be grown any place in the United States. With just a little bit of attention and full sunlight, you can grow a batch of berries that will make anyone's mouth water. Raspberries and the rest are just as easy. So when you prepare the soil for one you are ready to plant the rest.

Preparing the Patch

The berries are the heavy eaters of the garden. They like rich food, plenty of it, and an acid soil. To prepare the bed, apply a liberal quantity of cattle manure, fifty pounds per hundred square feet, fifty pounds of leaves and three pounds of 10-6-4 lawn food, all in the fall. Spade once and let set for the winter. Before the snows come in the North, or the rains in the South and West, top-dress the bed with twenty-five pounds of gypsum. This will help to loosen up heavy soil. When spring comes, turn the soil again and grade off with a crown to allow good drainage. Make sure that you have removed any tall weeds from the sides of the berry patches or you will start out on the wrong foot.

Do not apply food to the plants before or during fruiting time in the spring, as this will cause excess plant growth and reduce fruit production or cause poor quality.

Check the Time

Early spring is the only time to plant new berry plants. In the North, wait until late May when the soil is ready to go to work. As a rule, frost or snow won't harm newly planted berries as they are still a dormant plant. Never plant berries in snow country after the 15th of July as they cannot harden-off in time to get set for winter and will therefore end up freezing to death.

Just Right

It is of the utmost importance that you plant each type of berry at just the right depth, or you will slow up production or halt it altogether.

STRAWBERRIES

Plant so that the crown is just at soil level. If it is too high the roots will dry out; if too low, the crowns will rot.

RASPBERRIES

Plant them three inches deeper than they were grown. Cut the tops back to twelve inches and place the plants three feet apart.

BLACKBERRIES

Same as raspberries.

CURRANTS AND GOOSEBERRIES

Plant two-year-old plants. Cut long roots off and plant

three feet apart; cut tops back to six inches. Set new plants one to two inches deeper than they were previously planted.

GRAPES

Plant one- or two-year-old vines six feet apart and two inches deeper than they were in the nursery. Prune grapes in the dead of winter, leaving only pencil-size canes.

Mulch all berries with marsh hay when planting.

No Special Diet

Strawberries are to be fed with 10-6-4 during late August or early September. These plants make fruit buds in the fall for next year's crop. Grapes are fed just as they begin to grow, with a 4-12-4 food, as are the rest of the bush crops. Nothing fancy is necessary; anything that you use on the lawn or garden will do nicely.

Keep a Clean House

Your berry patch should have no competition from weeds. These culprits carry diseases, steal food and harbor insects that feast on your berries. You must keep your eyes open for the first sign of trouble and treat at once. To avoid troubles, remember to wash often.

Here are my choices for your berry patch:

STRAWBERRIES
BEST FLAVOR
Redglow
Fairfax
Armore
Sparkle
Pocahontas
Midway
Red Star
Sunrise

LARGE BERRIES
Robinson
Catskill

Empire
Pocahontas
Vesper

BEST YIELD
Catskill
Midway
Sunrise
Surecrop
Earlidawn
Pocahontas

FIRMNESS
Dixieland

Surecrop
Pocahontas

RASPBERRIES
Black—Bristol
Red—Taylor

BLACKBERRIES
Darrow

BOYSENBERRIES
Thornless

GRAPES
Blue—Concord
Red—Caco
White—Niagara
Black—Fredonia
Seedless—Interlaken

BLUEBERRIES
Earliblue
Blue Crop

Questions and Answers

Q. What's the best all-around strawberry?

A. I would say the Pocahontas, hands down. It is good to eat, preserve, freeze and whatever else you want to do with berries.

Q. Where is the best place to buy berry plants?

A. I have relied on Rayner Bros. of Salisbury, Maryland, for a number of years. Send for their free catalogue.

Q. Do you dormant-spray grapes?

A. You sure do, when they are dormant in the late fall, with lime sulpher solution. Wash first.

Q. What should you do to strawberries for the winter in Kansas?

A. Cover them with straw. Same with the rest of the snow states.

Q. The crickets eat more of my strawberries than I do. What can I use to stop them?

A. Soap and water followed with forty-four percent chlordane, applied to the soil.

Q. When do you prune raspberries?

A. In the spring. Cut out canes that are weak.

Q. We bought a farm with several blueberry bushes. They are overgrown and crowded. What should we do now?
A. In the early or late fall cut out one third of the oldest and heaviest wood; next season cut out another third of the next oldest wood and then get the baskets ready.

Q. How do you keep the birds out of the raspberries?
A. You can cover the berries with thin cheesecloth or aluminum pie tins. I raise raspberries myself, and I always seem to get my share.

Q. What would make strawberries taste flat?
A. The soil is too sweet. Add manure and peat to the beds to build up the acidity.

Q. What is the best strawberry for northern Wisconsin?
A. The best cold-weather berries are Robinson, Catskill, Midway or Sparkle. While I'm at it, the best southern are Albritton, Pocahontas and Dixieland.

14
House Plants: Living Room Landscape

The increased interest in house plants in the last few years has been astounding! Fifteen or twenty years ago, there were very few indoor gardeners. Those that there were had a very limited selection of plants to work with. In those days, indoor gardening was just a plant collection on a windowsill or in a vestibule. Things have changed. There are now more house plants than people. And the assortment is virtually unlimited in color range. Sizes, shapes and plant containers have kept pace also. With the proper selection of plants, you can accent a piece of furniture, change the character of a room, or flatter an entire interior. With the recent improvements in heating and lighting in today's homes and apartments, anyone can raise house plants, and without the proverbial green thumb! You only need a little knowledge and common sense.

Pick the Right Type

There are five basic types of house plants to choose from: foliage plants, flowering house plants, flowering pot plants, bulbs and corms, and cacti. The foliage plants are permanent residents. Flowering house plants, like African violets, are also permanent. Flowering pot plants are holiday plants which are temporary visitors, as are the bulb plants. The cacti are the fun plants and collectors' items. Decide what you wish to accomplish and follow suit with your selection.

Choose Carefully

The fun of indoor gardening is in choosing the most suitable plants from the large selection offered. But first let's lay down some ground rules. Rule number one, make sure that the plants you pick appeal to you and that you don't just select them because a person or book recommends them. Rule two, make sure that these plants are suitable for the conditions they must live in. Rule three, be sure that they are no more difficult to grow than the time and experience you have to offer. Ask yourself these questions before you make your final selection:

1. What shape plant do I want? Upright, bushy, trailing or climbing?

The uprights consist of aphelandra, codiaeum, cordyline, dracaena, *Ficus decora* (rubber plant), *Ficus lyrate*, Grevillea, pandanus and sansevieria.

The bushy plants are adiantum, azalea, begonia, coleus, fatsia, fittonia, maranta, neanthe and saintpaulia (African violet).

Trailing plants consist of begonia glaucophylla, campanula isophylla, columnea, *Ficus pumila, Fuchsia pendula,* helxine, *Saxifraga sarmentosa,* tradescantia, zebrina.

The climbing plants are cissus, *Cobaea scandens, Ficus pumila,* hedera, hoya, *Philodendron scandens,* rhoicissus, scindapsus and tetrastigma.

2. Do I want the plant to live in the same room permanently? If the answer is yes, then you must avoid flowering pot plants. They only bloom for a short while inside.

3. Do I want a plant with colorful foliage? Lots of house plants have colorful foliage and variegated leaves. This simply means that the leaves have multi-colored edges or spots. In that case, you would choose from this list: sansevieria, *Peperomia magnoliaefolia variegata,* dracaena, *Hedera helix, Zebrina pendula* or *Ficus pumila.* These plants require plenty of light. Other colors are available with nidularium, maranta, coleus, *Begonia rex,* codiaeum, cordyline, aphelandra and *Cissus discolor.*

4. How much time and effort will I be able to give? Some house plants are almost indestructible, while others

are best left to experienced green thumbs. If you are a newcomer to the Plant Kingdom, or you are interested in plants for interior design, then I would recommend that you select plants from the "easy group." The easy group of plants will stand a little cool weather and a certain amount of neglect or poor management.

The easy plants are hedera, *Cissus antarctica, Rhoicissus rhomboidea, Ficus pumila, Fiscus decora* (rubber plant), sansevieria (mother-in-law's tongue), *Philodendron scandens,* chlorophytum, tradescantia, cyperus, scindapsus, *Monstera deliciosa,* fatshedera, fatsia, helxine grevillea, tolmiea, *Saxifraga sarmentosa.*

Easy flowering plants are billbergia, clivia, geraniums, impatiens, fuchsia and *all of the cactus plants.*

5. What kind of living conditions am I going to offer my foliage friends? Here is a general description of growing conditions that we might find in most homes and apartments and the plants that will best fit those conditions.

Dim and cool: aspidistra, dizygothica, fatshedera, fatsia, ferns, *Ficus pumila,* hedera, helxine, maranta and philodendron. When I say cool, I mean in the fifty- to fifty-five-degree range, not cold like forty degrees.

Bright but no sunlight: *Cissus antarctica,* columnea, fuchsia, *Monstera deliciosa, Rhoicissus rhomboidea,* scindapsus, tetrastigma, tolmiea, foliage house plants with variegated leaves and most of the holiday plants.

Some sunlight each day: chlorophytum, cordyline, *Ficus decora,* peperomia, sansevieria, and most flowering house plants.

Bright sunny window: beloperone, cobaea, coleus, genista, geranium, impatiens, passiflora, cacti and succulents.

Little heat in the winter: aspidistra, billbergia, *Cissus antarctica,* chlorophytum, fatshedera, fatsia, hedera, philodendron scandens, *Saxifraga sarmentosa,* zebrina.

Homes with gas heat: Least affected are thick-leaved foliage house plants. All flowering plants (except impatiens and billbergia) should be avoided.

Poor humidity, dry: aechmea, billbergia, chlorophytum, clivia, *Ficus decora,* grevillea, pilea, sansevieria, vriesia, zebrina, cacti and succulents.

It is absolutely necessary for you to determine exactly what the climatic conditions of your home are, and not hedge on your evaluation. Should you have any doubts, then choose another plant. This will avert disappointment for both you and the plant.

Be a Tire Kicker

When you go buy a house plant, be as choosy as you would if you were buying a new car. You must remember that house plants are raised in greenhouses, where the air is warm and humid. The world outside is far less accommodating, so always buy from a reputable supplier who will have made sure that the plants have been properly "hardened off" and are able to stand the shock of the change. Of course, house plants can be bought at any time of the year, but it is best to buy delicate varieties in late spring or summer. Look over the plant carefully before buying; it should be sturdy with no damaged leaves, and it should be free from insects.

Wrap up your purchase before leaving the nursery and treat it gently for about a week. Keep it out of direct sunlight and drafts, and be careful not to give it too much heat or water. After this, it can be placed in its permanent quarters and treated normally. Certain plants, such as azalea and cyclamen, are purchased in flower during the winter months and require different treatment. Put them in their permanent quarters immediately and give them as much light as possible.

Landscaping Your Living Room

Every room in your house can accommodate a plant, planter or vase, but you should know which one will fit in each room the best. Plants serve a more important purpose in our lives than mere decoration. They are beneficial to our health in the purification of the air around us. Plants can brighten our spirits when we are down, busy our hands when we are idle, sharpen our creative abilities, keep us company when we are lonely and be a sounding board when we are mad.

Plants are an everyday part of our lives. Just look around. Here are some brief suggestions of how to use plants indoors:

A *Plant Window* is one of the most spectacular ways of displaying house plants. Instead of a windowsill there is the plant trough which runs along the full length of a large picture window. Into this trough is placed a wide variety of flowering and foliage plants, with the largest specimens often being used to frame the two sides.

A venetian blind is usually installed to provide protection against both sun and frost damage.

The floor-to-ceiling plant window is the most satisfactory method known of blending room and garden together.

A *Climbing Display* is useful to frame a window or to cover a metal or bamboo room-divider.

Where a dense screen is required, use tetrastigma or *Cissus antarctica*. If, on the other hand, you merely want to decorate the supports and not to cut out light or hide the view, then choose a small-leaved climber such as *Ficus pumila* or *Hedera helix*.

Some climbing plants are self-supporting; others may require tying loosely with raffia to the support.

A *Miniature Garden* differs from an "indoor garden" in that smaller plants are used, and a definite attempt is made to reproduce garden features on a small scale—paths, pools, mossy turf and even windmills and figurines! Cacti and succulents are sometimes used for miniature or "dish" gardens, but they should not be mixed with other types of indoor plants because of their need for dry conditions.

Single pots have a place in indoor plant arrangements. A single flowering plant can be used to provide a splash of vivid color to dramatize pastel furnishings; a large foliage plant will provide an ideal focal point. Pots with drainage holes should be stood on saucers which are deep enough to prevent water from running onto the surface beneath, and which are not that noticeable.

Pots without drainage holes should be provided with a bottom layer of crocks and lumps of charcoal. Be careful not to overwater.

Some flowering plants give their best display when not surrounded by other plants. Small and medium-sized foliage types, however, should be grouped together and not kept as a collection of isolated pots on shelf, table or windowsill.

Planters come in many forms. You can buy containers made of wire, split cane, pottery or plastic to hide ordinary clay pots, or you can use a wide variety of ordinary household objects, such as copper bowls and pans.

The best one to choose is a matter of personal taste, but remember that the plant should not have to compete with the pot hider for attention, so pick a container which is simple in shape and not too brightly colored. A pot hider should be taller than the pot it contains, and, where suitable, the space between them should be filled with damp peat.

Warm Up to Your Plants

I do not understand why most folks have so much trouble understanding the temperature range that plants like to grow in indoors. You only have to remember one fact: plants will be uncomfortable in any condition that makes you uncomfortable! They do not like drafts, cold or hot. They prefer the same comfort range that most people do, and that is sixty-five degrees to seventy-five degrees. To check for drafts, simply place a candle on a saucer and light it. Place the lighted candle in the spot where you intend to place your plant and watch the flame. If the flame is blown out or blows in one direction for a long period of time, do not make that spot a home for any of your foliage friends, or they'll perish. When the edges of the leaves are brown or black, your plant is in a draft and has caught cold. Move it!

Light Up Your Plant's Life

No matter how much light you have in a room, it is nothing like outside sunlight. However you can help. If you intend to decorate your home with plants, pick colors for the walls in white or cream, light blue, aqua or pale tan. When the foliage of your plants is bent over in one direction, you can bet it is trying to look out of the window. Turn it a little every few days so that all sides get some sunlight. But don't place plants in direct sunlight in front of a glass window, or the foliage will be burned. Filter the sunlight with a sheer curtain.

Other signs that the plant is getting poor light are: small blooms or no blooms at all, thin tall stems, small pale leaves.

A Vitamin Helps

Dissolve a child's vitamin tablet in one quart of water and feed plants three times each winter.

Knee Bends and Deep Breaths

Fresh air is the best thing you can give house plants. On a mild day, open doors and windows, and in the summer send your plants off to camp. The east side of your home is the best camping spot—warm fresh morning sun that's not too hot in the afternoon. Plants become stiff when they have been in all winter. To give them a little exercise, place the smaller ones on top of your radio or stereo, from time to time. The base vibrations will keep the circulation moving and, besides, they love music.

Plants Get Thirsty

Without water your plants will die, and that will be on your conscience, since they can't help themselves. It's best to water whenever the soil is dry to the touch, and that will be never if you water on a regular routine. The watering schedule should be based on the needs of the plant itself, the time of the year and the humidity in the room. When water runs right through the plant and pot, the soil has shrunk from the sides. When this happens, sink the pot in a room-temperature bucket of water with a pinch of weak tea added. When the water will not go into the soil at all, it is caked hard. Pierce the surface with a fork and sink in the same bucket.

Good and Bad Water

The best water is rain or melted snow. Water defrosted from your refrigerator is next best. The worst water for your plants is tap. Place a layer of agriculture charcoal over the top of the soil in your plants' pots to filter out the human additives. Since plants don't have teeth, they can do without the fluoride. The charcoal dressing will look nicer and remove smoke and food odors from your rooms.

Love Morning Showers

House plants love a warm shower; it starts their day out just right. Our homes are so dry that your plants wake up with their eyes stuck shut, nose dried up and their mouths full of cotton. You must control humidity, and this is done by showering, placing your plants on a layer of stone with the water level kept just below the bottom of the pot, or giving the foliage plants a steam bath twice a month. Place a brick or block in the middle of a bucket and place the plant on it. Then add steaming water to the bottom of the bucket. Do not let it touch the pot or plant. Let set for five or six minutes, then return it to its favorite spot.

Wash behind Their Ears

Clean plants are happy ones. Wash them twice a month with soap and water—two tablespoons of mild liquid soap in a half-gallon of room-temperature water. Rinse with the same temperature water and then spray with a weak solution of tea to act as a rubdown and antiseptic. This wash will keep the bugs away, and a pinch of ant powder to the soil will kill bugs already in the soil. I do not use any leaf polish of any kind. If I wanted unnatural, shiny leaves, I would buy plastic plants! Plants breathe through their leaves, so don't plug their noses.

Invited to Dinner

When you decided to ask the plants to live at your house, you also took on the responsibility of feeding them. All plants need food, and they must have a balanced diet. Nitrogen is a leaf builder. Phosphate is a root maker and potash promotes flowers.

If your plants do not get enough nitrogen, the foliage will be stunted, with small foliage and pale leaves. A lack of phosphate will be indicated by a lack of feeder roots, and potash deficiency will be recognizable by weak stem and small, poorly colored flowers. All plants need a vitamin shot once a season. They also need iron, which can be added by applying Green-Garde micronized iron. One tablespoon per five-inch pot in the early winter, and again in late spring.

The best time to feed plants is during the growing season when they are making flowers and new foliage. Do not feed them when they are resting or when they have a cold (draft symptoms). The best way to feed your chlorophyll colleagues is with a good, organic liquid, like Alaska fish fertilizer. I have a party for my plants a couple of times a season when I give all but the ferns a sip of beer. I add two ounces of week-old flat beer to a quart of room-temperature water and use this to water them. Once the alcohol has evaporated, you have the purest water and organic foods: hops, yeast, and malt. However, I do not give the "teetotaler" ferns and fern types any beer.

Overcrowded

If you are kind to your plants, they will grow right out of their pots. You will know this when you see the roots coming out of the bottom. When you do, move them. Be sure to water them the night before their move. Move them into the next size pot (a three inch to a four inch and so on). Use only clay pots. Cover the hole in the bottom with a partially flattened beer cap and add soil to the bottom to bring the plant soil up to within an inch of the top of the new pot. Place plant on top of the soil. Then press new soil around the sides, dress with charcoal, dampen and return to the old stand.

Keep Your Gift Plants Blooming

The biggest mistake most of us make when we receive a flowering plant as a gift is that we give it too much love, but not enough proper care.

Here are a few of the more popular gift plants and

their simple likes and dislikes. Heed these suggestions and you will be repaid with an abundance of blooming glory.

Chrysanthemums   Potted chrysanthemums are usually the longest-lasting flowering house plants. Keep yours in a good light and in the coolest spot you can find. Water it well and frequently (about every other day, or when the soil becomes dry). Spraying the foliage with water helps. After your plant has bloomed, cut it back to about eight inches and keep it moist, but not wet. Hardy varieties can be planted outside, but many of the varieties which you receive as flowering plants are not hardy and must be planted in well-protected spots and covered well if you attempt to carry them over the winter.

Azaleas   Azaleas need bright light, but not strong sun. The soil should be evenly moist and the temperature kept between fifty-five and sixty-five degrees. You'll have better luck in keeping your azalea if you remove the foil or other covering from the pot and submerge the pot in a pan of water every other day for fifteen to twenty minutes and then allow it to drain. Spray the foliage with water three or four times a week. If you would like to try to keep your azalea indefinitely, give it a chance to replenish its strength after it finishes blooming. In the summer, set the pot in the ground in semi-shade where it is protected from hot winds. Water it regularly and feed with special fertilizer for acid-loving plants. Bring it inside in early fall and place it in a cool, light place, keeping the soil moist but not wet. When buds show activity, provide more sun, water, and fertilizer.

Easter lilies   Keep your Easter lily in a cool spot, well out of the sun. Check it daily adding water when the soil is dry and sandy on top. Water well then, being sure the moisture goes to the bottom of the pot and drains. Remove blossoms as they fade and pinch out the yellow anthers as new buds open. Keep your plant watered and growing in good light after it has flowered. When it dies down and the weather warms, plant it outside in a sunny place. If you wish to try for bloom indoors again, plant the bulb in a pot with only two inches of soil beneath the bulb. Place it in your unheated garage until December, then bring it indoors and keep at a temperature no higher than sixty degrees.

Bulb plants The blooms on your bulb plant will last longer if you place the plant in a cool, light place. Water it when the soil starts to dry out, probably every day. Remove the old flowers when they have faded, but allow the foliage to mature by continuing to water the plant. As soon as the garden soil can be worked, the bulb can be removed from the pot and planted outdoors to provide enjoyment for you again next year in the garden.

Hydrangeas Your hydrangea will bloom for a long time if you keep it well-watered and out of direct sun. It is best to water it at least twice a day, or submerge the pot in a pan of water daily, let it soak for about ten minutes, and then drain. After your plant has finished blooming, cut back all of the stems with flowers and then plant it in your garden in a shady area. The stems that have not bloomed will often produce blooms the same summer. If you bring the plant back inside for winter, cut it back severely after it has bloomed, and re-pot in fresh planter mix. Keep it in full sun, give it a great deal of water, and feed with fish tablets once a week.

Gloxinia Gloxinias are unusual house plants with handsome, velvety flowers in striking colors. If you give them proper care, the plants will last for months. They require full light but should not be placed in direct sun. Keep the soil uniformly moist. When it starts to become dry, set the pot in about an inch of water until the soil becomes moist. If this is not convenient, water may be applied to the top of the soil; but avoid wetting the foliage.

Cyclamen To get the greatest enjoyment from this colorful plant, keep it in a cool, bright place. A temperature of fifty-five degrees at night and seventy degrees during the day is ideal. When the soil starts to dry out, apply enough water to wet it to the bottom. If it gets too dry and the flowers wilt, submerge the pot in water for about five minutes or until the soil is wet again.

Roses Place the plant in a cool, light spot. Keep the

soil uniformly moist. Water thoroughly when it starts to dry out. Cut off old blooms as they fade.

Cut Roses Cut an inch off the stems and place them in deep, warm water (ninety to one-hundred degrees) in a cool room for an hour or two before arranging. If they are in a container, fill it with water. Change the water daily or use a floral preservative. If the flowers are arranged in a solid material, keep this material moist.

Poinsettias Poinsettias can be enjoyed longer if these suggestions for their care are followed carefully. Check the soil every day and water when it's dry to the touch. Don't allow soil to dry out completely or remain soaked. Place near a warm, sunny window, but not touching the glass. Keep them away from extreme heat, cold or drafts. If you want to enjoy the plant another season, stop watering it and store it in a cool, dry place when the leaves fall. In spring, water it again and cut the stems back to six inches. Keep the stems pinched back as new leaves begin to form. From early October until blooming starts, place the plant in a dark closet (without a single flash of light) for twelve hours each day (8:00 PM until 8:00 AM) and keep in a sunny window for the other twelve hours of the day. Fertilize during active growth.

Plants Have a Personality

There has been much said and written about plant sensitivity. In my opinion, based on experience, plants do have feelings and will produce for someone they like and pout and be stubborn for someone they dislike. Anyone who is in doubt that plants are anything more than just a glob of green on the end of a stick, need only watch the Venus flytrap in action or see the sensitivity plant open and close to the human touch or go to sleep at night. Then they will soon change their minds. Anyone who says he has grown tomatoes and not talked to them at least once or twice, when they looked ill, isn't telling all. You will be in close contact with your house plants all winter, and will begin to feel an affection for each one of them. Remember, the feeling will be mutual. You are the provider, protector and confidant of your plants. Learn their language, that you might carry on an interesting conversation!

House Plant Identification

PROFESSIONAL NAME	HOME GARDEN NAME
Adiantum	MAIDENHAIR FERN
Aglaonema commutatum	CHINESE EVERGREEN
Asparagus plumosus	ASPARAGUS FERN
Aspidistra	PARLOUR PALM
Begonia	BEGONIA
Bougainvillea	BOUGAINVILLEA
Bromeliad	BROMELIADS
Calathea	CALATHEA
Chlorophytum	SPIDER PLANT
Cissus antarctica	KANGAROO VINE
Cissus discolor	CISSUS DISCOLOR
Codiaeum	CROTON
Coleus	FLAME NETTLE
Cordyline	CORDYLINE
Cryptanthus	EARTH STAR
Cyperus	UMBRELLA PLANT
Dieffenbachia	DUMB CANE
Dizygotheca	FINGER ARALIA
Dracaena	DRAGON PLANT
Fatshedera lizei	FATHEAD LIZZIE
Fatsia japonica	FIG-LEAF PALM
Ficus decora	RUBBER PLANT
Ficus lyrata	FIDDLE FIG
Ficus pumila	CLIMBING FIG
Ficus benjamina	WEEPING FIG
Fittonia	FITTONIA
Grevillea robusta	SILVER OAK
Hedera	ALL OF THE IVY FAMILY
Helxine soleirolii	MIND YOUR BUSINESS
Maranta	PRAYER PLANT
Monstera deliciosa	SWISS CHEESE PLANT
Neanthe elegans	DWARF PALM
Nidularium	BIRDS NEST BROMELIAD
Pandanus	SCREW-PINE
Peperomia	PEPPER ELDER
Philodendron	SWEETHEART VINE
Pilea cadierei	ALUMINUM PLANT
Platycerium bifurcatum	STAG-HORN FERN
Rhoes discolor	BOAT LILY
Rhoicissus rhomboidea	GRAPE IVY

PROFESSIONAL NAME	HOME GARDEN NAME
Sansevieria	MOTHER-IN-LAW'S TONGUE
Saxifraga sarmentosa	MOTHER OF THOUSANDS
Scindapsus	DEVIL'S IVY
Setcreasea purpurea	PURPLE TRAILER
Syngonium	GOOSE FOOT
Tetrastigma voinierianum	CHESTNUT VINE
Tolmiea menziesii	PICKABACK PLANT
Tradescantia	WANDERING JEW
Zebrina	PURPLE-LEAF WANDERING JEW

These are the most common and popular varieties. There are hundreds more and most without common names.

Questions and Answers

Q. Do we need a special soil mix to grow plants inside?

A. Not really, but it sure saves a lot of time, mess and effort. You could use any good garden loam heated up to 250 degrees for one hour to kill diseases and, hopefully, the bugs. I spend the fifty or sixty cents on a commercial mix just to avoid the mess.

Q. How do you get rid of red spiders on house plants once and for all?

A. Throw all of them out. . . . No, no! You won't ever get rid of them once and for all as long as you continue to add to your guest list of plants. Spray new plants with soap and water and any one of the house plant bombs.

Q. What makes foliage sort of mushy and yellow brown?

A. Too much time in the bathtub! A plant is getting too much water when it looks like this. Run it dry for a week or two.

Q. Why won't the flowers on a mum plant open?

A. Why should they? You are giving the plant everything it wants, so why should it end it all by opening and fading out. Shut off the water and watch it open up!

Q. Where do mealy bugs come from?
A. They are almost always born in the soil. You can touch them with a Q-tip dipped in alcohol and apply a pinch of chlordane to the soil.

Q. My husband would like a large plant for his office, but he won't take care of it. What can I buy that will have half a chance?
A. Purchase a fiddle-leaf fig. This is a man's plant. It can eat more cigarette and cigar ashes than an ashtray, drink more martinis, manhattans and beer than any human, and never waver. Your mother might give him a planter full of sansevieria (mother-in-law's tongue). It's so obnoxious and persistent, you just can't get rid of it.

Q. Why do house plants die so easily?
A. How high is high or long is long? There are about eight reasons that a plant can die: the soil is either too dry or too wet; too cold or too hot (direct sunshine); too dry or in a draft; gas fumes and no light. Check all of these reasons.

Q. How do you get rid of scale on house plants?
A. Dip a Q-tip in alcohol and rub the plant with it.

Q. What makes the leaves just plain droop?
A. Too much water, too dry, too much forced heat or sun. Mist spray.

Q. When the leaves on my plant turn light green but the veins stay dark green, what's up?
A. This plant needs iron, at least one ounce, and a slight meal.

15
Herbs and Other Things: The Spice of Life

From Out of the Thundering Past

Herbs have played a big part in man's past for generations. They have been influential in our romance, religion, health and superstition, and they still continue to influence our environment. With the move to improve our environment and health, we are returning to the use of certain herbs and plants to control insects and lengthen our own life span. One need only to visit a health food emporium and view the shelves, if one doubts that we are returning to the past.

Herbs do have a place in our everyday life and garden. They should be used to flavor our food, to avoid the artificial additives that are presently being offered to tenderize and jazz up our food. Herbs can add to the overall plan of our garden.

Throughout this book I have talked about the sights and sounds of the garden. Now I am going to talk about smell. To really enjoy a garden, one should be able to tilt back one's head, breathe deeply and fill the lungs with the fragrance of mint, bay, lavender or rue. This is when a garden really comes alive—dances, shouts and sings. To really wake up your garden and your life, plant herbs.

Spice Up Your Life

"Herb" is a word loosely used to describe certain plants which are used as aromatics. They may be used as perfumes, garment room deodorizers, food flavorings or medicines, as well as plant antagonists and pesticide bases.

With the right selection of herbs growing in your garden or on the windowsill of your kitchen, living room or bath, you would virtually eliminate the necessity of using aerosol room sprays. Of course, one of the greatest and most important uses of herbs is for the improvement in the taste of your everyday cooking. I am not going to go into a lengthy discussion or description on the design or layout of a formal herb garden. I am more interested in giving you a pointer or two that you can use to decorate, use in cooking and baking, and, to coin a word, to fragrantize.

I think that every vegetable garden should have a border. This is to make it look neat and as though it were designed to fit into the overall landscape, rather than be a dirt patch in the middle of a palace garden. For this border, I suggest that you use a bushy low-growing herb that can be picked and trimmed to be fat and low—perhaps parsley or many others. Check the back of the seed packets for heights. I have also used herbs as borders for my evergreen beds and flower beds. Here I look for fragrance and foliage appearance, trying to put a different smell all over the garden. I wish you could be at my home on a night when the oil torches are lit, and the colored floor lights are lit throughout the trees and evergreens. I'd love to watch you wander around to the spot that has your favorite fragrance. Then you would really understand the idea of "turning-on" without drugs!

Some of the other herbs should be inter-planted with your flowers and vegetables, to keep certain insects away or add flavor to another plant, because of its close proximity. A couple of examples: Plant the herb "chervil" next to radishes if you want them to be hot. Plant mint near windows and doors to keep ants out of the house.

Check the list for insect enemies and plants' friends.

For sniffers, here are a few of the aromatic herbs to plant throughout your garden. Rue, lavender, cotton, myrtle, bay, lad's-love, rosemary, smelly verbena, balm and bergamot. For the kitchen: fennel, chervil, basil, chive, parsley, mint, sage, thyme, caraway and borage, along with dill. For your health (These are a few that Grandma kept handy for home remedies): dill, tansy, feverfew, wormwood, St. Johnswort, castor oil, woodruff, mustard, licorice, pennyroyal, cinnamon, and mock-ginger.

If you think you are a good cook now, try adding some fresh herbs to your soups, salads, omelets, and roasts. And watch the praise fly!

Salads with a purpose: I have been asked many times about the so-called aphrodisiac qualities of many of the fruits, vegetables and herbs. I have heard the many stories and tales of the amorous qualities of many of the garden items, but I have learned from twenty years of marital bliss and four beautiful children, that love, affection, a warm kiss and a tender embrace are all the aphrodisiacs I will ever need. I had a discussion recently with a doctor friend of mine about this very subject, and the results were very interesting.

My friend informed me that if folks would eat plenty of fresh raw vegetables regularly, they would be in a good healthy state both mentally and physically. Therefore, they would be relaxed and in a commemorating mood with the one they love. But when you have indigestion and other discomforts, there is not too much of a chance for this affectionate communication. So the answer is to eat any and all of the fruits and vegetables that agree with you in good health. Sleep tight.

From the Gardener's Still

As you have already surmised from reading this book, I am not one to waste anything. I am especially diligent in this practice with my fruit and vegetable garden and try not to waste a thing by throwing it out. If we cannot eat it, can it, dry, or freeze it, we can brew it and come up with some of the finest wines this side of the Atlantic.

The choice of vegetables, fruit and flowers with which wine can be made is almost endless, but I am only going to list a few of the easier and more popular recipes that my neighbors, friends and I find tasty and worth the trouble.

FROM THE STILL OF MRS. POPOOFNICK: APPLE CRANBERRY WINE

FIRST WEEK

6 lbs. of apples, any tart variety   4 quarts of water
8 cups of cranberries

SECOND WEEK

8 cups of cane sugar
1 slice of whole wheat toast
1 oz. of wet yeast
2 cups of muscat raisins

Chop the cranberries very fine and put into canner kettle. Pour two quarts of boiling water over them. This will set the red color of the wine. Set aside to cool. Chop the apples up very fine and add to the cranberries along with the remaining two quarts of water. Cover and put in a warm place to ferment for one week.

Then strain through jelly bag, squeezing very dry. Return to canner kettle and add sugar; stir well so that it is all dissolved. Add the chopped raisins. Moisten the yeast with a few drops of water and spread on one side of the toast. Float toast, yeast side down, on the surface of the liquid. Set in a warm place to ferment for two more weeks. Stir twice a week.

At the end of this two-week period, strain again through jelly bag, squeezing quite dry. Return to canner kettle to settle two days longer. Then siphon off into clean sterilized bottles and cork lightly until fermentation ceases. After the wine has stopped all of its activity, cork tightly and seal with paraffin. Keep for at least four months before drinking.

BEET WINE

10 lbs. beets
1 lb. raisins
3 lemons (cut up)
8 lbs. sugar
1 pkg. powdered yeast

Boil beets until tender, add water to beet juice to make two gallons. Add above ingredients.

TO FIX YEAST:

½ cup lukewarm water
1 tsp. white sugar

Mix sugar and water (stir). Pour powdered yeast on top. Let stand for ten minutes. Pour yeast mixture over top of beet juice. Let stand for two weeks. Then strain and bottle.

Compliments of Mrs. Edward Bara. Parsnips, turnips or carrots may be substituted for beets in this recipe.

DANDELION WINE

1 quart dandelion blossoms
4 quarts water
½ cup tepid water
1 yeast cake
1 lb. seedless raisins
3 lbs. (6 cups) sugar
1 lemon
1 orange

Measure a generous quart of the dandelion blossoms, but do not use any of the stems. Put them into a large saucepan with the water and boil for thirty minutes. Pour through strainer, then strain through cheesecloth into a large stone jar. When cool, add the yeast cake dissolved in the tepid water, raisins, sugar, lemon and orange cut into small pieces including the skins.

Stir it every day for two weeks, then strain and let stand for a day to settle.

Now strain carefully through cheesecloth until clear. Bottle and seal.

This recipe can also be made with roses, violets, clover flowers or any other sweet blossoms.

POTATO CHAMPAGNE (4 WEEKS)

7 potatoes
7 oranges
7 lemons
7 lbs. sugar
7 quarts water
1 lb. raisins, ground
1 pkg. dry yeast
1 slice of toast

Peel and slice oranges, lemons and potatoes. Place in crock and add rest of ingredients. Mix well with wooden spoon. Place yeast on toast in water and remove in one week.

Let sit and strain in two weeks. Then strain again in three days. Then let sit three days, strain and bottle.

Compliments of my friend, Mrs. H. Swanson.

MINT WINE

1 quart fresh mint leaves
4 lbs. sugar
1 gallon water

Pour one gallon of cold water over the mint leaves, add four pounds of sugar, stir and cover. Let stand for ten days. Stir each day. Strain and balloon seal. After gasses no longer fill balloon, seal and set aside. Wine should be ready to drink in about four months.

There are many fine wine-making books in the library. Why not try a few more. Bottoms up.

Questions and Answers

Q. I would like to grow herbs on an apartment patio. We live in New York City.

A. It wouldn't matter if you lived in "Tim-buck-to," you can grow herbs any place. Why don't you get a clay strawberry jardiniere and plant parsley, chives, mint, sage, rosemary for fragrance, and thyme.

Q. We have a wild flower growing in our rock garden, with a tag on it, called *Galeopsis terrahit*. Can it be grown inside as a kitchen herb?

A. Who do you think you are kidding! The real name is common hemp nettle, and if you have any plans for spicing up your life with this, forget it. It is not "pot." You will get stung harvesting it and sick from the results.

Q. What are the three best salad herbs?

A. My wife makes super salads, and she adds thyme, basil and tarragon. Yummm.

Q. What do they rub a roast with before they roast?

A. First, I think your wedding thank-you notes are beautiful. The most common herb would be thyme, but your mother or mother-in-law would be glad to give you all of the culinary advice you will need, and will consider it an honor.

Q. What is the herb that tastes so strong in most Italian food?

A. Probably oregano. I like it in scrambled eggs, and on fish when caught fresh and pan-fried.

Q. Can I make up my own curry powder from an herb garden?

A. Well, you could, but you might run into trouble with

an herb called turmeric. But here are the other ingredients: coriander, black pepper, mustard, ginger, cumin, allspice, cardamon, cloves and anise.

Q. Which herbs do you use for preparing wild fowl?
A. Hunters use dirty hands, but you can try marjoram and sage.

Q. Is the marigold really an herb?
A. Why not, they used to use it to color butter, and it makes great wine.

Q. What is meant by balloon-sealing wine?
A. Instead of using the old-fashioned method of water sealing, which consisted of a complicated aparatus of corks and glass tubing to enable the gasses to escape, we now just place a child's balloon over the neck of the bottle. When the gasses fill the balloon, causing it to enlarge, we let them out and put the balloon over the bottle neck again. This process is repeated until no more gasses form, at which time the wine can be corked and stored.

Q. Can I use any kind of barrel to make wine?
A. The best kind of cask, as it is called by my good Italian winemaking teacher, is a new white oak barrel. Do not buy one that is charred or waxed inside. If you use either of these types you will smother the wine, and it will sour.

Q. Can you grow herbs in a barrel?
A. Sure you can, or in an old crock, wagon wheel, rubber tire, iron kettle or any other imaginative container.

Q. What medicinal purpose does ginger serve?
A. My grandma used to give us a cup of ginger tea after she had rubbed our chests with camphorated oil to sweat out a cold, and then put us to bed.

16

Solution to Pollution

Ecology!

What does it mean? I posed this question to men,
women, and school children of all ages. Do you know
what I got for an answer? "I don't know." "Would you
like to know?" I ask. "Not particularly." "Why not,
when your life may depend upon the ecological balances
we are all so nonchalantly upsetting and destroying?"
"Because I can't do anything to correct it; I am just one
person." Mr. and Mrs. America, that's where you're
wrong. You as individuals can do something about it.

If every one of us would take environmental improvement seriously and practice it in our daily lives at home
and work, pollution could become a thing of the past.

If you want to live out the rest of your natural life and
have your children and grandchildren and generations of
the future do the same in a clean, clear atmosphere, then
it's time you and I took the bull by the horn. How? Before you begin this clean-the-earth campaign, make sure
that your own skirts are clean.

You can practice ecology in your own garden by doing
what might seem like small things, but things which, if
practiced by everyone, would amount to a lot more than
a "hill of beans."

Let's begin. Don't burn grass clippings or leaves. They
are the best sources of green manure and compost. Simply
make alternating layers of soil and grass or leaves, turning the pile several times a season. In the fall or spring,
spade it back into the ground. Next, put two or three
layers of newspapers on the ground beneath natural
mulches like wood chips, bark, ground corn-cob and leaf

mulch, instead of the commercially sold plastic which does not break down and return to the soil. Just a few short years ago, anyone who practiced organic gardening was considered a kook, and if you referred to the Farmer's Almanac as a reference guide without making it appear a joke, you were put in the same category. Now the organic kook is a *practicing ecologist* and the Farmer's Almanac is crammed with *technical information*.

You housewives of America and the rest of the world can help too. Stop buying and using non bio-degradable detergents. It's not worth the pennies you save to jeopardize your future health. Do not patronize cleaners which use cleaning solvents containing hydrocarbons. Think anti-pollution and you will get in the habit of living.

And now, Mr. America, let's get around to the sports and camping. One only needs to walk the banks or wade the streams of this country to soon become disenchanted with the image of the outdoor enthusiasts. Beer and pop bottles, garbage and trash, literally cover the shore lines and nature trails, left by unconcerned hunters and campers. But I would bet you dollars to donuts that their guns are spic and span. Another example of the concern of the sportsman to eliminate pollution and improve our environment is the littered and contaminated condition in which they left the shore line and tributary banks of Lake Michigan after the first coho salmon season. There are, I am sure, many exceptions to the incidents I have just described, but these exceptions are not enough. All of the campers and hunters and hikers must pitch in to prevent this mass destruction of our natural forests, lakes and waterways. These are just simple, commonsense steps that one can take; they are not the complete answer to ecology and pollution control, for that still ends up in the hands of the politicians, and they themselves are polluters blowing a lot of hot air.

I asked one of our federal legislators what he was doing to help find the solution to pollution. He informed me that he came out against the use of DDT, and agrees that the weed killer 2, 4, 5 DDT should be banned, along with all of the rest of the harmful chemicals. I also asked him to define ecology. He couldn't. I asked if he was aware that they found some harmful quantities of DDT in mother's milk. Was he going to suggest that they ban this?

Toilet paper has recently come under fire also, along with soda pop, face creams, canned food, fresh fruit, fish, poultry and a whole list of other products. What an arsenal for the local wind warmers running for office who end up after the election as more "yack than shack." Banning and outlawing is not the answer. If each man, woman and child would practice the anti-litter lesson that we were taught; if ministers would preach, teachers and parents scold; then, we *might* have a chance! But the big word is IF. The industrialist says, "Wait a minute, why blame us?" The urban communities say, "Why blame us?" and the politicians, farmers and homeowners all ask the same question, "Why blame us?" We are all to blame for the toxic turmoil present in our sky, streams and soil, for we have abused and misused Mother Nature. Even the kindest parent finds it necessary to be firm from time to time, and the subject of pollution is one that we must all become firm about. For if we don't become firm with ourselves, Mother Nature will make it virtually impossible for us to survive.

The solution to pollution does not lie in blaming the other guy or passing the buck. It lies in first understanding what ecology, environmental control and pollution really mean and where they begin, and then determining what steps we can take to correct them.

In concluding this book, I would like to refer to the beginning, the Book of Genesis, verses 11–13 and 26–31, which tell us that we were created in God's image and He is the *Creator!*

May you enjoy the best that Mother Nature can provide, with your own helping hand.

him to define ecology. He couldn't. I asked if he was aware that they found some harmful quantities of DDT in mother's milk. Was he going to suggest that they ban this?

Toilet paper has recently come under fire also, along with soda pop, face creams, canned food, fresh fruit, fish, poultry and a whole list of other products. What an arsenal for the local wind warmers running for office who end up after the election as more "yack than shack." Banning and outlawing is not the answer. If each man, woman and child would practice the anti-litter lesson that we were taught; if ministers would preach, teachers and parents scold; then, we *might* have a chance! But the big word is IF. The industrialist says, "Wait a minute, why blame us?" The urban communities say, "Why blame us?" and the politicians, farmers and homeowners all ask the same question, "Why blame us?" We are all to blame for the toxic turmoil present in our sky, streams and soil, for we have abused and misused Mother Nature. Even the kindest parent finds it necessary to be firm from time to time, and the subject of pollution is one that we must all become firm about. For if we don't become firm with ourselves, Mother Nature will make it virtually impossible for us to survive.

The solution to pollution does not lie in blaming the other guy or passing the buck. It lies in first understanding what ecology, environmental control and pollution really mean and where they begin, and then determining what steps we can take to correct them.

In concluding this book, I would like to refer to the beginning, the Book of Genesis, verses 11–13 and 26–31, which tell us that we were created in God's image and He is the *Creator!*

May you enjoy the best that Mother Nature can provide, with your own helping hand.

Index

Acti-Dione 25, 26, 27, 171
Aerating, lawn 7-8
Air-layering 157
Ajuga 89
Alaska, suitable annuals 185
Alder shrub, speckled 156
Almond tree 138
Aluminum foil collar 214
Amid-Thin 128
Andora junipers (spreading ever-
    green) 60
Annuals
    Cutting and pinching back
        181
    Feeding 179-80
    Landscaping 176-77, 178-79
    Mulching 186
    Planting 178
    Selection of plants 177-78,
        183-84
    Soap and water treatment
        180
    Soil preparation 178, 179
    Varieties (names) 181-83,
        184, 185, 186
    Watering 180, 186
Anthracnoses (fungus disease)
    119
Ants 45, 47, 58, 93
Aphids
    Evergreens 95
    Flowering shrubs 150
    Roses 170
Apple-cranberry wine (recipe)
    255
Apple tree
    Dwarf 137
    Flowering 112, 114
    Mice, protection from 142
    Transplanting 142
    Varieties (names) 137, 138,
        142
Apricot tree 137
Aquatic weeds 51
Aramite 170
Arborvitae 66, 88, 117
Armyworms 45
Ash tree 116
Asiatic garden beetle larvae 47
Aspen tree, quaking 118
Asters 193
Automatic feeding, lawns 54
Automatic water timers 54-55
Avocado tree 140-41, 143
Azaleas
    Indoors 237, 244
    Outdoors 61, 89, 94, 156

Bag worms 89
Balloon-sealing wine bottles 258
Balsam-apple 224
Bamboo stakes 197
Banvel 58
Bare root trees 120
Bark, split 118
Bark, torn 118
Bay tree, sweet 114
Beans 213
Bee hives 143
Beech tree 116
Beer, houseplants 243
Beet wine (recipe) 255
Beets 213
Bent (grasses) 38

Bermuda grass 32, 39
Berries
    Feeding 230
    Mulching 230
    Preparation for planting 228-29
    Time to plant 229
    Varieties (names) 230-31; see also specific names, i.e., strawberries
Biennials and perennials
    Characteristics 188-89
    Dividing 190-91
    Feeding 189-90
    Landscaping 189
    Planting 189, 192, 193
    Second bloomings 192
    Soap and water treatment 191
    Soil types 192
    Sowing seed 192
    Transplanting 192-93
    Varieties (names) 191
    Watering 191
Birch tree 116, 118
Birds 90, 147-48, 232
Bittersweet, how to dry 94
Black Leaf Forty 89
Black locust 118
Black plastic 210
Black spot 170, 172
Black walnut tree 138
Blackberries 229, 231
Blossom-end rot 216
Blueberries
    As ground cover 157
    Cultivation 232
    Varieties (names) 231
Bone meal 199
Bordeaux mix 119
Borers 121-22, 130
Borgo 121
Bottle-brush shrub 156
Box elder bugs 45
Boxwood 95, 151
Boysenberries 231
Broad-leafed evergreens 60
Broad-leafed weeds (Dicot) 23
Brown patch 25-26

Brussel sprouts 213
Buckhorn 23
Bulbs
    Diseases 202
    Dormant treatment 201, 203
    Feeding 199
    Growing indoors 200-01
    House plants 234, 245
    Landscaping 196-97
    Mulching 199, 202
    New bulb treatment 202
    Planting, how 198-99
    Planting, when 198
    Planting, where 198
    Sizes 203
    Soap and water treatment 199, 202
    Timetable for blooming 197-98
    Varieties (names) 197-98
Burning bush shrub 151
Burning lawn 56
Bushy house plants 235
Butternut tree 138

Cabbage 213
Cabbage worms 216
Cacti, house plants 234
Calamondin lemon tree 140
Calcium, lawns 57
Camphor tree 116
Canadian hemlock 88
Cane borers 170
Captan 170
Carob tree 113
Carolina silverbell tree 132
Carpenter ants 93
Carrots 215
Cauliflower 213
Cedar tree
    Aphids 95
    Cuttings 88
    Varieties (names) 112, 116
Celery 213
Centipedes 45
Cherry tree
    Flowering 114-15, 117, 124, 128, 130

Poisonous twigs 142
Varieties (names) 137, 138
Chervil 253
Chestnut tree 113, 138
Chickweed 23
Chiggers 45
Chimotto orange tree 140
Chinch bugs 46
Chinese lantern 193
Chlordane 30, 47, 48, 49, 58,
93, 94, 107, 122, 129, 132,
150, 199, 202, 216, 222, 231,
249
Chlorosis 53, 91, 108, 172
Christmas trees 90, 95
Chrysanthemums 190, 193
Chrysanthemums, house plants
244, 248
Citrus trees
How to plant 140
Varieties (names) 140; see
also specific names, i.e.,
Valencia orange
Clay soil 19, 49, 67, 131, 172,
192
Clematis vines 224, 225
Climbing ground covers 224-25
Climbing house plants 235
Climbing roses 161, 169
Clover
Ground cover 58
Weed 23
Coconut palm tree 116
Coddling moths 139
Coffee grounds, use on ever-
greens 94
Compost 58, 178, 185, 208, 259
Composting 259
Conifers, see evergreens
Cork tree 116
Corn 213
Cornell University mixture 148
Cottony maple scale 117
Crab apple tree
Edible 138
Flowering 114, 128, 132
Crab grass 22, 50
Crape myrtle tree 114, 116
Creeping ground covers 224

Crickets 231
Crimson star (red clematis) 224
Crocuses 201, 202
Cross-pollinating fruit trees 137
Crown-vetch 225
Cucumbers 213, 217
Currants 157, 229-30
Curry powder, herb ingredients
257-58
Cuttings, flowering shrubs 151-
53
Cuttings, roses 174
Cut worms 45, 214-15
Cyanamid 55-56
Cyclamen, house plant 237, 245

Daffodils 198, 200, 201
Dallis grass 22
Dandelion 23
Dandelion wine (recipe) 256
Date palm tree 116
DDT 67, 173-74, 260-61
Deer 92
Delphinium 192
Devil grass 50
Dibrome 67
Dichondra 33, 42, 58
Dicot weeds (broadleaf) 23
Diquat weed killers 51
Diseases
Evergreens 75-77, 79-80,
91, 94
Flowering trees 129-30, 132
House plants 249
Lawns 24-27, 49, 51; see
also specific diseases, i.e.,
leaf spot
Roses 170, 171; see also
specific diseases, i.e., rose
scale
Shade trees 107, 119, 121;
see also specific diseases,
i.e., Dutch elm
Vegetables 216
Dogs
Lawn damage 25, 48
Protecting evergreens 89
Dogwood shrub, red twig 156

Dogwood tree 112, 113, 127, 129, 130
Dollar spot 26
Dormant spraying
    Grapes 231
    Roses 166, 170
    Trees 103, 117, 119, 128, 139, 141
Drain tile, lawn areas 54
Drying annuals 185
Dundee (upright junipers) 60
Dutch elm disease 107, 121
Dwarf fruit trees 137-38

Earthworms (lawn) 56
Earwigs 46
Easter lilies 202, 244-45
Eggplant 213
Elm tree 117
Espaliered trees 130-31
Eucalyptus tree 114, 116
Eureka lemon tree 140
European chafer larvae 47
Evergreens
    Catalogs available for plant selection 84-87
    Diseases and prevention 75-77
    Feeding 73, 74-75
    How to choose 62-63, 68-69
    How to plant 67, 70-73, 92
    Insects and insect control 77-79
    Landscaping 61-62, 64, 87
    Mulches 94
    Pools and landscaping 64-67
    Preparation of planting beds 67-68
    Pruning and trimming 79-81
    Re-landscaping 83-84
    Soap and water treatment 76, 77, 78, 90, 94
    Transplanting 81-83
    Tieing 93
    Transporting from nursery 69

Watering 91
When to plant 88
Wind screens 93

Fading out 25
Fairy rings 26-27
Fels Naptha soap 139
Fertilizers
    Berries and grapes 230
    Bulbs 199
    Citrus trees 140
    Evergreens 73, 74-75
    Flowers 180, 189-90
    Ground covers 225
    Lawn 19-21, 51-52, 53, 58
    Roses 164, 172
    Shrubs, flowering 150
    Trees, flowering 127
    Trees, shade 105-06, 120
Fescue (grasses) 38, 39, 56
Fiddle-leaf fig (house plant) 249
Field timothy 58
Fig tree 130
Fir tree, Douglas 117
Fish emulsion 75, 180, 190
Fish fertilizer, liquid 53, 243
Floribunda roses 160, 168-69
Flowering almond 157
Flowering cherry tree 124, 128
Flowering crab tree 128, 129-30, 132
Flowering house plants 234
Flowering pot plants 234
Flowering shrubs
    Air-layering 157
    Birds and shrubs 147-48
    Care 146-47
    Colors 153
    Cuttings 151-53, 157
    Cuttings, in water 156
    Feeding 150
    Hedges 150-51
    Insects and insect control 149-50
    Planting 148
    Pruning and trimming 148-49, 156
    Root pruning 150

Soap and water treatment
149-50
Uses 146
Varieties (names) 153-55
Flowering trees
Diseases 129-30, 132
Feeding 127
How to buy 125-26
How to plant 126
Insects 128, 129, 132
Pruning and trimming 127,
130, 131
Uses 125
Varieties (names) 113-15
Flowers, annuals
Cutting and pinching back
181
Feeding 179-80
Landscaping 176-77, 178
Planting 179
Selection of plants 177-78,
183, 184
Soap and water treatment
180
Soil preparation 178, 179
Varieties (names) 181-83,
184
Watering 180, 186
Flowers, perennials and
biennials
Characteristics 188
Dividing 190-91
Feeding 189-90
Landscaping 189
Planting 189, 192-93
Second bloomings 192
Soap and water treatment
191
Soil types 192
Sowing seed 192
Transplanting 192-93
Varieties (names) 191
Watering 191
Flying ants 58
Foliage house plants 234
Footprints on lawn 57
Forcing annual flowers 184
Forsythia 151, 156
Foxtails 22

Fruit, small
Feeding 230
Mulching 230
Preparation for planting
228-29
Time to plant 229
Varieties (names) 230-31;
see also specific names,
i.e., strawberries
Fruit trees
Citrus (varieties) 140
Citrus flowering trees 113,
114
Cross-pollinating 137
Dwarf 137-38
How to buy 135-36
How to plant 136-37
How to plant citrus 140
Insects and insect control
139
Nut trees 138-39
Shade trees, non-edible
(varieties) 112, 128
Soap and water treatment
139
Varieties (names) 137-38;
see also specific types,
i.e., cherry trees
Watering 142
Fullers rose beetles 170
Fungus (Anthracnoses) 119

Galeopsis Terrabit 257
Gall, insect 90
Garden Preen 130
Geographical zone map for
planting 111
Ginkgo tree 116
Gladiolus 203
Gloxinia (house plant) 245
Goldenchain tree 127, 131-32
Gooseberries 157, 229-30
Goosegrass 22
Grandiflora roses 161, 168
Grapes
Feeding 230
How to plant 230
Pruning 230

Grapes *(Continued)*
  Spraying 231
  Varieties (names) 231
Grass, bank areas 58
Grass seed, shade 49
Grasshoppers 46
Grassy weeds (Monocot) 22-23
Gravel 163
Grease spot (lawn) 26
Green Garde 172, 243
Green moss (lawn) 49, 51
Ground covers
  As mulch 89
  Bulbs, flowers, fruits and
    vegetables 89, 182-83,
    220, 221, 224, 225
  Feeding 225
  Mulching 89, 223, 224
  Pruning 225
  Soap and water treatment
    222
  Soil preparation 222
  Sun tolerant plants 225
  Supports for vines 223,
    225
  Time to plant 222
  Uses 220, 221
  Varieties (names) 223-24
Ground ivy 23
Grubs 50, 93-94, 132, 139
Gypsum, uses
  Annuals 178
  Berries and grapes 229
  Bulbs 199
  Evergreens 66, 92
  Lawns 25, 36, 48, 49, 51
  Roses 163
  Vegetables 208

Hanging flower baskets, water-
  ing 186
Hardwood cuttings (shrubs) 152-
  53
Hardy annuals 183
Harlequin bugs 171
Hawthorn tree 112, 113
Hazelnut tree 138
Hedges
  Evergreen 88

Fast growing 118
  Flowering shrubs 151
  Roses 173
Hemlock tree 117
Henbit 23
Herbs
  Borders 253
  Patio herb garden 257
  Varieties (names) 253, 254,
    257, 258
Hetzi juniper 95
Hickory nut tree 138
Holly 95
Holly tree 112
Hollyhocks 192
House plants
  Air 240
  Basic shapes 235
  Basic types 234
  Climatic conditions 236-37
  Colorful foliage 235
  Ease of maintenanace 235-
    36
  Easy flowering 236
  Feeding 240
  Indoor landscaping 237-39
  Purchase and care 237
  Selection 234-35
  Soap and water treatment
    241-42, 248
  Transplanting 243
  Varieties (names) 247-48
  Water 241
Hyacinths 198, 200, 201
Hybrid perpetual roses 161
Hybrid polyantha roses 161
Hybrid tea roses 161, 167-68
Hydrangea (bush) 155, 156
Hydrangea (house plant) 245

Iceland poppies 192
Insects and insect control
  Evergreens 89, 90, 93-94,
    95
  Flowering shrubs 149-50
  Flowering trees 128-29,
    130, 132
  Fruit trees 139, 140
  House plants 248, 249

Lawns 27-30, 31, 45-48, 50, 56, 58; see also specific insects, i.e., sod web-worms

Roses 169-71; see also specific insects, i.e., thrips

Shade trees 107, 118, 119, 121-22

Vegetables 214-15, 216

Iris, dividing 190-91

Iron chelates 108

Iron (lawns) 53

Irrigation, lawns 53

Isotox 169, 170

Jacaranda tree 114

Jack-o-lantern 215

Jack pine (disease) 94

Japanese beetle larvae 47

Japanese beetles 171

Japanese maple tree 132

Japanese yew tree 92

June bloomers (roses) 161

Junipers 60, 224

Katsura tree 116

Kentucky blue grass 33, 38, 42

Kentucky coffee tree 116, 132

Kentucky 31 grass 56

Knotweed 23

Kumquat tree 140

Laburnum tree 114

Landscaping 61-62, 64-67, 83-84, 87, 90, 91, 93, 100-01, 176-77, 178, 189, 196-97

Laurel fig tree, Indian 116

Lavender shrub 156

Lawn moths 46

Lawn mower blades 55

Lawn mowers, riding 54

Lawns

    Aerating 7-8

    Common problems 48-58; see also specific problem, i.e., dog damage

    Diseases 24-27; see also specific diseases, i.e., leaf spot

Fertilizers 19-21, 51, 52, 53, 58

Gypsum, uses of 25, 36, 48, 49, 51

Insect infestation and treatment 45-48

Insects and control 27-30, 31, 45-48; see also specific insects, i.e., ants

Leveling uneven lawns 8-9

Mowers (types) 12-13

Mowing 9-13, 55

Seeding (new lawns) 31-39; see also specific seed types, i.e., Kentucky blue grass

Seeding (established lawns) 39-42

Soap and water treaatment 5-6, 28, 29, 40, 56, 58

Sodding 43-45

Sprinklers 17-19

Thatch 3-5

Varieties (names) 38-39

Watering 13-17

Weeds, control 23-24, 50, 51

Weeds, identification 22-23; see also specific weeds, i.e., knotweed

Lead arsenate 170

Leaf-cutting bees 171

Leaf feeding, roses 172

Leaf mulch 222

Leaf rollers 169-70

Leaf spot, lawns 25

Lemon cucumbers 217

Lemon tree 140; see also varieties, i.e., Meyer lemon

Lettuce 213

Leveling uneven lawns 8-9

Lighting, artificial 142

Lilac bush 156-57

Lilac, Japanese tree 115

Lime 52, 94

Lime-sulphur solution 139, 231

Lime tree 140

Limestone, ground cover 90

Linden tree 115

Liquid lawn food 52
Locust tree 116, 118
London plane tree 117
Loquat tree 112
Lupine 193

Magnolia tree 114, 128, 131
Malathion
    Annuals 180
    Evergreens 78, 89, 90, 94, 95
    Flowering shrubs 150
    Flowering trees 130
    Lawns 30, 58
    Roses 169, 170, 171
    Shade trees 103, 107, 119
Mandarin orange tree 140
Manure 52-53, 162, 208, 228, 232
Manzate 170
Maple bladder gall 119
Maple tree 113, 115, 117, 118, 132
Marigolds 95, 215, 258
Meadow grass, rough stalk 38
Mealy bugs (house plants) 249
Melon 213
Merion grass 33, 34, 38, 42
Meyer lemon tree, dwarf 140
Mice 92, 129, 142, 222
Mildew
    Lawns 49-50
    Roses 171
    Zinnias 180
Millipedes 46
Milorganite 26
Miniature roses 161
Mint 253
Mint wine (recipe) 256
Mockorange shrub 155
Mole crickets 48
Moles 49, 222
Monocot weeds (grassy) 22, 23
Monrovia Nursery 88
Morning glory 129-30, 224
Mosquitoes 46, 185
Moss, lawns 49, 51
Moth crystals 89, 122, 128, 130, 141

Mountain-ash tree 112, 115
Mountain laurel 89, 94
Mowers (types) 12-13
Mowing lawns 9-13, 55
Mulching
    Annuals 185-86
    Berries 230
    Bulbs 199, 202
    Evergreens 94
    Ground covers 89, 223, 224
    Roses 166, 171, 172
    Trees (old) 143
    Vegetables 210, 215
Multiflora rosa shrub 151

Nareissi 200
Natriphene 171
Navel orange tree 140
Nectarine tree 141-42
Needle drop 79
Nicotine sulphate 139, 170
Night watering (lawns) 54
Nimble-will 23
Nut grass 22
Nut trees, 138-39; see also specific varieties, i.e., almond tree

Oak leaf mulch 143, 150, 172, 202, 215
Oak tree 117
Olive tree 116
Orange trees 140
    As flowering trees 113, 114; see also specific varieties, i.e., Valencia orange tree
Orchard grass 23
Orchards, saving old 141
Orchid tree 113, 131
Oregano 257
Oxalis 23

Pachysandra 89
Pagoda tree 112, 115, 117
Painted daisies 192
Painting trees 122, 129
Palm tree 110, 116, 117, 121
Palm wine 121
Palmolive Green soap, see soap and water treatment

Panogen Turf Fungicide 26
Pansies 192
Para Scaleicide 91
Parabenzine 170
Parabenzine moth crystals 89, 122, 128, 130, 141
Parabenzine paint 122
Parsley 253
Paul's scarlet hawthorne tree 128, 129
Peach trees (varieties) 137, 138
Peach trees, flowering 114
Peach trees, protect from rabbits 141
Pear trees 137, 138, 139
Pear trees, flowering 115
Peas 213
Peat moss 120, 163, 178, 199, 208, 222, 232
Pecan tree 138
Penngift 225
Peonies 190, 192
Pepper tree 112
Peppermint 224
Peppers 213-14
Perennials and biennials
    Characteristics 188
    Dividing 190-91
    Feeding 189-90
    Landscaping 189
    Planting 190, 192, 193
    Second bloomings 192
    Soap and water treatment 191
    Soil types 192
    Sowing seed 192
    Transplanting 192
    Varieties (names) 191
    Watering 191
Petunias 181, 184
Phaltan 170
Photinia tree 112, 114
Pieris japonica 89
Pine bark mulch 172
Pine tree 60, 116
Pistachio tree, Chinese 117
Plantain 23
Plastic bags 171
Plastic covers 224

Plastic mulch 90
Plum trees 137, 138
Plum trees, flowering 114, 131
Poinsettias (house plants) 246
Poisonous cherry tree twigs 142
Pollution 259-61
Pools and landscaping 64-67
Poplar tree 117, 118
Potato champagne (recipe) 256
Poultry manure 90
Privet 151
Privet tree 114
Pruning and trimming
    Berries and grapes 229-30, 231
    Evergreens 80-81
    Flowering shrubs 148-53, 156
    Flowering trees 128, 130, 131
    Ground covers 225
    Roses 165-66, 173, 174
    Shade trees 103-05, 119-20
Pumpkins 215
Purple leaf plum tree 127, 131
Purslane 23
Pussy willow 156
Pyracantha 94
Pyrethum 30, 79

Quack grass 51
Quaking aspen 118
Queen palm 121

Rabbits 92, 118, 129, 141, 215
Radishes 214, 215, 216
Rain tree 114
Rainwater (lawns) 53
Rayner Bros. 231
Raspberries 229, 231, 232
Real Kill 79, 184
Recipes 255-56
Redbud tree 113, 116, 127, 129
Red clematis 224
Red spider mites 130, 139, 170
Red spiders 89, 248
Red spiraea shrub 151
Red top grass 39

Red twig dogwood shrub 156
Redi-Earth 136, 148, 216
Redwood mulch 172
Redwood tree, dawn 116
Rhododendrons 61, 89, 94, 156
Rock gardens 91
Root feeders 92, 108, 172
Root maggots 215
Root-pruning 91, 150
Rootone 151, 174
Rose beds, size 172
Rose canker 170
Rose chafers 170
Rose collars 173
Rose cuts, sealing 173
Rose cuttings 174
Rose dust 169, 170, 171, 180
Rose midges 171
Rose scale 170
Rose slugs 170
Rose suckers 166
Roses
    Classification 160-61
    Cut roses, care 246
    Diseases and insects 169-
        71; see also specific
        name, i.e., thrips
    Feeding 164, 172
    House plants 245-46
    Mulches 166, 171, 172
    Planting, how 163-64, 173
    Planting, when 163
    Planting, where 162-63, 173
    Preparation of soil 162-63
    Pruning and cutting back
        165-66, 173, 174
    Size of bed 172
    Soap and water treatment
        165
    Varieties (names) 161-62,
        167-69
    Watering 164-65, 172
Roses, grades 174
Roses, leaf feeding 172
Rough lemon tree 140
Rust, lawns 26
Rust, roses 170
Rye grass 33, 39, 42, 49

St. Augustine grass 33, 39
Salt 216
Salt damage to lawn 48
Sandy soil 49, 67, 118
Scale, evergreens 91
Scale, house plants 249
Scoring trees 106
Scotch pine 90
Sea lavender 193
Seeding, lawns 31-34
Serviceberry tree 112, 113
Sevin 58, 128, 170, 171, 180,
    210
Shade trees
    Care of during construc-
        tion 109-10
    Chlorosis (lack of iron)
        108
    Diseases 107, 119, 121
    Feeding 105-06, 120
    Flowering trees (varieties)
        113-15
    Foliage, attractive (vari-
        eties) 115-17
    Fruit trees (varieties) 112
    How to plant 102-03, 120
    Insects 107, 121-22
    Landscaping 100-01
    Palm trees 110-12, 121
    Pruning and trimming 103-
        05, 119-20
    Scoring 106
    Soap and water treatment
        107, 117, 119
    Standard shade trees (vari-
        eties) 115-17
    Transplanting 108, 120
    Transporting from nursery
        101-02
    Uses 100
    Varieties (names) 112-17
Shrubs, flowering
    Air-layering 157
    Birds and shrubs 147-48
    Care 146-47
    Colors 153
    Cuttings 151-53, 157
    Cuttings, in water 156

Feeding 150
Hedges 150-51
Insects and insect control 149-50
Planting 148
Pruning 148-49, 156
Root pruning 150
Soap and water treatment 149-50
Uses 146
Varieties (names) 153-55
Silica gel 185
Silk tree 113
Silver maple 117
Silver poplar 118
Silverbell tree 114
Slugs 46
Snails 46
Snow mold (lawns) 26
Snowbell tree 115
Soap and water treatment
Annuals 180
Biennials and perennials 191
Bulbs 199, 202
Evergreens 76, 77-78, 90, 94
Flowering shrubs 149-50
Flowering trees 132
Fruit trees 139, 141
Ground covers 222
Lawns 5-6, 28, 40, 56, 58
Roses 165, 170
Shade trees 107, 117, 119
Strawberries 231
Sod webworms 46, 48
Sodding, lawns 43-45
Softwood cuttings (shrubs) 151-52
Sorrel tree 114
Sour milk, as pest control 139
Spearmint plants 139
Speckled alder shrub 156
Speedwell 193
Spiders 46-47, 89, 248
Spinach 214
Spiraea shrub 151
Spring kill 166

Sprinklers, lawn 17-18
Sprinkling systems 53, 54
Spruce tree 60, 116
Squash 214
Statice 193
Stewartia tree 115
Stone chips 130
Strawberries 229, 230, 231, 232
Strawberry tree 112, 129
Stump nott 121
Sumac tree 157
Sure-Nox-Em 170
Sweet-gum tree 116
Sweet peas 224
Swimming pool water 58
Sycamore tree 117, 119
Symbiosis 209-10

Tangerine tree 140
Tarnished plant bugs 170
Tedion 170
10-6-4 lawn food 228
Tent worms 118-19
Thatch, lawn 3-4
Thistle 23
Thrips 169
Ticks 47
Timothy grass 23
Toadstools (lawn) 26
Tomato plants
Blossom-end rot 216
Cultivation of soil (not recommended) 215
Cut worms 214-15
Grow with evergreens 91
Pinching 217
Type for patio 215
Varieties (names) 214
Toyon tree 112, 114
Trailing annuals 186
Trailing house plants 235
Transplanting, evergreens 81-82
Transplanting, shade trees 108, 120
Tree cuts, sealing 129
Tree roses 161
Tree stump, removing 121
Tree Tangle Foot 122

Trees, flowering
  Diseases 129-30, 132
  Feeding 127
  How to buy 125-26
  How to plant 126
  Insects 128-29, 132
  Pruning and trimming 128, 130, 131
  Uses 125
  Varieties (names) 113-15, 127-28
Trees, fruit
  Citrus (varieties) 140
  Cross-pollinating 137
  Dwarf 137-38
  How to buy 135-36
  How to plant 136
  How to plant citrus 140
  Insects and insect control 139
  Nut trees 138-39
  Shade trees, non-edible (varieties) 112, 127-28
  Soap and water treatment 139
  Varieties (names) 137-38; see also specific types, i.e., cherry tree
  Watering 142
Trees, shade
  Care of during construction 109-10
  Chlorosis (lack of iron) 108
  Diseases 107, 119, 121
  Feeding 105-06, 120
  Flowering trees (varieties) 113-15
  Foliage, attractive 115-17
  Fruit trees (varieties) 112
  How to plant 102, 120
  Insects 107, 121-22
  Landscaping 100-01
  Palm trees 110-12, 116, 117, 121
  Pruning and trimming 103-05, 119-20
  Scoring 106
  Soap and water treatment 107, 117, 119
  Standard shade trees (varieties) 115-17
  Transplanting 108, 120
  Transporting from nursery 101-02
  Uses 100
  Varieties (names) 110-17
Trellises, roses 173
Tulip tree 114
Tulips 198, 200, 201, 202, 203
Tupelo tree 112
Turf dye, lawn 55
Twelve-spotted cucumber beetle 171
2,4-D weed killer 23, 24, 50-51

Upright house plants 235

Valencia orange tree 140
Vegetables
  Crop rotation 216
  Growing order (by names) 212-13
  Mulching 210, 215
  Patio vegetable garden 216
  Preparation of planting area 207
  Preparation of soil 207-08
  Quick growing plants 216
  Size of garden 208
  Staking plants 210
  Sunshine 215
  Symbiosis (combination of compatible vegetables) 209-210
  Thinning plants 211
  Varieties 213-14; see also names of specific vegetables, i.e., beans
  Watering 211
Veronica 193
Vinca 89
Vines 225
Vitamins (house plants) 240
Volk oil 103, 139

Walnut tree 138
Water damage to lawn 48

Watering
  Flowers 180, 186, 191
  Fruit trees 142
  House plants 241
  Lawns 14-17, 53, 54
  Vegetables 211
Wattle tree 113
Weed killers 23-24, 44, 50-51, 119, 171-72, 179
Weed sprayer, how to clean 50
Weeds, lawn 22-24, 50, 51
Weeping trees 130, 132
Weeping willow tree 117
Wheat flour, as pest control 139
White fringed beetle larvae 48
White poplar tree 118
Whitebud tree 113
Wild garlic 95, 165

Wilt-Pruf 89, 95, 120
Wind screen for evergreens 93
Windsor grass 33
Wine barrels 258
Wisteria vine 221, 225
Wisteria tree 131
Witchgrass 23
Wood chip mulch 172, 210
Wrapping trees 118, 130

Yellow-wood tree 113
Yew tree 60, 66, 91, 92
Yucca candle 94

Zelkova tree 117
Zinnia, mildew 180
Zone map for planting 111
Zoysia grass 33, 39, 55